THREE PLAYS ABOUT CRIME AND CRIMINALS

is in *The American National Theatre and Academy* (ANTA) *of Distinguished Plays*.

ANTA is an organization of theatre services, information and activities, congressionally chartered and independently financed by its members and interested donors. Its aim is ". . . to extend the living theatre beyond its present limitations by bringing the best in the theatre to every state in the Union."

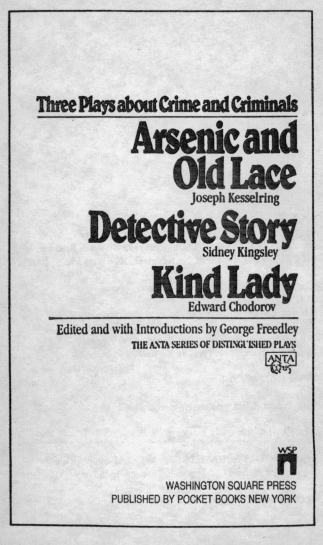

Three Plays about Crime and Criminals

Arsenic and Old Lace
Joseph Kesselring

Detective Story
Sidney Kingsley

Kind Lady
Edward Chodorov

Edited and with Introductions by George Freedley

THE ANTA SERIES OF DISTINGUISHED PLAYS

ANTA

WSP

WASHINGTON SQUARE PRESS
PUBLISHED BY POCKET BOOKS NEW YORK

A Washington Square Press Publication of
POCKET BOOKS, a division of Simon & Schuster, Inc.
1230 Avenue of the Americas, New York, N.Y. 10020

ISBN: 0-671-47229-1

First Pocket Books printing November, 1962

20   19   18   17

WASHINGTON SQUARE PRESS, WSP and colophon are
registered trademarks of Simon & Schuster, Inc.

Printed in the U.S.A.

CONTENTS

Any group that wishes to
produce any of these plays
will find production information
for each play on page 279.

ARSENIC AND OLD LACE

Joseph Kesselring was born in New York City on June 21, 1902. From 1922 to 1924 he was a professor of music in Newton, Kansas. From 1925 to 1933 he was a short-story writer, an actor and a producer of vaudeville sketches. He began his career as a writer of full-length plays with *Aggie Appleby, Maker of Men* (1933), followed by *There's Wisdom in Women* (1935), *Cross-Town* (1937), *Maggie McGilligan* (1942) and *Four Twelves Are 48* (1950).

Arsenic and Old Lace, imaginatively directed by Bretaigne Windust and skillfully produced by the eminent playwrights Howard Lindsay and Russel Crouse, was produced on August 18, 1941, at the Fulton Theatre (now the Helen Hayes) and ran for three and a half years. The play repeated the length of run (1332 performances) in London starting in December, 1942.

Brooks Atkinson in *The New York Times,* August 19, 1941, stated: "Let's not exaggerate! At some time there may have been a funnier murder charade than *Arsenic and Old Lace,* which was acted at the Fulton last evening. But the supposition is purely academic. Joseph Kesselring has written one so funny none of us will ever forget it." On the same date John Mason Brown wrote in the New York *Evening Post:* "The evening is at once so side-splitting and terrific that it can be guaranteed to make even dramatic critics care about the theatre."

"And that indeed is the joke which the author prolongs with wonderful ingenuity through three whole acts. *Arsenic and Old Lace* is a prime expression of the extravaganza and burlesque in which the Americans excel—a Runyon plot in a Mary Petty setting," remarked *New Statesman and Nation* on January 2, 1943.

The January 13, 1943, *Sketch* added: "The grim joke is really funny, and the perfect timing of the accomplished cast makes this fantastic skit on thrillers go with tremendous vim."

Further Reading

Clark, Barrett H., and Freedley, George. *A History of Modern Drama*. New York: Appleton-Century, 1947, p. 738.

Freedley, George, and Reeves, John Adams. *A History of the Theatre*, rev. ed. New York: Crown, 1955, p. 687.

Gassner, John. (ed.). *Best Plays of the Modern American Theatre, 2nd Series, 1939–1946*. New York: Crown, 1947, pp. 459–510.

Mantle, Burns. (ed.). *The Best Plays of 1940–1941*. New York: Dodd, Mead, 1941, pp. 165–203.

Shipley, Joseph T. *Guide to Great Plays*. Washington: Public Affairs, 1956, p. 381. " 'The funniest play about murder ever written,' as the Baltimore *Sun* (March 26, 1941) called it, *Arsenic and Old Lace* has audiences on both sides of the ocean half-seas over with applause at poisoning."

Arsenic and Old Lace

ACT I

SCENE: *It is late afternoon in September. The time is the present. The living room of the old Brewster home in Brooklyn, N.Y., is just as Victorian as the two sisters,* ABBY *and* MARTHA BREWSTER, *who occupy the house with their nephew,* TEDDY.

There is a staircase leading to the upper floor, broken by a landing with a window looking out on the front porch. At the top of the stairs, a balcony with a door leading to bedrooms and an archway beyond which are stairs to the top floor. There is a large window, a long window seat below it. A door leads to the cellar, another to the kitchen, and the main door of the house, which opens onto the porch. When the curtain rises, ABBY BREWSTER, *a plump little darling in her late sixties, is presiding at the tea table. The table is lighted by candles. Seated in armchair at her left is the* REV. DR. HARPER, *and on her right, standing, her nephew,* TEDDY, *whose costume includes a frock coat and pince-nez attached to a black ribbon.* TEDDY *is in his forties and*

*has a large black mustache, and his manner and make-up
suggest Theodore Roosevelt.*

ABBY: Yes, indeed, my sister Martha and I have been talking
all week about your sermon last Sunday. It's really wonderful, Dr. Harper—in only two short years you've taken on
the spirit of Brooklyn.

HARPER: That's very gratifying, Miss Brewster.

ABBY: You see, living here next to the church all our lives,
we've seen so many ministers come and go. The spirit of
Brooklyn we always say is friendliness—and your sermons
are not so much sermons as friendly talks.

TEDDY: Personally, I've always enjoyed my talks with Cardinal
Gibbons—or have I met him yet?

ABBY: No, dear, not yet. (*Changing the subject.*) Are the biscuits good?

TEDDY (*he sits on sofa*): Bully!

ABBY: Won't you have another biscuit, Dr. Harper?

HARPER: Oh, no, I'm afraid I'll have no appetite for dinner
now. I always eat too many of your biscuits just to taste
that lovely jam.

ABBY: But you haven't tried the quince. We always put a little
apple in with it to take the tartness out.

HARPER: No, thank you.

ABBY: We'll send you over a jar.

HARPER: No, no. You keep it here so I can be sure of having
your biscuits with it.

ABBY: I do hope they don't make us use that imitation flour
again. I mean with this war trouble. It may not be very
charitable of me, but I've almost come to the conclusion
that this Mr. Hitler isn't a Christian.

HARPER (*with a sigh*): If only Europe were on another planet!

TEDDY (*sharply*): Europe, sir?

HARPER: Yes, Teddy.

TEDDY: Point your gun the other way!

HARPER: Gun?

ABBY (*trying to calm him*): Teddy.

TEDDY: To the West! There's your danger! There's your enemy! Japan!

HARPER: Why, yes—yes, of course.

ABBY: Teddy!

TEDDY: No, Aunt Abby! Not so much talk about Europe and more about the canal!

ABBY: Well, let's not talk about war. Will you have another cup of tea, dear?

TEDDY: No, thank you, Aunt Abby.

ABBY: Dr. Harper?

HARPER: No, thank you. I must admit, Miss Abby, that war and violence seem far removed from these surroundings.

ABBY: It *is* peaceful here, isn't it?

HARPER: Yes—peaceful. The virtues of another day—they're all here in this house. The gentle virtues that went out with candlelight and good manners and low taxes.

ABBY (*glancing about her contentedly*): It's one of the oldest houses in Brooklyn. It's just as it was when Grandfather Brewster built and furnished it—except for the electricity—and we use it as little as possible. It was Mortimer who persuaded us to put it in.

HARPER (*beginning to freeze*): Yes, I can understand that. Your nephew Mortimer seems to live only by electric light.

ABBY: The poor boy has to work so late. I understand he's taking Elaine with him to the theatre again tonight. Teddy, your brother Mortimer will be here a little later.

TEDDY (*baring his teeth in a broad grin*): Dee-lighted!

ABBY (*to Harper*): We're so happy it's Elaine Mortimer takes to the theatre with him.

HARPER: Well, it's a new experience for me to wait up until three o'clock in the morning for my daughter to be brought home.

ABBY: Oh, Dr. Harper, I hope you don't disapprove of Mortimer.

HARPER: Well—

ABBY: We'd feel so guilty if you did—sister Martha and I. I mean since it was here in our home that your daughter met Mortimer.

HARPER: Of course, Miss Abby. And so I'll say immediately that I believe Mortimer himself to be quite a worthy gentleman. But I must also admit that I have watched the growing intimacy between him and my daughter with some trepidation. For one reason, Miss Abby.

ABBY: You mean his stomach, Dr. Harper?

HARPER: Stomach?

ABBY: His dyspepsia—he's bothered with it so, poor boy.

HARPER: No, Miss Abby, I'll be frank with you. I'm speaking of your nephew's unfortunate connection with the theatre.

ABBY: The theatre! Oh, no, Dr. Harper! Mortimer writes for a New York newspaper.

HARPER: I know, Miss Abby, I know. But a dramatic critic is constantly exposed to the theatre, and I don't doubt but what some of them do develop an interest in it.

ABBY: Well, not Mortimer. You need have no fear of that. Why, Mortimer hates the theatre.

HARPER: Really?

ABBY: Oh, yes! He writes awful things about the theatre. But you can't blame him, poor boy. He was so happy writing about real estate, which he really knew something about, and then they just made him take this terrible night position.

HARPER: My! My!

ABBY: But, as he says, the theatre can't last much longer anyway and in the meantime it's a living. (*Complacently.*) Yes, I think if we give the theatre another year or two, perhaps . . . (*A knock on door.*) Well, now, who do you suppose that is? (*They all rise as* ABBY *goes to door;* TEDDY *starts for door at same time, but* ABBY *stops him.*) No, thank you, Teddy. I'll go. (*She opens door to admit two* COPS, OFFICERS BROPHY *and* KLEIN.) Come in, Mr. Brophy.

BROPHY: Hello, Miss Brewster.

ABBY: How are you, Mr. Klein?

KLEIN: Very well, Miss Brewster.

(*The* COPS *cross to* TEDDY *who is standing near desk, and salute him.* TEDDY *returns salute.*)

TEDDY: What news have you brought me?

BROPHY: Colonel, we have nothing to report.

TEDDY: Splendid! Thank you, gentlemen! At ease!

(COPS *relax;* ABBY *has closed door, and turns to them.*)

ABBY: You know Dr. Harper.

KLEIN: Sure! Hello, Dr. Harper.

BROPHY (*turns to* ABBY, *doffing cap*): We've come for the toys for the Christmas Fund.

ABBY: Oh, yes.

HARPER (*standing below table*): That's a splendid work you men do—fixing up discarded toys to give poor children a happier Christmas.

KLEIN: It gives us something to do when we have to sit around the station. You get tired playing cards and then you start cleaning your gun, and the first thing you know you've shot yourself in the foot. (KLEIN *drifts around to window seat.*)

ABBY (*crossing to* TEDDY): Teddy, go upstairs and get that big box from your Aunt Martha's room. (TEDDY *crosses upstage toward stairs.* ABBY *speaks to* BROPHY.) How is Mrs. Brophy today? Mrs. Brophy has been quite ill, Dr. Harper.

BROPHY (*to* HARPER): Pneumonia!

HARPER: I'm sorry to hear that.

TEDDY (*reaching first landing on stairs where he stops and draws an imaginary sword; shouting*): CHARGE! (*He charges up stairs and exits off balcony. The others pay no attention to this.*)

BROPHY: Oh, she's better now. A little weak still—

ABBY (*starting toward kitchen*): I'm going to get you some beef broth to take to her.

BROPHY: Don't bother, Miss Abby! You've done so much for her already.

ABBY (*at kitchen door*): We made it this morning. Sister Martha is taking some to poor Mr. Benitzky right now. I won't be a minute. Sit down and be comfortable, all of you.

(*She exits into kitchen.*)

(HARPER *sits again.* BROPHY *crosses to table and addresses the other two.*)

BROPHY: She shouldn't go to all that trouble.

KLEIN: Listen, try to stop her or her sister from doing something nice—and for nothing! They don't even care how you vote. (*He sits on window seat.*)

HARPER: When I received my call to Brooklyn and moved next door my wife wasn't well. When she died and for months before—well, if I know what pure kindness and absolute generosity are, it's because I've known the Brewster sisters.

(*At this moment* TEDDY *steps out on balcony and blows a bugle call. They all look.*)

BROPHY (*stepping upstage; remonstrating*): Colonel, you promised not to do that.

TEDDY: But I have to call a Cabinet meeting to get the release of those supplies. (TEDDY *wheels and exits.*)

BROPHY: He used to do that in the middle of the night. The neighbors raised cain with us. They're a little afraid of him, anyway.

HARPER: Oh, he's quite harmless.

KLEIN: Suppose he does think he's Teddy Roosevelt. There's a lot worse people he could think he was.

BROPHY: Damn shame—a nice family like this hatching a cuckoo.

KLEIN: Well, his father—the old girls' brother—was some sort of a genius, wasn't he? And their father—Teddy's grandfather—seems to me I've heard he was a little crazy too.

BROPHY: Yeah—he was crazy like a fox. He made a million dollars.

HARPER: Really? Here in Brooklyn?

BROPHY: Yeah. Patent medicine. He was a kind of a quack of some sort. Old Sergeant Edwards remembers him. He used the house here as a sort of a clinic—tried 'em out on people.

KLEIN: Yeah, I hear he used to make mistakes occasionally, too.

BROPHY: The department never bothered him much because he was pretty useful on autopsies sometimes. Especially poison cases.

KLEIN: Well, whatever he did he left his daughters fixed for life. Thank God for that—

BROPHY: Not that they ever spend any of it on themselves.

HARPER: Yes, I'm well acquainted with their charities.

KLEIN: You don't know a tenth of it. When I was with the Missing Persons Bureau I was trying to trace an old man that we never did find—(*Rises.*)—do you know there's a renting agency that's got this house down on its list for furnished rooms? They don't rent rooms—but you can bet that anybody who comes here lookin' for a room goes away with a good meal and probably a few dollars in their kick.

BROPHY: It's just their way of digging up people to do some good to.

(MARTHA BREWSTER *enters.* MARTHA *is also a sweet elderly woman with Victorian charm. She is dressed in the old-fashioned manner of* ABBY, *but with a high lace collar that covers her neck.* MEN *all rise.*)

MARTHA (*at door*): Well, now, isn't this nice? (*Closes door.*)

BROPHY (*crosses to* MARTHA): Good afternoon, Miss Brewster.

MARTHA: How do you do, Mr. Brophy? Dr. Harper. Mr. Klein.

KLEIN: How are you, Miss Brewster? We dropped in to get the Christmas toys.

MARTHA: Oh, yes, Teddy's Army and Navy. They wear out. They're all packed. (*She turns to stairs.* BROPHY *stops her.*)

BROPHY: The Colonel's upstairs after them—it seems the Cabinet has to O.K. it.

MARTHA: Yes, of course. I hope Mrs. Brophy's better?

BROPHY: She's doin' fine, ma'am. Your sister's getting some soup for me to take to her.

MARTHA: Oh, yes, we made it this morning. I just took some to a poor man who broke ever so many bones.

ABBY (*enters from kitchen carrying a covered pail*): Oh, you're back, Martha. How was Mr. Benitzky?

MARTHA: Well, dear, it's pretty serious, I'm afraid. The doctor was there. He's going to amputate in the morning.

ABBY (*hopefully*): Can we be present?

MARTHA (*disappointment*): No. I asked him but he says it's against the rules of the hospital. (MARTHA *crosses to sideboard, puts pail down. Then puts cape and hat on small table.*)

(TEDDY *enters on balcony with large cardboard box and comes downstairs to desk, putting box on stool.* KLEIN *crosses to toy box, while* HARPER *speaks.*)

HARPER: You couldn't be of any service—and you must spare yourselves something.

ABBY (*to* BROPHY): Here's the broth, Mr. Brophy. Be sure it's good and hot.

BROPHY: Yes, ma'am.

KLEIN: This is fine—it'll make a lot of kids happy. (*Lifts out toy soldier.*) That O'Malley boy is nuts about soldiers.

TEDDY: That's General Miles. I've retired him. (KLEIN *removes ship.*) What's this! The *Oregon!*

MARTHA: Teddy, dear, put it back.

TEDDY: But the *Oregon* goes to Australia.

ABBY: Now, Teddy—

TEDDY: No, I've given my word to Fighting Bob Evans.

MARTHA: But, Teddy—

KLEIN: What's the difference what kid gets it—Bobby Evans, Izzy Cohen? (*Crosses to door with box, opens door.* BROPHY *follows.*) We'll run along, ma'am, and thank you very much.

ABBY: Not at all. (*The* COPS *stop in doorway, salute* TEDDY *and exit.* ABBY *crosses and shuts door as she speaks.* TEDDY *starts upstairs.*) Good-by.

HARPER (*crosses to sofa, gets hat*): I must be getting home.

ABBY: Before you go, Dr. Harper—

TEDDY (*has reached stair landing*): CHARGE! (*He dashes*

upstairs. At top he stops and with a sweeping gesture over the balcony rail, invites all to follow him as he speaks.) Charge the blockhouse! (*He dashes through door, closing it after him.*)

(HARPER *looks after him.* MARTHA *is fooling with a pin on her dress.* ABBY *stands to the right of* HARPER.)

HARPER: The blockhouse?

MARTHA: The stairs are always San Juan Hill.

HARPER: Have you ever tried to persuade him that he wasn't Teddy Roosevelt?

ABBY: Oh, no!

MARTHA: He's so happy being Teddy Roosevelt.

ABBY: Once, a long time ago (*She walks across to* MARTHA.), remember, Martha? We thought if he would be George Washington it might be a change for him—

MARTHA: But he stayed under his bed for days and just wouldn't be anybody.

ABBY: And we'd so much rather he'd be Mr. Roosevelt than nobody.

HARPER: Well, if he's happy—and what's more important you're happy—(*He takes blue-backed legal paper from inside pocket.*) you'll see that he signs these.

MARTHA: What are they?

ABBY: Dr. Harper has made all arrangements for Teddy to go to Happy Dale Sanitarium after we pass on.

MARTHA: But why should Teddy sign any papers now?

HARPER: It's better to have it all settled. If the Lord should take you away suddenly perhaps we couldn't persuade Teddy to commit himself and that would mean an unpleasant legal procedure. Mr. Witherspoon understands they're to be filed away until the time comes to use them.

MARTHA: Mr. Witherspoon? Who's he?

HARPER: He's the superintendent of Happy Dale.

ABBY (*to* MARTHA): Dr. Harper has arranged for him to drop in tomorrow or the next day to meet Teddy.

HARPER (*going to door and opening it*): I'd better be running along or Elaine will be over here looking for me.

ABBY (*calls out after him*): Give our love to Elaine—and Dr. Harper, please don't think harshly of Mortimer because he's a dramatic critic. Somebody has to do those things. (ABBY *closes door, comes back into room.*)

MARTHA (*at sideboard, puts legal papers on it; notices tea things on table*): Did you just have tea? Isn't it rather late?

ABBY (*as one who has a secret*): Yes—and dinner's going to be late too.

(TEDDY *enters on balcony, starts downstairs to first landing.* MARTHA *steps to* ABBY.)

MARTHA: So? Why?

ABBY: Teddy! (TEDDY *stops on landing.*) Good news for you. You're going to Panama and dig another lock for the canal.

TEDDY: Dee-lighted! That's bully! Just bully! I shall prepare at once for the journey. (*He turns to go upstairs, stops as if puzzled, hurries back to landing, cries CHARGE! and rushes up and off.*)

MARTHA (*elated*): Abby! While I was out?

ABBY (*taking* MARTHA'S *hand*): Yes, dear! I just couldn't wait for you. I didn't know when you'd be back and Dr. Harper was coming.

MARTHA: But all by yourself?

ABBY: Oh, I got along fine!

MARTHA: I'll run right downstairs and see. (*She starts happily for cellar door.*)

ABBY: Oh, no, there wasn't time, and I was all alone.

MARTHA (*looks around room toward kitchen*): Well—

ABBY (*coyly*): Martha—just look in the window seat. (MARTHA *almost skips to window seat, and just as she gets there a knock is heard on door. She stops. They both look toward door.* ABBY *hurries to door and opens it.* ELAINE HARPER *enters.* ELAINE *is an attractive girl in her twenties; she looks surprisingly smart for a minister's daughter.*) Oh, it's Elaine. (*Opens door.*) Come in, dear.

ELAINE: Good afternoon, Miss Abby. Good afternoon, Miss Martha. I thought Father was here.

MARTHA (*stepping to left of table*): He just this minute left. Didn't you meet him?

ELAINE (*pointing to window*): No, I took the short cut through the cemetery. Mortimer hasn't come yet?

ABBY: No, dear.

ELAINE: Oh? He asked me to meet him here. Do you mind if I wait?

MARTHA: Not at all.

ABBY: Why don't you sit down, dear?

MARTHA: But we really must speak to Mortimer about doing this to you.

ELAINE (*sits in chair*): Doing what?

MARTHA: Well, he was brought up to know better. When a gentleman is taking a young lady out he should call for her at her house.

ELAINE (*to both*): Oh, there's something about calling for a girl at a parsonage that discourages any man who doesn't embroider.

ABBY: He's done this too often—we're going to speak to him.

ELAINE: Oh, please don't. After young men whose idea of night life was to take me to prayer meeting, it's wonderful to go to the theatre almost every night of my life.

MARTHA: It's comforting for us too, because if Mortimer has to see some of those plays he has to see—at least he's sitting next to a minister's daughter. (MARTHA *steps to back of table.*)

(ABBY *crosses to back of table, starts putting tea things on tray.* ELAINE *and* MARTHA *help.*)

ABBY: My goodness, Elaine, what must you think of us—not having tea cleared away by this time. (*She picks up tray and exits to kitchen.*)

(MARTHA *blows out one candle and takes it to sideboard.* ELAINE *blows out other, takes it to sideboard.*)

MARTHA (*as* ABBY *exits*): Now don't bother with anything in the kitchen until Mortimer comes, and then I'll help you. (*To* ELAINE.) Mortimer should be here any minute now.

ELAINE: Yes. Father must have been surprised not to find me at home. I'd better run over and say good night to him. (*She crosses to door.*)

MARTHA: It's a shame you missed him, dear.

ELAINE (*opening door*): If Mortimer comes you tell him I'll be right back. (*She has opened door, but sees* MORTIMER *just outside.*) Hello, Mort!

MORTIMER (*entering*): Hello, Elaine. (*As he passes her going toward* MARTHA, *thus placing himself between* ELAINE *and* MARTHA, *he reaches back and pats* ELAINE *on the fanny . . . then embraces* MARTHA.) Hello, Aunt Martha.

MARTHA (*exiting to kitchen, calling as she goes*): Abby, Mortimer's here!

(ELAINE *slowly closes door.*)

MORTIMER (*turning*): Were you going somewhere?

ELAINE: I was just going over to tell Father not to wait up for me.

MORTIMER: I didn't know that was still being done, even in Brooklyn. (*He throws his hat on sofa.*)

(ABBY *enters from kitchen.* MARTHA *follows, stays in doorway.*)

ABBY (*crosses to* MORTIMER): Hello, Mortimer.

MORTIMER (*embraces and kisses her*): Hello, Aunt Abby.

ABBY: How are you, dear?

MORTIMER: All right. And you look well. You haven't changed much since yesterday.

ABBY: Oh, my goodness, it was yesterday, wasn't it? We're seeing a great deal of you lately. (*She crosses and starts to sit in chair.*) Well, come, sit down. Sit down.

MARTHA (*stops her from sitting*): Abby—haven't we something to do in the kitchen?

ABBY: Huh?

MARTHA: You know—the tea things.

ABBY (*suddenly seeing* MORTIMER *and* ELAINE, *and catching on*): Oh, yes! Yes! Yes! The tea things— (*She backs toward kitchen.*) Well—you two just make yourselves at home. Just—

MARTHA: —make yourselves at home.

(*They exit through kitchen door,* ABBY *closing door.*)

ELAINE (*stepping to* MORTIMER, *ready to be kissed*): Well, can't you take a hint?

MORTIMER (*complaining*): No . . . that was pretty obvious. A lack of inventiveness, I should say.

ELAINE (*only slightly annoyed as she crosses to table, and puts handbag on it*): Yes—that's exactly what you'd say.

MORTIMER (*at desk, fishing various pieces of note paper from his pockets, and separating dollar bills that are mixed in with papers*): Where do you want to go for dinner?

ELAINE (*opening bag, looking in hand mirror*): I don't care. I'm not very hungry.

MORTIMER: Well, I just had breakfast. Suppose we wait until after the show?

ELAINE: But that'll make it pretty late, won't it?

MORTIMER: Not with the little stinker we're seeing tonight. From what I've heard about it we'll be at Blake's by ten o'clock.

ELAINE: You ought to be fair to these plays.

MORTIMER: Are these plays fair to me?

ELAINE: *I've* never seen you walk out on a musical.

MORTIMER: That musical isn't opening tonight.

ELAINE (*disappointed*): No?

MORTIMER: Darling, you'll have to learn the rules. With a musical there are always four changes of title and three postponements. They liked it in New Haven but it needs a lot of work.

ELAINE: Oh, I was hoping it was a musical.

MORTIMER: You have such a light mind.

ELAINE: Not a bit. Musicals somehow have a humanizing effect on you. (*He gives her a look.*) After a serious play we join the proletariat in the subway and I listen to a lecture on the drama. After a musical you bring me home in a taxi (*Turning away.*) and you make a few passes.

MORTIMER: Now wait a minute, darling, that's a very inaccurate piece of reporting.

ELAINE (*leaning against end of table*): Oh, I will admit that after the Behrman play you told me I had authentic beauty —and that's a hell of a thing to say to a girl. It wasn't until after our first musical you told me I had nice legs. And I have too.

MORTIMER (*stares at her legs a moment, then walks over and kisses her*): For a minister's daughter you know a lot about life. Where'd you learn it?

ELAINE (*casually*): In the choir loft.

MORTIMER: I'll explain that to you sometime, darling—the close connection between eroticism and religion.

ELAINE: Religion never gets as high as the choir loft. (*Crosses below table, gathers up bag.*) Which reminds me, I'd better tell Father please not to wait up for me tonight.

MORTIMER (*almost to himself*): I've never been able to rationalize it.

ELAINE: What?

MORTIMER: My falling in love with a girl who lives in Brooklyn.

ELAINE: Falling in love? You're not stooping to the articulate, are you?

MORTIMER (*ignoring this*): The only way I can regain my self-respect is to keep you in New York.

ELAINE (*a few steps toward him*): Did you say keep?

MORTIMER: No, no. I've come to the conclusion that you're holding out for the legalities.

ELAINE (*crossing to him as he backs away*): I can afford to be a good girl for quite a few years yet.

MORTIMER (*stops and embraces her*): And I can't wait that long. Where could we be married in a hurry—say tonight?

ELAINE: I'm afraid Father will insist on officiating.

MORTIMER (*turning away from her*): Oh, God! I'll bet your father could make even the marriage service sound pedestrian.

ELAINE: Are you by any chance writing a review of it?

MORTIMER: Forgive me, darling. It's an occupational disease. (*She smiles at him lovingly and walks toward him. He meets her halfway and they forget themselves for a moment in a sentimental embrace and kiss. When they come out of it, he turns away from her quickly.*) I may give that play tonight a good notice.

ELAINE: Now, darling, don't pretend you love me that much.

MORTIMER (*looks at her with polite lechery, then starts toward her*): Be sure to tell your father not to wait up tonight.

ELAINE (*aware that she can't trust either of them, and backing upstage*): I think tonight I'd better tell him to wait up.

MORTIMER (*following her*): I'll telephone Winchell to publish the banns.

ELAINE (*backing*): Nevertheless—

MORTIMER: All right, everything formal and legal. But not later than next month.

ELAINE (*runs into his arms*): Darling! I'll talk it over with Father and set the date.

MORTIMER: No—we'll have to see what's in rehearsal. There'll be a lot of other first nights in October.

(TEDDY *enters from balcony and comes downstairs dressed in tropical clothes and a solar topee. At foot of stairs he sees* MORTIMER, *crosses to him and shakes hands.*)

TEDDY: Hello, Mortimer!

MORTIMER (*gravely*): How are you, Mr. President?

TEDDY: Bully, thank you. Just bully! What news have you brought me?

MORTIMER: Just this, Mr. President—the country is squarely behind you.

TEDDY (*beaming*): Yes, I know. Isn't it wonderful? (*He shakes* MORTIMER'S *hand again.*) Well, good-by. (*He*

crosses to ELAINE *and shakes hands with her.*) Good-by.
(*He goes to cellar door.*)

ELAINE: Where are you off to, Teddy?

TEDDY: Panama. (*He exits through cellar door, shutting it.*
ELAINE *looks at* MORTIMER *inquiringly.*)

MORTIMER: Panama's the cellar. He digs locks for the canal
down there.

(ELAINE *takes his arm and they stroll to the table.*)

ELAINE: You're so sweet with him—and he's very fond of you.

MORTIMER: Well, Teddy was always my favorite brother.

ELAINE (*stopping and turning to him*): Favorite? Were there
more of you?

MORTIMER: There's another brother—Jonathan.

ELAINE: I never heard of him. Your aunts never mention him.

MORTIMER: No, we don't like to talk about Jonathan. He left
Brooklyn very early—by request. Jonathan was the kind of
boy who liked to cut worms in two—with his teeth.

ELAINE: What became of him?

MORTIMER: I don't know. He wanted to become a surgeon
like Grandfather but he wouldn't go to medical school first
and his practice got him into trouble.

ABBY (*enters from kitchen*): Aren't you two going to be late
for the theatre?

MORTIMER (*his arm around* ELAINE's *neck; looks at his wrist
watch*): We're skipping dinner. We won't have to start for
half an hour.

ABBY (*backing away*): Well, then I'll leave you two alone
together again.

ELAINE: Don't bother, darling. (*Moving in front of* MORTI-
MER.) I'm going to run over to speak to Father. (*To*
MORTIMER.) Before I go out with you he likes to pray over
me a little. (*She runs to door and opens it, keeping her
hand on outside doorknob.*) I'll be right back—I'll cut
through the cemetery.

MORTIMER (*crosses to her, puts his hand on hers*): If the

prayer isn't too long, I'd have time to lead you beside distilled waters.

(ELAINE *laughs and exits.* MORTIMER *shuts door.*)

ABBY (*happily*): Mortimer, that's the first time I've ever heard you quote the Bible. We knew Elaine would be a good influence for you.
MORTIMER (*laughs, then turns to* ABBY): Oh, by the way— I'm going to marry her.
ABBY: What? Oh, darling! (*She runs and embraces him. Then she dashes toward kitchen door as* MORTIMER *crosses to window and looks out.*) Martha, Martha! (MARTHA *enters from kitchen.*) Come right in here. I've got the most wonderful news for you—Mortimer and Elaine are going to be married.
MARTHA: Married? Oh, Mortimer! (*She runs over to* MORTIMER, *who is looking out window, embraces and kisses him.* ABBY *comes to his left. He has his arms around both of them.*)
ABBY: We hoped it would happen just like this.
MARTHA: Well, Elaine must be the happiest girl in the world.
MORTIMER (*pulls curtain back, looks out window*): Happy! Just look at her leaping over those gravestones. (*As he looks out window* MORTIMER's *attention is suddenly drawn to something.*) Say! What's that?
MARTHA (*looking out over his shoulder*): What's what, dear?
MORTIMER: See that statue there. That's a *horundinida carnina.*
MARTHA: Oh, no, dear—that's Emma B. Stout ascending to heaven.
MORTIMER: No, no—standing on Mrs. Stout's left ear. That bird—that's a red-crested swallow. I've only seen one of those before in my life.
ABBY (*crosses around above table and pushes chair into table*): I don't know how you can be thinking about a bird now—what with Elaine and the engagement and everything.

MORTIMER: It's a vanishing species. (*He turns away from window.*) Thoreau was very fond of them. (*He crosses to desk to look through various drawers and papers.*) By the way, I left a large envelope around here last week. It was one of the chapters of my book on Thoreau. Have you seen it?

MARTHA (*pushing armchair into table*): Well, if you left it here it must be here somewhere.

ABBY: When are you going to be married? What are your plans? There must be something more you can tell us about Elaine.

MORTIMER: Elaine? Oh, yes, Elaine thought it was brilliant. (*He crosses to sideboard, looks through cupboards and drawers.*)

MARTHA: What was, dear?

MORTIMER: My chapter on Thoreau. (*He finds a bundle of papers in a drawer and takes them to table and looks through them.*)

ABBY: Well, when Elaine comes back I think we ought to have a little celebration. We must drink to your happiness. Martha, isn't there some of that Lady Baltimore cake left?

(*During last few speeches MARTHA has picked up pail from sideboard and her cape, hat and gloves from table.*)

MARTHA: Oh, yes!

ABBY: And I'll open a bottle of wine.

MARTHA (*as she exits to kitchen*): Oh, and to think it happened in this room!

MORTIMER (*has finished looking through papers, is gazing around room*): Now where could I have put that?

ABBY: Well, with your fiancée sitting beside you tonight, I do hope the play will be something you can enjoy for once. It may be something romantic. What's the name of it?

MORTIMER: *Murder Will Out.*

ABBY: Oh dear! (*She disappears into kitchen as MORTIMER goes on talking.*)

MORTIMER: When the curtain goes up the first thing you'll

see will be a dead body. (*He lifts window seat and sees one. Not believing it, he drops window seat again and starts downstage. He suddenly stops, then goes back, throws window seat open and stares in. He goes slightly mad for a moment. He backs away, then hears* ABBY *humming on her way into the room. He drops window seat again and holds it down, staring around the room.* ABBY *enters carrying a silencer and tablecloth which she puts on armchair, then picks up bundle of papers and returns them to drawer in sideboard.* MORTIMER *speaks in a somewhat strained voice.*) Aunt Abby!

ABBY (*at sideboard*): Yes, dear?

MORTIMER: You were going to make plans for Teddy to go to that . . . sanitarium—Happy Dale—

ABBY (*bringing legal papers from sideboard to* MORTIMER): Yes, dear, it's all arranged. Dr. Harper was here today and brought the papers for Teddy to sign. Here they are.

MORTIMER (*takes them from her*): He's got to sign them right away.

ABBY (*arranging silencer on table;* MARTHA *enters from kitchen door with table silver and plates on a tray, and sets tray on sideboard*): That's what Dr. Harper thinks. Then there won't be any legal difficulties after we pass on.

MORTIMER: He's got to sign them this minute! He's down in the cellar—get him up here right away.

MARTHA (*unfolding tablecloth*): There's no such hurry as that.

ABBY: No. When Teddy starts working on the canal you can't get his mind on anything else.

MORTIMER: Teddy's got to go to Happy Dale now—tonight.

MARTHA: Oh, no, dear, that's not until after we're gone.

MORTIMER: Right away, I tell you! Right away!

ABBY (*turning to* MORTIMER): Why, Mortimer, how can you say such a thing? Why, as long as we live we'll never be separated from Teddy.

MORTIMER (*trying to be calm*): Listen, darlings, I'm frightfully sorry, but I've got some shocking news for you. (*The* AUNTS *stop work and look at him with some interest.*) Now we've all got to try and keep our heads. You know we've sort of humored Teddy because we thought he was harmless.

MARTHA: Why he *is* harmless!

MORTIMER: He *was* harmless. That's why he has to go to Happy Dale. Why he has to be confined.

ABBY (*stepping to* MORTIMER): Mortimer, why have you suddenly turned against Teddy? Your own brother?

MORTIMER: You've got to know sometime. It might as well be now. Teddy's—killed a man!

MARTHA: Nonsense, dear.

MORTIMER (*rises and points to window seat*): There's a body in the window seat!

ABBY: Yes, dear, we know.

MORTIMER (*does a double-take as* ABBY *and* MARTHA *busy themselves again at table*): You *know?*

MARTHA: Of course, dear, but it has nothing to do with Teddy. (*Gets tray from sideboard—arranges silver and plates on table.*)

ABBY: Now, Mortimer, just forget about it—forget you ever saw the gentleman.

MORTIMER: *Forget?*

ABBY: We never dreamed you'd peek.

MORTIMER: But who is he?

ABBY: His name's Hoskins—Adam Hoskins. That's really all I know about him—except that he's a Methodist.

MORTIMER: That's all you know about him? Well, what's he doing here? What happened to him?

MARTHA: He died.

MORTIMER: Aunt Martha, men don't just get into window seats and die.

ABBY: No, he died first.

MORTIMER: Well, how?

ABBY: Oh, Mortimer, don't be so inquisitive. The gentleman died because he drank some wine with poison in it.

MORTIMER: How did the poison get in the wine?

MARTHA: Well, we put it in wine because it's less noticeable— when it's in tea it has a distinct odor.

MORTIMER: *You* put it in the wine?

ABBY: Yes. And I put Mr. Hoskins in the window seat because Dr. Harper was coming.

MORTIMER: So you knew what you'd done! You didn't want Dr. Harper to see the body!

ABBY: Well, not at tea—that wouldn't have been very nice. Now, Mortimer, you know the whole thing, just forget about it. I do think Martha and I have the right to our own little secrets. (*She crosses to sideboard to get two goblets from cupboard as* MARTHA *comes to table from sideboard with salt dish and pepper shaker.*)

MARTHA: And don't you tell Elaine! (*She gets third goblet from sideboard, then turns to* ABBY *who takes tray from sideboard.*) Oh, Abby, while I was out I dropped in on Mrs. Schultz. She's much better but she would like us to take Junior to the movies again.

ABBY: Well, we must do that tomorrow or next day.

MARTHA: Yes, but this time we'll go where we want to go. (*She starts for kitchen door.* ABBY *follows.*) Junior's not going to drag me into another one of those scary pictures. (*They exit into kitchen as* MORTIMER *wheels around and looks after them.* ABBY *shuts door.*)

MORTIMER (*dazed, looks around the room; his eyes come to rest on phone on desk; he crosses to it and dials a number; into phone*): City desk! . . . Hello, Al. Do you know who this is? . . . That's right. Say, Al, when I left the office, I told you where I was going, remember? Well, where did I say? . . . Uh-huh. Well, it would take me about half an hour to get to Brooklyn. What time have you got? (*He looks at his watch.*) That's right. I must be here. (*He hangs up, sits for a moment, then suddenly leaps off stool toward kitchen.*) Aunt Abby! Aunt Martha! Come in here! (*The two* AUNTS *bustle in.* MARTHA *has tray with plates, cups, saucers and soup cups.*) What are we going to do? What are we going to do?

MARTHA: What are we going to do about what, dear?

MORTIMER (*pointing to window seat*): There's a body in there.

ABBY: Yes—Mr. Hoskins.

MORTIMER: Well, good heavens, I can't turn you over to the police! But what am I going to do?

MARTHA: Well, for one thing, dear, stop being so excited.

ABBY: And for pity's sake stop worrying. We told you to forget the whole thing.

MORTIMER: Forget! My dear Aunt Abby, can't I make you realize that something has to be done?

ABBY (*a little sharply*): Now, Mortimer, you behave yourself. You're too old to be flying off the handle like this.

MORTIMER: But Mr. Hotchkiss—

ABBY (*on her way to sideboard, stops and turns to MORTIMER*): Hoskins, dear. (*She continues on her way to sideboard and gets napkins and rings from drawer. MARTHA puts her tray, with cups and plates, on table. MORTIMER continues speaking through this.*)

MORTIMER: Well, whatever his name is, you can't leave him there.

MARTHA: We don't intend to, dear.

ABBY (*crossing to table with napkins and rings*): No, Teddy's down in the cellar now digging the lock.

MORTIMER: You mean you're going to bury Mr. Hotchkiss in the cellar?

MARTHA (*stepping to him*): Oh, yes, dear—that's what we did with the others.

MORTIMER (*walking away*): No! You can't bury Mr.— (*Double-take; turns back to them.*)—others?

ABBY: The other gentlemen.

MORTIMER: When you say others—do you mean—others? More than one others?

MARTHA: Oh, yes, dear. Let me see, this is eleven. (*To ABBY.*) Isn't it, Abby?

ABBY: No, dear, this makes twelve.

(*MORTIMER backs away from them, stunned, toward phone stool at desk.*)

MARTHA: Oh, I think you're wrong, Abby. This is only eleven.

ABBY: No, dear, because I remember when Mr. Hoskins first
came in, it occurred to me that he would make just an
even dozen.

MARTHA: Well, you really shouldn't count the first one.

ABBY: Oh, *I* was counting the first one. So that makes it
twelve.

(*Phone rings.* MORTIMER, *in a daze, turns toward it and without picking up receiver, speaks.*)

MORTIMER: Hello! (*He comes to, picks up receiver.*) Hello.
Oh, hello, Al. My, it's good to hear your voice.

ABBY (*still holding out for a "twelve" count*): Well, anyway,
they're all down in the cellar—

MORTIMER (*to* AUNTS): Ssshhh— (*Into phone, as* AUNTS
*cross to sideboard and put candelabras from top to bottom
shelf.*) Oh, no, Al, I'm sober as a lark. I just called you
because I was feeling a little Pirandello—Piran—you
wouldn't know, Al. Look, I'm glad you called. Get hold of
George right away. He's got to review the play tonight. I
can't make it. No, Al, you're wrong. I'll tell you all about it
tomorrow. Well, George has got to cover the play tonight!
This is my department and I'm running it! You get ahold
of George! (*He hangs up and sits a moment trying to collect
himself.*) Now let's see, where were we? (*He suddenly
leaps from stool.*) TWELVE!

MARTHA: Yes, Abby thinks we ought to count the first one
and that makes twelve. (*She goes back to sideboard.*)

MORTIMER (*placing a chair; then takes* MARTHA'S *hand, leads
her to chair and sets her in it*): All right—now—who was
the first one?

ABBY (*crossing from above table to* MORTIMER): Mr. Midgely. He was a Baptist.

MARTHA: Of course, I still think we can't claim full credit for
him because he just died.

ABBY: Martha means without any help from us. You see, Mr.
Midgely came here looking for a room—

MARTHA: It was right after you moved to New York.

ABBY: And it didn't seem right for that lovely room to be go-

ing to waste when there were so many people who needed
it—

MARTHA: He was such a lonely old man. . . .

ABBY: All his kith and kin were dead and it left him so for-
lorn and unhappy—

MARTHA: We felt so sorry for him.

ABBY: And then when his heart attack came—and he sat
dead in that chair (*Pointing to armchair.*) looking so peaceful—remember, Martha—we made up our minds then
and there that if we could help other lonely old men
to that same peace—we would!

MORTIMER (*all ears*): He dropped dead right in that chair!
How awful for you!

MARTHA: Oh, no, dear. Why, it was rather like old times.
Your grandfather always used to have a cadaver or two
around the house. You see, Teddy had been digging in
Panama and he thought Mr. Midgely was a yellow fever
victim.

ABBY: That meant he had to be buried immediately.

MARTHA: So we all took him down to Panama and put him
in the lock. (*She rises, puts her arm around* ABBY.) Now
that's why we told you not to worry about it because we
know exactly what's to be done.

MORTIMER: And that's how all this started—that man walking in here and dropping dead.

ABBY: Of course, we realized we couldn't depend on that
happening again. So—

MARTHA (*crosses to* MORTIMER): You remember those jars
of poison that have been up on the shelves in Grandfather's laboratory all these years—?

ABBY: You know your Aunt Martha's knack for mixing things.
You've eaten enough of her piccalilli.

MARTHA: Well, dear, for a gallon of elderberry wine I take
one teaspoonful of arsenic, then add a half teaspoonful of
strychnine and then just a pinch of cyanide.

MORTIMER (*appraisingly*): Should have quite a kick.

ABBY: Yes! As a matter of fact one of our gentlemen found
time to say "How delicious!"

MARTHA: Well, I'll have to get things started in the kitchen.
ABBY (*to* MORTIMER): I wish you could stay for dinner.
MARTHA: I'm trying out a new recipe.
MORTIMER: I couldn't eat a thing.

(MARTHA *goes out to kitchen.*)

ABBY (*calling after* MARTHA): I'll come and help you, dear.
   (*She pushes chair into table.*) Well, I feel so much better
   now. Oh, you have to wait for Elaine, don't you? (*She
   smiles.*) How happy you must be. (*She goes to kitchen
   doorway.*) Well, dear, I'll leave you alone with your
   thoughts. (*She exits, shutting door.*)

(*The shutting of the door wakes* MORTIMER *from his trance.
   He crosses to window seat, kneels down, raises cover, looks
   in. Not believing, he lowers cover, rubs his eyes, raises
   cover again. This time he really sees Mr. Hoskins. Closes
   window seat hastily, rises, steps back. Runs over and closes
   drapes over window. Backs up to table. Sees water glass
   on table, picks it up, raises it to lips, suddenly remembers
   that poisoned wine comes in glasses, puts it down quickly.
   Crosses to cellar door, opens it.* ELAINE *enters; he closes
   cellar door with a bang. As* ELAINE *puts her bag on top
   of desk he looks at her, and it dawns on him that he knows
   her. He speaks with faint surprise.*)

MORTIMER: Oh, it's you.
ELAINE (*crosses to him, takes his hand*): Don't be cross,
   darling! Father could see that I was excited—so I told him
   about us and that made it hard for me to get away. But
   listen, darling—he's not going to wait up for me tonight.
MORTIMER (*looking at window seat*): You run along home,
   Elaine, and I'll call you up tomorrow.
ELAINE: Tomorrow!
MORTIMER (*irritated*): You know I always call you up every
   day or two.
ELAINE: But we're going to the theatre tonight.
MORTIMER: No—no we're not!

ELAINE: Well, why not?

MORTIMER (*turning to her*): Elaine, something's come up.

ELAINE: What, darling? Mortimer—you've lost your job!

MORTIMER: No—no—I haven't lost my job. I'm just not covering that play tonight. (*Pushing her.*) Now you run along home, Elaine.

ELAINE: But I've got to know what's happened. Certainly you can tell me.

MORTIMER: No, dear, I can't.

ELAINE: But if we're going to be married—

MORTIMER: Married?

ELAINE: Have you forgotten that not fifteen minutes ago you proposed to me?

MORTIMER (*vaguely*): I did? Oh—yes! Well, as far as I know that's still on. (*Urging her to go again.*) Now you run along home, Elaine. I've got to do something.

ELAINE: Listen, you can't propose to me one minute and throw me out of the house the next.

MORTIMER (*pleading*): I'm not throwing you out of the house, darling. Will you get out of here?

ELAINE: No, I won't get out of here. (MORTIMER *crosses toward kitchen.* ELAINE *crosses below to window seat.*) Not until I've had some kind of explanation. (ELAINE *is about to sit on window seat.* MORTIMER *grabs her by the hand. Phone rings.*)

MORTIMER: Elaine! (*He goes to phone, dragging* ELAINE *with him.*) Hello! Oh, hello, Al. Hold on a minute, will you? All right, it's important! But it can wait a minute, can't it? Hold on! (*He puts receiver on desk. Takes* ELAINE's *bag from top of desk and hands it to her. Then takes her by hand and leads her to door and opens it.*) Look, Elaine, you're a sweet girl and I love you. But I have something on my mind now and I want you to go home and wait until I call you.

ELAINE (*in doorway*): Don't try to be masterful.

MORTIMER (*annoyed to the point of being literate*): When we're married and I have problems to face I hope you're less tedious and uninspired!

ELAINE: And when we're married *if* we're married—I hope I find you adequate! (*She exits.* MORTIMER *runs out on porch after her.*)

MORTIMER: Elaine! Elaine! (*He runs back in, shutting door, crosses and kneels on window seat to open window. Suddenly remembers contents of window seat and leaps off it. Dashes into kitchen but remembers Al is on phone, re-enters immediately and crosses to phone.*) Hello, Al? Hello . . . hello. . . . (*He pushes hook down and starts to dial when doorbell rings. He thinks it's the phone.* ABBY *enters from kitchen.*) Hello. Hello, Al?

ABBY (*crossing to door and opening it*): That's the doorbell, dear, not the telephone. (MORTIMER *pushes hook down . . . dials.* MR. GIBBS *steps in doorway.*) How do you do? Come in.

GIBBS: I understand you have a room to rent.

(MARTHA *enters from kitchen. Puts Lazy Susan on sideboard, then goes to table.*)

ABBY: Yes. Won't you step in?

GIBBS (*stepping into room*): Are you the lady of the house?

ABBY: Yes, I'm Miss Brewster. And this is my sister, another Miss Brewster.

GIBBS: My name is Gibbs.

ABBY (*easing him to chair*): Oh, won't you sit down? I'm sorry we were just setting the table for dinner.

MORTIMER (*into phone*): Hello—let me talk to Al again. City desk. AL!! CITY DESK! WHAT? I'm sorry, wrong number. (*He hangs up and starts dialing again as* GIBBS *looks at him.* GIBBS *turns to* ABBY.)

GIBBS: May I see the room?

MARTHA: Why don't you sit down a minute and let's get acquainted.

GIBBS: That won't do much good if I don't like the room.

ABBY: Is Brooklyn your home?

GIBBS: Haven't got a home. Live in a hotel. Don't like it.

MORTIMER (*into phone*): Hello. City desk.

MARTHA: Are your family Brooklyn people?

GIBBS: Haven't got any family.

ABBY (*another victim*): All alone in the world?

GIBBS: Yep.

ABBY: Well, Martha— (MARTHA *goes happily to sideboard, gets bottle of wine from cupboard and a wineglass, and sets them on table.* ABBY *eases* GIBBS *into chair and continues speaking to him.*) Well, you've come to just the right house. Do sit down.

MORTIMER (*into phone*): Hello, Al? Mort. We got cut off. Al, I can't cover the play tonight—that's all there is to it, I can't!

MARTHA: What church do you go to? There's an Episcopal church practically next door. (*Her gesture toward window brings her to window seat and she sits.*)

GIBBS: I'm Presbyterian. Used to be.

MORTIMER (*into phone*): What's George doing in Bermuda? (*Rises and gets loud.*) Certainly I told him he could go to Bermuda—it's my department, isn't it? Well, you've got to get somebody. Who else is there around the office? (*He sits on second chair.*)

GIBBS (*annoyed; rises and walks in front of table*): Is there always this much noise?

MARTHA: Oh, he doesn't live with us.

(ABBY *sits.*)

MORTIMER (*into phone*): There must be somebody around the place. Look, Al, how about the office boy? You know, the bright one—the one we don't like? Well, you look around the office, I'll hold on.

GIBBS: I'd really like to see the room.

ABBY: It's upstairs. Won't you try a glass of our wine before we start up?

GIBBS: Never touch it.

MARTHA: We make this ourselves. It's elderberry wine.

GIBBS (*to* MARTHA): Elderberry wine. Hmmph. Haven't tasted elderberry wine since I was a boy. Thank you. (*He pulls armchair around and sits as* ABBY *uncorks bottle and starts to pour wine.*)

MORTIMER (*into phone*): Well, there must be some printers around. Look, Al, the fellow who sets my copy. He ought to know about what I'd write. His name is Joe. He's the third machine from the left. But, Al, he might turn out to be another Burns Mantle!

GIBBS (*to* MARTHA): Do you have your own elderberry bushes?

MARTHA: No, but the cemetery is full of them.

MORTIMER (*into phone*): No, I'm not drinking, but I'm going to start now.

GIBBS: Do you serve meals?

ABBY: We might, but first just see whether you like our wine.

(MORTIMER *hangs up, puts phone on top of desk. He sees wine on table. Goes to sideboard, gets glass, brings it to table and pours drink.* GIBBS *has his glass in hand and is getting ready to drink.*)

MARTHA (*sees* MORTIMER *pouring wine*): Mortimer! Eh eh eh eh! (GIBBS *stops and looks at* MARTHA. MORTIMER *pays no attention.*) Eh eh eh eh!

(*As* MORTIMER *raises glass to lips* ABBY *reaches up and pulls his arm down.*)

ABBY: Mortimer. Not that. (MORTIMER, *still dumb, puts his glass down on table. Then he suddenly sees* GIBBS *who has just got glass to his lips and is about to drink. He points across table at* GIBBS *and gives a wild cry.* GIBBS *looks at him, putting his glass down.* MORTIMER, *still pointing at* GIBBS, *goes around table toward him.* GIBBS, *seeing a madman, rises slowly and backs toward door, then turns and runs for it,* MORTIMER *following him.* GIBBS *opens door and* MORTIMER *pushes him out, closing door after him. Then he turns and leans on door in exhausted relief. Meantime,* MARTHA *has risen and crossed to armchair, while* ABBY *has risen and crossed to the center of the room.*)

ABBY (*greatly disappointed*): Now you've spoiled everything. (*She goes to sofa and sits.*)

(MARTHA *sits in armchair.* MORTIMER *looks from one to the other . . . then speaks to* ABBY.)

MORTIMER: You can't do things like that. I don't know how to explain this to you, but it's not only against the law. It's wrong! (*To* MARTHA.) It's not a nice thing to do. (MARTHA *turns away from him as* ABBY *has just done.*) People wouldn't understand. (*Points to door after* GIBBS.) *He* wouldn't understand.

MARTHA: Abby, we shouldn't have told Mortimer!

MORTIMER: What I mean is—well, this has developed into a very bad habit.

ABBY (*rises*): Mortimer, we don't try to stop you from doing things you like to do. I don't see why you should interfere with us.

(*Phone rings.* MORTIMER *answers.* MARTHA *rises.*)

MORTIMER: Hello? (*It's* AL *again.*) All right, I'll see the first act and I'll pan the hell out of it. But look, Al, you've got to do something for me. Get hold of O'Brien—our lawyer, the head of our legal department. Have him meet me at the theatre. Now, don't let me down. O.K. I'm starting now. (*He hangs up and turns to* AUNTS.) Look, I've got to go to the theatre. I can't get out of it. But before I go will you promise me something?

MARTHA: We'd have to know what it was first.

MORTIMER: I love you very much and I know you love me. You know I'd do anything in the world for you and I want you to do just this little thing for me.

ABBY: What do you want us to do?

MORTIMER: Don't *do* anything. I mean don't do *anything*. Don't let anyone in this house—and leave Mr. Hoskins right where he is.

MARTHA: Why?

MORTIMER: I want time to think—and I've got quite a little to think about. You know I wouldn't want anything to happen to you.

ABBY: Well, what on earth could happen to us?

MORTIMER (*beside himself*): Anyway—you'll do this for me, won't you?

MARTHA: Well—we were planning on holding services before dinner.

MORTIMER: Services!

MARTHA (*a little indignant*): Certainly. You don't think we'd bury Mr. Hoskins without a full Methodist service, do you? Why he was a Methodist.

MORTIMER: But can't that wait until I get back?

ABBY: Oh, then you could join us.

MORTIMER (*going crazy himself*): Yes! Yes!

ABBY: Oh, Mortimer, you'll enjoy the services—especially the hymns. (*To* MARTHA.) Remember how beautifully Mortimer used to sing in the choir before his voice changed?

MORTIMER: And remember, you're not going to let anyone in this house while I'm gone—it's a promise!

MARTHA: Well—

ABBY: Oh, Martha, we can do that now that Mortimer's co-operating with us. (*To* MORTIMER.) Well, all right, Mortimer.

(MORTIMER *heaves a sigh of relief. Crosses to sofa and gets his hat. Then on his way to opening door, he speaks.*)

MORTIMER: Have you got some paper? I'll get back just as soon as I can. (*Taking legal papers from coat pocket as he crosses.*) There's a man I've got to see.

(ABBY *has gone to desk for stationery. She hands it to* MORTIMER.)

ABBY: Here's some stationery. Will this do?

MORTIMER (*taking stationery*): That'll be fine. I can save

time if I write my review on the way to the theatre. (*He
exits.*)

(*The* Aunts *stare after him.* Martha *crosses and closes door.*
Abby *goes to sideboard and brings two candelabras to
table, then gets matches from sideboard—lights candles.*)

Martha: Mortimer didn't seem quite himself today.

Abby (*lighting candles*): Well, that's only natural—I think I
know why.

Martha (*lighting floor lamp*): Why?

Abby: He's just become engaged to be married. I suppose
that always makes a man nervous.

Martha (*during this speech she goes to first landing and
closes drapes over window, then comes downstairs and
turns off remote switch*): Well, I'm so happy for Elaine—
and their honeymoon ought to give Mortimer a real vacation. I don't think he got much rest this summer.

Abby: Well, at least he didn't go kiting off to China or Spain.

Martha: I could never understand why he wanted to go to
those places.

Abby: Well, I think to Mortimer the theatre has always
seemed pretty small potatoes. He needs something big to
criticize—something like the human race. (*She sets the
candelabras on the table.*)

Martha: Oh, Abby, if Mortimer's coming back for the
services for Mr. Hoskins, we'll need another hymnal.
There's one in my room. (*She starts upstairs.*)

Abby: You know, dear, it's really my turn to read the services,
but since you weren't here when Mr. Hoskins came I want
you to do it.

Martha (*pleased*): That's very nice of you, dear—but, are
you sure you want me to?

Abby: It's only fair.

Martha: Well, I think I'll wear my black bombazine and
Mother's old brooch. (*She starts up again when doorbell
rings.*)

ABBY (*crossing as far as desk*): I'll go, dear.

MARTHA (*hushed*): We promised Mortimer we wouldn't let anyone in.

ABBY (*trying to peer through curtained window in door*): Who do you suppose it is?

MARTHA: Wait a minute, I'll look. (*She turns to landing window and peeks out the curtains.*) It's two men—and I've never seen them before.

ABBY: Are you sure?

MARTHA: There's a car at the curb—they must have come in that.

ABBY: Let me look! (*She hurries upstairs. There is a knock on door. ABBY peeks out the curtains.*)

MARTHA: Do you recognize them?

ABBY: They're strangers to me.

MARTHA: We'll just have to pretend we're not at home. (*The two of them huddle back in corner of landing.*)

(*Another knock at the door, the knob is turned, and door swings slowly open. A tall man walks in, looking about the room. He has assurance and ease, as though the room were familiar to him. There is something sinister about the man—something that brings a slight chill in his presence. It is in his walk, his bearing, and his strange resemblance to Boris Karloff. From stair landing ABBY and MARTHA watch him, almost afraid to speak. Having completed his survey of the room, the man turns and addresses someone outside the front door.*)

JONATHAN: Come in, Doctor. (DR. EINSTEIN *enters. He is somewhat ratty in appearance. His face wears the benevolent smirk of a man who lives in a pleasant haze of alcohol. There is something about him that suggests the unfrocked priest. He stands just inside the door, timid but expectant.*) This is the home of my youth. As a boy I couldn't wait to escape from this place—now I'm glad to escape back into it.

EINSTEIN (*shutting door, his back to* AUNTS): Yah, Chonny,
it's a fine hide-out.

JONATHAN: The family must still live here. There's something
so unmistakably Brewster about the Brewsters. I hope
there's a fatted calf awaiting the return of the prodigal.

EINSTEIN: Yah, I'm hungry. (*He suddenly sees the fatted
calf in the form of the two glasses of wine on table.*) Look,
Chonny, drinks! (*He runs over to table.*)

JONATHAN: As though we were expected. A good omen.

(*They raise glasses to their lips as* ABBY *steps down a couple
of stairs and speaks.*)

ABBY: Who are you? What are you doing here?

(*They both put glasses down.* EINSTEIN *picks up his hat from
armchair, ready to run for it.* JONATHAN *turns to* ABBY.)

JONATHAN: Why, Aunt Abby! Aunt Martha! It's Jonathan.

MARTHA (*frightened*): You get out of here.

JONATHAN (*crossing to* AUNTS): I'm Jonathan—your nephew,
Jonathan.

ABBY: Oh, no, you're not. You're nothing like Jonathan, so
don't pretend you are! You just get out of here!

JONATHAN (*coming closer*): But I am Jonathan. And this
(*Indicating* EINSTEIN.) is Dr. Einstein.

ABBY: And he's not Dr. Einstein either.

JONATHAN: Not Dr. Albert Einstein—Dr. Herman Einstein.

ABBY (*down another step*): Who are you? You're not our
nephew, Jonathan.

JONATHAN (*peering at* ABBY's *outstretched hand*): I see
you're still wearing the lovely garnet ring that Grandma
Brewster bought in England. (ABBY *gasps, looks at ring.*)
And you, Aunt Martha, still the high collar—to hide the
scar where Grandfather's acid burned you.

(MARTHA's *hand goes to her throat. The* AUNTS *look at* JONA-
THAN. MARTHA *comes down a few steps to behind* ABBY.)

MARTHA: His voice is like Jonathan's.

ABBY (*stepping down to stage floor*): Have you been in an accident?

JONATHAN (*his hand goes to side of his face*): No—(*He clouds.*)—my face—Dr. Einstein is responsible for that. He's a plastic surgeon. He changes people's faces.

MARTHA (*comes down to* ABBY): But I've seen that face before (*To* ABBY.) Abby, remember when we took the little Schultz boy to the movies and I was so frightened? It was that face!

(JONATHAN *grows tense and looks toward* EINSTEIN. EINSTEIN *addresses* AUNTS.)

EINSTEIN: Easy, Chonny—easy! (*To* AUNTS.) Don't worry, ladies. The last five years I give Chonny three new faces. I give him another one right away. This last face—well, I saw that picture too—just before I operate. And I was intoxicated.

JONATHAN (*with a growing and dangerous intensity as he walks toward* EINSTEIN): You see, Doctor—you see what you've done to me. Even my own family—

EINSTEIN (*to calm him*): Chonny—you're home—in this lovely house— (*To* AUNTS.) How often he tells me about Brooklyn—about this house—about his aunts that he lofes so much. (*To* JONATHAN.) They know you, Chonny. (*To* ABBY, *as he leads her toward* JONATHAN.) You know it's Jonathan. Speak to him. Tell him so. (*He drifts beyond table.*)

ABBY: Well—Jonathan—it's been a long time—what have you been doing all these years?

MARTHA: Yes, Jonathan, where have you been?

JONATHAN (*recovering his composure*): Oh, England, South Africa, Australia—the last five years Chicago. Dr. Einstein and I were in business there together.

ABBY: Oh, we were in Chicago for the World's Fair.

MARTHA (*for want of something to say*): Yes—we found Chicago awfully warm.

EINSTEIN: Yah—it got hot for us too.

JONATHAN (*turning on the charm as he crosses above* ABBY, *placing himself between the* AUNTS): Well, it's wonderful to be in Brooklyn again. And you—Abby—Martha—you don't look a day older. Just as I remembered you—sweet —charming—hospitable. (*The* AUNTS *don't react too well to this charm.*) And dear Teddy—(*He indicates with his hand a lad of eight or ten.*)—did he get into politics? (*He turns to* EINSTEIN.) My little brother, Doctor, was determined to become President.

ABBY: Oh, Teddy's fine! Just fine! And Mortimer's well too.

JONATHAN (*a bit of a sneer*): I know about Mortimer. I've seen his picture at the head of his column. He's evidently fulfilled all the promise of his early nasty nature.

ABBY (*defensively*): We're very fond of Mortimer.

(*There is a slight pause. Then* MARTHA *speaks uneasily as she gestures toward door.*)

MARTHA: Well, Jonathan, it's very nice to have seen you again.

JONATHAN (*expanding*): Bless you, Aunt Martha. (*Crosses and sits in chair.*) It's good to be home again.

(*The* AUNTS *look at each other with dismay.*)

ABBY: Well, Martha, we mustn't let what's on the stove boil over. (*She starts to kitchen, then sees* MARTHA *isn't following. She crosses back and tugs at* MARTHA, *then crosses toward kitchen again.* MARTHA *follows, then speaks to* JONATHAN.)

MARTHA: Yes, if you'll excuse us for a minute, Jonathan. Unless you're in a hurry to go somewhere.

(JONATHAN *looks at her balefully.* MARTHA *walks around table, takes bottle of wine and puts it back in sideboard, then exits with* ABBY. ABBY, *who has been waiting in kitchen doorway for* MARTHA, *closes door after them.* EINSTEIN *crosses to behind* JONATHAN.)

EINSTEIN: Well, Chonny, where do we go from here? We got to think fast. The police. The police have got pictures of that face. I got to operate on you right away. We got to find some place for that—and we got to find a place for Mr. Spenalzo too.

JONATHAN: Don't waste any worry on that rat.

EINSTEIN: But, Chonny, we got a hot stiff on our hands.

JONATHAN (*flinging hat onto sofa*): Forget Mr. Spenalzo.

EINSTEIN: But you can't leave a dead body in the rumble seat. You shouldn't have killed him, Chonny. He's a nice fellow —he gives us a lift—and what happens?

JONATHAN (*remembering bitterly*): He said I looked like Boris Karloff! (*He starts for* EINSTEIN.) That's your work, Doctor. You did that to me!

EINSTEIN (*he's backed away from table*): Now, Chonny— we find a place somewhere—I fix you up quick!

JONATHAN: Tonight!

EINSTEIN: Chonny—I got to eat first. I'm hungry—I'm weak.

(*The* AUNTS *enter from kitchen.* ABBY *comes to* JONATHAN. MARTHA *remains in kitchen doorway.*)

ABBY: Jonathan—we're glad that you remembered us and took the trouble to come in and say hello. But you were never happy in this house and we were never happy while you were in it—so, we've just come in to say good-by.

JONATHAN (*takes a menacing step toward* ABBY; *then decides to try the charm again*): Aunt Abby, I can't say that your feeling toward me comes as a surprise. I've spent a great many hours regretting the many heartaches I must have given you as a boy.

ABBY: You were quite a trial to us, Jonathan.

JONATHAN: But my great disappointment is for Dr. Einstein. (EINSTEIN *is a little surprised.*) I promised him that no matter how rushed we were in passing through Brooklyn, I'd take the time to bring him here for one of Aunt Martha's homecooked dinners.

MARTHA (*rises to this a bit*): Oh . . .

ABBY: I'm sorry. I'm afraid there wouldn't be enough.

MARTHA: Abby, it's a pretty good-sized pot roast.

JONATHAN: Pot roast!

MARTHA: I think the least we can do is to—

JONATHAN: Thank you, Aunt Martha! We'll stay to dinner.

ABBY (*backing to kitchen door and not at all pleased*): Well, we'll hurry it along.

MARTHA: Yes! (*She exits into kitchen.*)

ABBY (*stopping in doorway*): Oh, Jonathan, if you want to freshen up—why don't you use the washroom in Grand-father's old laboratory?

JONATHAN (*crossing to her*): Is that still there?

ABBY: Oh, yes. Just as he left it. Well, I'll help Martha get things started—since we're all in a hurry. (*She exits into kitchen.*)

EINSTEIN: Well, we get a meal anyway.

JONATHAN: Grandfather's laboratory! (*Looks upstairs.*) And just as it was. Doctor, a perfect operating room.

EINSTEIN: Too bad we can't use it.

JONATHAN: After you've finished with me— Why, we could make a fortune here. The laboratory—that large ward in the attic—ten beds, Doctor—and Brooklyn is crying for your talents.

EINSTEIN: Vy vork yourself up, Chonny? Anyway, for Brook-lyn I think we're a year too late.

JONATHAN: You don't know this town, Doctor. Practically everybody in Brooklyn needs a new face.

EINSTEIN: But so many of the old faces are locked up.

JONATHAN: A very small percentage—and the boys in Brook-lyn are famous for paying generously to stay out of jail.

EINSTEIN: Take it easy, Chonny. Your aunts—they don't want us here.

JONATHAN: We're here for dinner, aren't we?

EINSTEIN: Yah—but after dinner?

JONATHAN (*crossing to sofa*): Leave it to me, Doctor. I'll handle it. Why, this house'll be our headquarters for years.

EINSTEIN: Oh, that would be beautiful, Chonny! This nice

quiet house. Those aunts of yours—what sweet ladies. I love them already. I get the bags, yah?

JONATHAN (*stopping him*): Doctor! We must wait until we're invited.

EINSTEIN: But you chust said that—

JONATHAN: We'll be invited.

EINSTEIN: And if they say no—?

JONATHAN: Doctor—two helpless old women—? (*He sits on sofa.*)

EINSTEIN (*takes bottle flask from hip pocket and unscrews cork as he crosses to window seat*): It's like comes true a beautiful dream— Only I hope you're not dreaming. (*He stretches out on window seat, taking a swig from bottle.*) It's so peaceful.

JONATHAN (*stretched out on sofa*): That's what makes this house so perfect for us—it's so peaceful.

(TEDDY *enters from cellar, blows a terrific blast on his bugle, as* JONATHAN *sits up.* TEDDY *marches to stairs and on up to first landing as the two men look at his tropical garb with some astonishment.*)

TEDDY: CHARGE! (*He rushes up the stairs and off.*)

(JONATHAN *watches him from foot of stairs.* EINSTEIN, *sitting on window seat, takes a hasty swig from his flask.*)

ACT II

SCENE: *The same. Later that night.* JONATHAN, *with an after-dinner cigar, is occupying armchair left of table, completely at his ease.* ABBY *and* MARTHA, *seated on window seat, are giving him a nervous attention in the attitude of people who wish their guests would go home.* EINSTEIN *is relaxed and happy in chair right of table. Dinner dishes have been cleared. There is a red cloth on the table, with a saucer to serve as ash tray for* JONATHAN. *The room is in order. All doors are closed, as are drapes over windows.*

JONATHAN: Yes, Aunties, those five years in Chicago were amongst the busiest and happiest of my life.

EINSTEIN: And from Chicago we go to South Bend, Indiana. (*He shakes his head as though he wishes they hadn't.*)

JONATHAN (*gives him a look*): They wouldn't be interested in our experience in Indiana.

ABBY: Well, Jonathan, you've led a very interesting life, I'm sure—but we really shouldn't have allowed you to talk so late. (*She starts to rise.* JONATHAN *seats her just by the tone of his voice.*)

JONATHAN: My meeting Dr. Einstein in London, I might say, changed the whole course of my life. You remember I had been in South Africa, in the diamond business—then Amsterdam, the diamond market. I wanted to go back to South Africa—and Dr. Einstein made it possible for me.

EINSTEIN: A good job, Chonny. (*To* AUNTS.) When we take off the bandages—his face look so different, the nurse had to introduce me.

JONATHAN: I loved that face. I still carry the picture with me. (*He produces snapshot-size picture from inside coat pocket, looks at it a moment, then hands it to* MARTHA. *She looks at it and hands it to* ABBY.)

ABBY: This looks more the way you used to look, but still I wouldn't know you.

JONATHAN: I think we'll go back to that face, Doctor.

EINSTEIN: Yah, it's safe now.

ABBY (*rising*): Well, I know you both want to get to—where you're going.

JONATHAN (*relaxing even more*): My dear aunts—I'm so full of that delicious dinner I'm unable to move a muscle.

EINSTEIN (*relaxing too*): Yah, it's nice here.

MARTHA (*rises*): After all—it's very late and—

(TEDDY *enters on balcony wearing his solar topee, carrying a book, open, and another topee.*)

TEDDY (*descending stairs*): I found it! I found it!

JONATHAN: What did you find, Teddy?

TEDDY: The story of my life—my biography. Here's the picture I was telling you about, General. (*He lays open book on table showing picture to* EINSTEIN.) Here we are, both of us. "President Roosevelt and General Goethals at Culebra Cut." That's me, General, and that's you.

EINSTEIN (*looks at picture*): My, how I've changed.

TEDDY (*looks at* EINSTEIN, *a little puzzled, but makes adjustment*): Well, you see that picture hasn't been taken yet. We haven't even started work on Culebra Cut. We're still digging locks. And now, General, we will both go to Panama and inspect the new lock. (*Hands him topee.*)

ABBY: No, Teddy—not to Panama.

EINSTEIN: We go some other time. Panama's a long way off.

TEDDY: Nonsense, it's just down in the cellar.

JONATHAN: The cellar?

MARTHA: We let him dig the Panama Canal in the cellar.

TEDDY (*severely*): General Goethals, as President of the United States, Commander in Chief of the Army and Navy and the man who gave you this job, I demand that you accompany me on the inspection of the new lock.

JONATHAN: Teddy! I think it's time you went to bed.

TEDDY: I beg your pardon! (*He walks to* JONATHAN, *putting on his pince-nez as he crosses.*) Who are you?

JONATHAN: I'm Woodrow Wilson. Go to bed.

TEDDY: No—you're not Wilson. But your face is familiar. Let me see— You're not anyone I know now. Perhaps later— On my hunting trip to Africa—yes, you look like someone I might meet in the jungle.

(JONATHAN *stiffens.* ABBY *crosses in front of* TEDDY, *getting between him and* JONATHAN.)

ABBY: It's your brother, Jonathan, dear.

MARTHA (*rising*): He's had his face changed.

TEDDY: So that's it—a nature faker!

ABBY: And perhaps you had better go to bed, Teddy—Jonathan and his friend have to go back to their hotel.

JONATHAN (*rising*): General Goethals (*To* EINSTEIN.), inspect the canal.

EINSTEIN (*rising*): All right, Mr. President. We go to Panama.

TEDDY: Bully! Bully! (*He crosses to cellar door, opens it.*) Follow me, General. (EINSTEIN *goes up to left of* TEDDY; TEDDY *taps solar topee in* EINSTEIN's *hand, then taps his own head.*) It's down south you know. (*He exits downstairs.*)

(EINSTEIN *puts on topee, which is too large for him. Then turns in cellar doorway.*)

EINSTEIN: Well—bon voyage. (*He exits, closing door.*)

JONATHAN: Aunt Abby, I must correct your misapprehension. You spoke of our hotel. We have no hotel. We came directly here—

MARTHA: Well, there's a very nice little hotel just three blocks down the—

JONATHAN (*cutting her off*): Aunt Martha, this is my home.

ABBY: But, Jonathan, you can't stay here. We need our rooms.

JONATHAN: You need them?

ABBY: Yes, for our lodgers.

JONATHAN (*alarmed*): Are there lodgers in this house?

MARTHA: Well, not just now, but we plan to have some.

JONATHAN (*cutting her off again*): Then my old room is still free.

ABBY: But, Jonathan, there's no place for Dr. Einstein.

JONATHAN (*crosses to table, drops cigar ashes into saucer*): He'll share the room with me.

ABBY: No, Jonathan, I'm afraid you can't stay here.

(JONATHAN *grinds cigar out in saucer, then starts toward* AUNTS. *They back around table,* MARTHA *first.* JONATHAN *turns back and crosses around table to* ABBY.)

JONATHAN: Dr. Einstein and I need a place to sleep. You

remembered, this afternoon, that as a boy I could be disagreeable. It wouldn't be very pleasant for any of us if—

MARTHA (*frightened*): Perhaps we'd better let them stay here tonight—

ABBY: Well, just overnight, Jonathan.

JONATHAN: That's settled. Now, if you'll get my room ready—

MARTHA (*starting upstairs, ABBY following*): It only needs airing out.

ABBY: We keep it ready to show our lodgers. I think you and Dr. Einstein will find it comfortable.

(JONATHAN *follows them to first landing and leans on newel post.* AUNTS *are on balcony.*)

JONATHAN: You have a most distinguished guest in Dr. Einstein. I'm afraid you don't appreciate his skill. But you will. In a few weeks you'll see me looking like a very different Jonathan.

MARTHA: He can't operate on you here.

JONATHAN (*ignoring her*): When Dr. Einstein and I get organized—when we resume practice— Oh, I forgot to tell you. We're turning Grandfather's laboratory into an operating room. We expect to be quite busy.

ABBY: Jonathan, we will not let you turn this house into a hospital.

JONATHAN (*laughing*): A hospital—heavens no! It will be a beauty parlor.

EINSTEIN (*enters excitedly from cellar*): Hey, Chonny, down in the cellar— (*He sees* AUNTS *and stops.*)

JONATHAN: Dr. Einstein—my dear aunts have invited us to live with them.

EINSTEIN: Oh, you fixed it?

ABBY: Well, you're sleeping here tonight.

JONATHAN: Please get our room ready immediately.

MARTHA: Well—

ABBY: For tonight.

(*They exit through arch.* JONATHAN *comes to foot of stairs.*)

EINSTEIN: Chonny, when I go down in the cellar, what do you think I find?

JONATHAN: What?

EINSTEIN: The Panama Canal.

JONATHAN (*disgusted*): The Panama Canal.

EINSTEIN: It just fits Mr. Spenalzo. It's a hole Teddy dug. Six feet long and four feet wide.

JONATHAN (*gets the idea; opens cellar door and looks down*): Down there!

EINSTEIN: You'd think they knew we were bringing Mr. Spenalzo along. That's hospitality.

JONATHAN (*closing cellar door*): Rather a good joke on my aunts—their living in a house with a body buried in the cellar.

EINSTEIN: How do we get him in?

JONATHAN: Yes. We can't just walk him through the door. (*He sees window in wall.*) We'll drive the car up between the house and the cemetery—then when they've gone to *bed*, we'll bring Mr. Spenalzo in through the window.

EINSTEIN (*taking out bottle flask*): Bed! Just think, we've got a bed tonight! (*He starts swigging.*)

JONATHAN (*grabbing his arm*): Easy, Doctor. Remember you're operating tomorrow. And this time you'd better be sober.

EINSTEIN: I fix you up beautiful.

JONATHAN: And if you don't— (*Gives* EINSTEIN *shove to door.*)

ABBY (*entering on balcony with* MARTHA): Jonathan! Your room is ready.

JONATHAN: Then you can go to bed. We're moving the car up behind the house.

MARTHA: It's all right where it is—until morning.

JONATHAN (*at opened door*): I don't want to leave it in the street—that might be against the law. (*He exits.*)

(EINSTEIN *follows him out, closing door.* ABBY *and* MARTHA *start downstairs and reach below table.*)

MARTHA: Abby, what are we going to do?

ABBY: Well, we're not going to let them stay more than one night in this house for one thing. What would the neighbors think? People coming in here with one face and going out with another.

MARTHA: What are we going to do about Mr. Hoskins?

ABBY (*crosses to window seat; MARTHA follows*): Oh, Mr. Hoskins. It can't be very comfortable for him in there. And he's been so patient, the poor dear. Well, I think Teddy had better get Mr. Hoskins downstairs right away.

MARTHA (*adamant*): Abby—I will not invite Jonathan to the funeral services.

ABBY: Oh, no. We'll wait until they've gone to bed and then come down and hold the services.

TEDDY (*enters from cellar, gets book from table*): General Goethals was very pleased. He says the Canal is just the right size.

ABBY: Teddy! Teddy, there's been another yellow fever victim.

TEDDY (*takes off pince-nez*): Dear me—this will be a shock to the General.

MARTHA: Then we mustn't tell him about it.

TEDDY (*to MARTHA*): But it's his department.

ABBY: No, we mustn't tell him, Teddy. It would just spoil his visit.

TEDDY: I'm sorry, Aunt Abby. It's out of my hands—he'll have to be told. Army regulations, you know.

ABBY: No, Teddy, we *must* keep it a secret.

MARTHA: Yes!

TEDDY (*he loves them*): A state secret?

ABBY: Yes, a state secret.

MARTHA: Promise?

TEDDY (*what a silly request*): You have the word of the President of the United States. (*Crosses his heart.*) Cross my heart and hope to die. (*He spits.*) Now let's see—(*Puts pince-nez on, then puts arms around both AUNTS.*) how are we going to keep it a secret?

ABBY: Well, Teddy, you go back down in the cellar and

when I turn out the lights—when it's all dark—you come up and take the poor man down to the Canal. (*Urging him to cellar door, which he opens.*) Now go along, Teddy.

MARTHA: And we'll come down later and hold services.

TEDDY (*in doorway*): You may announce the President will say a few words. (*He starts, then turns back.*) Where is the poor devil?

MARTHA: He's in the window seat.

TEDDY: It seems to be spreading. We've never had yellow fever there before. (*He exits, closing door.*)

ABBY: Martha, when Jonathan and Dr. Einstein come back, let's see if we can get them to go to bed right away.

MARTHA: Yes. Then by the time they're asleep, we'll be dressed for the funeral. (*Sudden thought.*) Abby, I've never even seen Mr. Hoskins.

ABBY: Oh, my goodness, that's right—you were out. Well, you just come right over and see him now. (*They go to window seat, ABBY first.*) He's really very nice looking—considering he's a Methodist. (*As they go to lift window seat, JONATHAN throws window open from outside with a bang. AUNTS scream and draw back. JONATHAN puts his head in through drapes.*)

JONATHAN: We're bringing—the luggage through here.

ABBY: Jonathan, your room's waiting for you. You can go right up.

(*Two dusty bags and a large instrument case are passed through window by EINSTEIN. JONATHAN puts them on floor.*)

JONATHAN: I'm afraid we don't keep Brooklyn hours—but you two run along to bed.

ABBY: Now, you must be very tired, both of you—and we don't go to bed this early.

JONATHAN: Well, you should. It's time I came home to take care of you.

MARTHA: We weren't planning to go until—

JONATHAN (*stronger*): Aunt Martha, did you hear me say

go to bed! (AUNT MARTHA *starts upstairs as* EINSTEIN *comes in through window and picks up two bags.* JONATHAN *takes instrument case and puts it on top of window seat.*) The instruments can go to the laboratory in the morning. (EINSTEIN *starts upstairs.* JONATHAN *closes window.* MARTHA *is part way upstairs as* EINSTEIN *passes her.*) Now, then, we're all going to bed. (*He crosses as* ABBY *goes to light switch.*)

ABBY: I'll wait till you're up, then turn out the lights.

(JONATHAN, *going upstairs, sees* EINSTEIN *pausing at balcony door.* MARTHA *is almost up to balcony.*)

JONATHAN: Another flight, Doctor. (*To* MARTHA.) Run along, Aunt Martha. (MARTHA *hurries into doorway.* EINSTEIN *goes through arch to third floor.* JONATHAN *continues on to end of balcony.* ABBY *is at light switch.*) All right, Aunt Abby.

ABBY (*stalling; looks toward cellar door*): I'll be right up.

JONATHAN: Now, Aunt Abby. Turn out the lights!

(ABBY *turns switch, plunging stage into darkness except for spot shining down stairway from arch.* ABBY *goes upstairs to her door where* MARTHA *is waiting. She takes a last frightened look at* JONATHAN *and exits.* MARTHA *closes door.* JONATHAN *goes off through arch, closing that door. A street light shines through main door on stage floor.* TEDDY *opens cellar door, then turns on cellar light, outlining him in doorway. He crosses to window seat and opens it—the window seat cover gives out its usual rusty squeak. He reaches in and pulls Mr. Hoskins. He gets Mr. Hoskins over his shoulder and, leaving window seat open, crosses to cellar door and goes down into cellar with Mr. Hoskins. Closes door.* JONATHAN *and* EINSTEIN *come through arch. It is dark. They light matches and listen at the aunts' door for a moment.* EINSTEIN *speaks.*)

EINSTEIN: All right, Chonny.

(*The matches go out.* JONATHAN *lights another and they come down to foot of stairs.*)

JONATHAN: I'll get the window open. You go around and hand him through.

EINSTEIN: No, he's too heavy for me. You go outside and push—I stay here and pull. Then together we get him down to Panama.

JONATHAN: All right. (*He blows out match, crosses and opens door.*) I'll take a look around outside the house. When I tap on the glass, you open the window.

EINSTEIN: All right. (JONATHAN *exits, closing door.* EINSTEIN *lights match. He bumps into table and match goes out. He feels his way from there. We hear ejaculations and noise.* EINSTEIN *has fallen into window seat. In window seat he lights another match and slowly rises up to a sitting position and looks around. He blows out match and hauls himself out of window seat.*) Who left dis open? Dummkopf! (*We hear the creak of the cover as he closes it. In the darkness we hear a tap on window.* EINSTEIN *opens it. Then in a hushed voice.*) Chonny? O.K. Allez Oop. Wait—wait a minute. You lost a leg somewhere. Ach—now I got him. Come on—ugh—(*He falls on floor and there is a crash of a body and the sound of a "Sshhhh" from outside.*) That was me, Chonny. I schlipped.

JONATHAN: Be more careful.

(*Pause.*)

EINSTEIN: Well, his shoe came off. . . . All right, Chonny. I got him! (*There is a knock at door.*) Chonny! Somebody at the door! Go quick. NO. I manage here—go quick!

(*A second knock at door. A moment's silence and we hear the creak of window seat as* EINSTEIN *puts Mr. Spenalzo in Mr. Hoskins' place. A third knock, as* EINSTEIN *struggles with body. A fourth knock and then the creak of the window seat as* EINSTEIN *closes it. He scurries around to*

beside desk, keeping low to avoid being seen through door.
ELAINE *enters, calling softly.*)

ELAINE: Miss Abby! Miss Martha! (*In the dim path of light she calls toward balcony.*) Miss Abby! Miss Martha! (*Suddenly* JONATHAN *steps through door and closes it. The noise swings* ELAINE *around and she gasps.*) Uhhh! Who is it? Is that you, Teddy? (JONATHAN *comes toward her as she backs into chair.*) Who *are* you?

JONATHAN: Who are *you?*

ELAINE: I'm Elaine Harper—I live next door!

JONATHAN: Then what are you doing here?

ELAINE: I came over to see Miss Abby and Miss Martha.

JONATHAN (*to* EINSTEIN, *without turning;* EINSTEIN *has crept to light switch after passing* JONATHAN *in dark*): Turn on the lights, Doctor. (*The lights go on.* ELAINE *gasps as she sees* JONATHAN *and sits in chair.* JONATHAN *looks at her for a moment.*) You chose rather an untimely moment for a social call. (*He crosses toward window seat, looking for Spenalzo, but doesn't see him. He looks up, behind table. Looks out window, then comes back into the room.*)

ELAINE (*trying to summon courage*): I think you'd better explain what *you're* doing here.

JONATHAN: We happen to live here.

ELAINE: You *don't* live here. I'm in this house every day and I've never seen you before. (*Frightened.*) Where are Miss Abby and Miss Martha? What have you done to them?

JONATHAN: Perhaps we'd better introduce ourselves. This— (*Indicating.*)—is Dr. Einstein.

ELAINE (*looks at* EINSTEIN): Dr. Einstein? (*She turns back to* JONATHAN. EINSTEIN, *behind her back, is gesturing to* JONATHAN *the whereabouts of Spenalzo.*)

JONATHAN: A surgeon of great distinction—(*He looks under table for Spenalzo, and not finding him—*) and something of a magician.

ELAINE: And I suppose you're going to tell me you're Boris Kar——

JONATHAN: I'm Jonathan Brewster.

ELAINE (*drawing back almost with fright*): Oh—you're Jonathan!

JONATHAN: I see you've heard of me.

(EINSTEIN *drifts to front of sofa.*)

ELAINE: Yes—just this afternoon for the first time.

JONATHAN (*stepping toward her*): And what did they say about me?

ELAINE: Only that there was another brother named Jonathan —that's all that was said. (*Calming.*) Well, that explains everything. Now that I know who you are—(*Running to door.*) I'll be running along back home. (*The door is locked. She turns to* JONATHAN.) If you'll kindly unlock the door.

(JONATHAN *goes to her, then, before reaching her, he turns to door and unlocks it.* EINSTEIN *drifts down to chair. As* JONATHAN *opens door part way,* ELAINE *starts toward it. He turns and stops her with a gesture.*)

JONATHAN: "That explains everything"? Just what did you mean by that? Why did you come here at this time of night?

ELAINE: I thought I saw someone prowling around the house. I suppose it was you.

JONATHAN (*closes door and locks it, leaving key in lock*): You thought you saw someone prowling around the house?

ELAINE: Yes—weren't you outside? Isn't that your car?

JONATHAN: You saw someone at the car?

ELAINE: Yes.

JONATHAN (*coming toward her as she backs away*): What else did you see?

ELAINE: Just someone walking around the house to the car.

JONATHAN: What else did you see?

ELAINE: Just that—that's all. That's why I came over here. I wanted to tell Miss Abby to call the police. But if it was you, and that's your car, I don't need to bother Miss Abby.

I'll be running along. (*She takes a step toward door. He steps in her path.*)

JONATHAN: What was the man doing at the car?

ELAINE (*excited*): I don't know. You see I was on my way over here.

JONATHAN: I think you're lying.

EINSTEIN: I think she tells the truth, Chonny. We let her go now, huh?

JONATHAN: I think she's lying. Breaking into a house this time of night. I think she's dangerous. She shouldn't be allowed around loose. (*He seizes* ELAINE's *arm. She screams.*)

ELAINE: Take your hands off me—

JONATHAN: Doctor—

(*As* EINSTEIN *starts,* TEDDY *enters from cellar, shutting door. He looks at* JONATHAN, *then speaks to* EINSTEIN.)

TEDDY (*simply*): It's going to be a private funeral. (*He goes upstairs to first landing.* ELAINE *crosses to desk, dragging* JONATHAN *with her.*)

ELAINE: Teddy! Teddy! Tell these men who I am.

TEDDY (*turns and looks at her*): That's my daughter—Alice. (*Dashing upstairs.*) CHARGE!

ELAINE (*struggling to get away from* JONATHAN): No! No! Teddy!

(JONATHAN *has* ELAINE's *arm twisted in back of her, his other hand is over her mouth.*)

JONATHAN: Doctor! Your handkerchief! (*As* EINSTEIN *hands him a handkerchief,* JONATHAN *releases his hand from* ELAINE's *mouth to take it. She screams. He puts his hand over her mouth again; spies the cellar door and speaks to* EINSTEIN.) The cellar!

(EINSTEIN *runs and opens cellar door. Then he runs back and turns off light switch, putting stage in darkness.* JONA-

THAN *pushes* ELAINE *through cellar doorway.* EINSTEIN
runs back and down cellar stairs with ELAINE. JONATHAN
shuts door, remaining on stage as the AUNTS *enter on balcony above in their mourning clothes. Everything is in
complete darkness except for street lamp.*)

ABBY: What's the matter?
MARTHA: What's happening down there? (MARTHA *shuts her
door and* ABBY *puts on lights from switch on balcony. They
look down at the room a moment, then come downstairs,
speaking as they come.*)
ABBY: What's the matter? (*Reaching foot of stairs as she sees*
JONATHAN.) What are you doing?
JONATHAN: We caught a burglar—a sneak thief. Go back to
your room.
ABBY: We'll call the police.
JONATHAN: We've called the police. We'll handle this. Go
back to your room. Do you hear me?

(*The doorbell rings, followed by several knocks.* ABBY *runs
and opens door.* MORTIMER *enters with suitcase. At the
same time,* ELAINE *runs out of cellar and into* MORTIMER'S
arms. JONATHAN *makes a grab for* ELAINE *but misses.* EIN-
STEIN *sneaks behind* JONATHAN.)

ELAINE: Mortimer! (*He drops suitcase.*) Where have you
been?
MORTIMER: To the Nora Bayes Theatre and I should have
known better. (*He sees* JONATHAN.) My God! I'm still there.
ABBY: This is your brother Jonathan—and this is Dr. Ein-
stein.
MORTIMER (*surveys his* AUNTS *all dressed in black*): I know
this isn't a nightmare, but what is it?
JONATHAN: I've come back home, Mortimer.
MORTIMER (*looking at him, and then to* ABBY): Who did
you say this was?
ABBY: It's your brother Jonathan. He's had his face changed.
Dr. Einstein performed the operation.

MORTIMER (*taking a closer look at* JONATHAN): Jonathan! Jonathan, you always were a horror, but do you have to look like one?

(JONATHAN *takes a step toward him.* EINSTEIN *pulls on his sleeve.* ELAINE *and* MARTHA *draw back to desk.*)

EINSTEIN: Easy, Chonny! Easy.

JONATHAN: Mortimer, have you forgotten the things I used to do to you when we were boys? Remember the time you were tied to the bedpost—the needles under your fingernails—?

MORTIMER: By God, it is Jonathan. Yes, I remember. I remember you as the most detestable, vicious, venomous form of animal life I ever knew.

(JONATHAN *grows tense.* ABBY *steps between them.*)

ABBY: Now don't you two boys start quarrelling again the minute you've seen each other.

MORTIMER: There won't be any fight, Aunt Abby. Jonathan, you're not wanted here—get out!

JONATHAN: Dr. Einstein and I have been invited to stay.

MORTIMER: Not in this house.

ABBY: Just for tonight.

MORTIMER: I don't want him anywhere near me.

ABBY: But we did invite them for tonight, and it wouldn't be very nice to go back on our word.

MORTIMER (*unwillingly*): All right, tonight. But the first thing in the morning—out! (*He picks up his suitcase.*) Where are they sleeping?

ABBY: We put them in Jonathan's old room.

MORTIMER: That's my old room. (*Starts upstairs.*) I'm sleeping in that room. I'm here to stay.

MARTHA: Oh, Mortimer, I'm so glad.

EINSTEIN: Chonny, we sleep down here.

MORTIMER: You bet your life you sleep down here.

EINSTEIN (*to* JONATHAN): You sleep on the sofa and I sleep on the window seat.

(*At the mention of window seat,* MORTIMER *has reached the landing; after hanging his hat on hall tree, he turns and comes slowly downstairs, speaking as he reaches the floor and crossing over to window seat.*)

MORTIMER: The window seat! Oh, well, let's not argue about it. That window seat's good enough for me for tonight. I'll sleep on the window seat. (*As* MORTIMER *crosses above table,* EINSTEIN *makes a gesture as though to stop him from going to window seat, but he's too late. He turns to* JONATHAN *as* MORTIMER *sits on window seat.*)

EINSTEIN: You know, Chonny—all this argument—it makes me think of Mr. Spenalzo.

JONATHAN: Spenalzo! (*He looks around for Spenalzo again. Realizing it would be best for them to remain downstairs, he speaks to* MORTIMER.) Well, now, Mortimer— It really isn't necessary to inconvenience you like this—we'll sleep down here.

MORTIMER (*rising*): Jonathan, your sudden consideration for me is very unconvincing.

EINSTEIN (*goes upstairs to landing*): Come along, Chonny. We get our things out of the room, eh?

MORTIMER: Don't bother, Doctor!

JONATHAN: By the way, Doctor, I've completely lost track of Mr. Spenalzo.

MORTIMER: Who's this Mr. Spenalzo?

EINSTEIN (*from landing*): Just a friend of ours Chonny's been looking for.

MORTIMER: Well, don't bring anyone else in here!

EINSTEIN: It's all right, Chonny. While we pack I tell you all about it. (*He goes on up and through arch.* JONATHAN *starts upstairs.*)

ABBY: Mortimer, you don't have to sleep down here. I can go in with Martha and you can take my room.

JONATHAN (*he has reached the balcony*): No trouble at all,

Aunt Abby. We'll be packed in a few minutes. And then you can have the room, Mortimer. (*He exits through arch.*)

(MORTIMER *walks to sofa.* MARTHA *crosses to armchair and as* MORTIMER *speaks she picks up sport shoe belonging to Spenalzo, that* EINSTEIN *put there in blackout scene, unnoticed by anyone. She pretends to dust hem of her dress.*)

MORTIMER: You're just wasting your time—I told you I'm sleeping down here.

ELAINE (*leaps up from stool into* MORTIMER's *arms*): Mortimer!

MORTIMER: What's the matter with you, dear?

ELAINE (*semi-hysterical*): I've almost been killed.

MORTIMER: You've almost been— (*He looks quickly at the* AUNTS.) Abby! Martha!

MARTHA: No! It was Jonathan.

ABBY: He mistook her for a sneak thief.

ELAINE: No, it was more than that. He's some kind of maniac. Mortimer, I'm afraid of him.

MORTIMER: Why, darling, you're trembling. (*Seats her on sofa. To* AUNTS.) Have you got any smelling salts?

MARTHA: No, but do you think some hot tea, or coffee—?

MORTIMER: Coffee. Make some for me, too—and some sandwiches. I haven't had any dinner.

MARTHA: We'll make something for both of you.

(MORTIMER *starts to question* ELAINE *as* ABBY *takes off her hat and gloves and puts them on sideboard. Talks to* MARTHA *at the same time.*)

ABBY: Martha, we can leave our hats downstairs here, now.

MORTIMER (*turns and sees her*): You weren't going out somewhere, were you? Do you know what time it is? It's after twelve. (*The word twelve rings a bell.*) TWELVE! (*He turns to* ELAINE.) Elaine, you've got to go home!

ELAINE: Whaa-t?

ABBY: Why, you wanted some sandwiches for you both. It won't take a minute. (*She exits into kitchen.*)

(MORTIMER *is looking at* ELAINE *with his back to* MARTHA. MARTHA *crosses over to him with shoe in hand by her side.*)

MARTHA: Why, don't you remember—we wanted to celebrate your engagement? (*She punctuates the word "engagement" by pointing the shoe at* MORTIMER's *back. She looks at the shoe in amazement, wondering how it ever got in her hand. She stares at it a moment [the other two do not see it, of course], then puts it on top of the table. Finally dismissing it she turns to* MORTIMER *again.*) That's what we'll do, dear. We'll make a nice supper for both of you. (*She starts out kitchen door, then turns back.*) And we'll open a bottle of wine! (*She exits kitchen door.*)

MORTIMER (*vaguely*): All right. (*Suddenly changes his mind and runs to kitchen door.*) No WINE! (*He closes the door and comes back as* ELAINE *rises from the sofa to him. She is still very upset.*)

ELAINE: Mortimer! What's going on in this house?

MORTIMER (*suspicious*): What do you mean—what's going on in this house?

ELAINE: You were supposed to take me to dinner and the theatre tonight—you called it off. You asked me to marry you—I said I would—and five minutes later you threw me out of the house. Tonight, just after your brother tries to strangle me, you want to chase me home. Now, listen, Mr. Brewster—before I go home, I want to know where I stand. Do you love me?

MORTIMER (*taking her hands*): I love you very much, Elaine. In fact I love you so much I can't marry you.

ELAINE: Have you suddenly gone crazy?

MORTIMER: I don't think so but it's just a matter of time. (*They both sit on sofa as* MORTIMER *begins to explain.*) You see, insanity runs in my family. (*He looks upstairs and toward kitchen.*) It practically gallops. That's why I can't marry you, dear.

ELAINE: Now wait a minute, you've got to do better than that.

MORTIMER: No, dear—there's a strange taint in the Brewster blood. If you really knew my family it's—well—it's what you'd expect if Strindberg had written *Hellzapoppin*.

ELAINE: Now just because Teddy is a little—

MORTIMER: No, it goes way back. The first Brewster—the one who came over on the *Mayflower*. You know in those days the Indians used to scalp the settlers—he used to scalp the Indians.

ELAINE: Mortimer, that's ancient history.

MORTIMER: No, the whole family. . . (*He rises and points to a picture of Grandfather over the sideboard.*) Take my grandfather—he tried his patent medicines out on dead people to be sure he wouldn't kill them.

ELAINE: He wasn't so crazy. He made a million dollars.

MORTIMER: And then there's Jonathan. You just said he was a maniac—he tried to kill you.

ELAINE (*rises, crosses to him*): But he's your brother, not you. I'm in love with you.

MORTIMER: And there's Teddy, too. You *know* Teddy. He thinks he's Roosevelt. No, dear, no Brewster should marry. I realize now that if I'd met my father in time I'd have stopped him.

ELAINE: Now, darling, all this doesn't prove *you're* crazy. Look at your aunts—they're Brewsters, aren't they?—and the sanest, sweetest people I've ever known.

MORTIMER (*walking to window seat, speaking as he goes*): Well, even they have their peculiarities.

ELAINE (*turning*): Yes, but what lovely peculiarities! Kindness, generosity—human sympathy—

(MORTIMER *sees* ELAINE'S *back is to him. He lifts window seat to take a peek, and sees Mr. Spenalzo instead of Mr. Hoskins. He puts window seat down again and staggers to table, and leans on it.*)

MORTIMER (*to himself*): There's another one!

ELAINE (*turning to* MORTIMER): Oh, Mortimer, there are
  plenty of others. You can't tell me anything about your
  aunts.

MORTIMER: I'm not going to. (*Crossing to her.*) Look, Elaine,
  you've got to go home. Something very important has just
  come up.

ELAINE: Up, from where? We're here alone together.

MORTIMER: I know I'm acting irrationally, but just put it down
  to the fact that I'm a mad Brewster.

ELAINE: If you think you're going to get out of this by pre-
  tending you're insane—you're crazy. Maybe you're not
  going to marry me, but I'm going to marry you. I love you,
  you dope.

MORTIMER (*urging her to door*): Well, if you love me will you
  get the hell out of here!

ELAINE: Well, at least take me home, won't you? I'm afraid.

MORTIMER: Afraid! A little walk through the cemetery?

ELAINE (*crosses to door, then changing tactics, turns to* MOR-
  TIMER): Mortimer, will you kiss me good night?

MORTIMER (*holding out arms*): Of course, dear. (*What*
  MORTIMER *plans to be a desultory peck,* ELAINE *turns into
  a production number. He comes out of it with no less of
  poise.*) Good night, dear. I'll call you up in a day or two.

ELAINE (*walks to door in a cold fury, opens it and turns to*
  MORTIMER): You—you critic! (*She slams door after her.*)

(MORTIMER *looks at the door helplessly, then turns and stalks
  to the kitchen door.*)

MORTIMER (*in doorway*): Aunt Abby! Aunt Martha! Come in
  here!

ABBY (*offstage*): We'll be in in a minute, dear.

MORTIMER: Come in here now! (*He stands down by window
  seat.*)

ABBY (*enters from kitchen*): Yes, dear, what is it? Where's
  Elaine?

MORTIMER: I thought you promised me not to let anyone in
  this house while I was gone!

(*The following speeches overlap.*)

ABBY: Well, Jonathan just walked in—
MORTIMER: I don't mean Jonathan—
ABBY: And Dr. Einstein was with him—
MORTIMER: I don't mean Dr. Einstein. Who's that in the
    window seat?
ABBY: We told you—Mr. Hoskins.

(MORTIMER *throws open the window seat and steps back.*)

MORTIMER: It is *not* Mr. Hoskins.

(ABBY, *a little puzzled, walks to window seat and looks in;
    then speaks very simply.*)

ABBY: Who can that be?
MORTIMER: Are you trying to tell me you've never seen
    this man before?
ABBY: I certainly am. Why, this is a fine how do you do! It's
    getting so anybody thinks he can walk into this house.
MORTIMER: Now Aunt Abby, don't you try to get out of this.
    That's another one of your gentlemen!
ABBY: Mortimer, how can you say such a thing! That man's
    an impostor! And if he came here to be buried in our cellar
    he's mistaken.
MORTIMER: Oh, Aunt Abby, you admitted to me that you put
    Mr. Hoskins in the window seat.
ABBY: Yes, I did.
MORTIMER: Well, this man couldn't have just got the idea
    from Mr. Hoskins. By the way—where is Mr. Hoskins? (*He
    looks toward cellar door.*)
ABBY: He must have gone to Panama.
MORTIMER: Oh, you buried him?
ABBY: No, not yet. He's just down there waiting for the
    services, poor dear. We haven't had a minute what with
    Jonathan in the house. (*At the mention of* JONATHAN'S
    name, MORTIMER *closes the window seat.*) Oh, dear. We've

always wanted to hold a double funeral (*Crossing to kitchen door.*) but I will not read services over a total stranger.

MORTIMER (*going up to her*): A stranger! Aunt Abby, how can I believe you? There are twelve men in the cellar and you admit you poisoned them.

ABBY: Yes, I did. But you don't think I'd stoop to telling a fib. Martha! (*She exits into kitchen.*)

(*At the same time* JONATHAN *enters through the arch onto balcony and comes down quickly to foot of stairs. He sees* MORTIMER *and crosses to him.*)

JONATHAN: Oh, Mortimer—I'd like to have a word with you.

MORTIMER (*standing up to him*): A word's about all you'll have time for, Jonathan, because I've decided you and your doctor friend are going to have to get out of this house just as quickly as possible.

JONATHAN (*smoothly*): I'm glad you recognize the fact that you and I can't live under the same roof—but you've arrived at the wrong solution. Take your suitcase and get out! (*He starts to walk by* MORTIMER, *anxious to get to the window seat, but* MORTIMER *makes a big sweep around table and comes back to him.*)

MORTIMER: Jonathan! You're beginning to bore me. You've played your one-night stand in Brooklyn—move on!

JONATHAN: My dear Mortimer, just because you've graduated from the back fence to the typewriter, don't think you've grown up. . . . (*He takes a sudden step around* MORTIMER *and gets to the window seat and sits.*) I'm staying, and you're leaving—and I mean now!

MORTIMER (*crossing to him*): If you think I can be frightened —if you think there's anything I fear—

JONATHAN (*he rises, they stand facing each other*): I've lived a strange life, Mortimer. But it's taught me one thing—to be afraid of nothing! (*They glare at each other with equal courage when* ABBY *marches in from kitchen, followed by* MARTHA.)

ABBY: Martha, just look and see what's in that window seat.

(*Both* MEN *throw themselves on the window seat simultaneously.*)

MORTIMER:
JONATHAN: } Now, Aunt Abby!

(MORTIMER *turns his head slowly to* JONATHAN, *light dawning on his face. He rises with smiling assurance.*)

MORTIMER: Jonathan, let Aunt Martha see what's in the window seat. (JONATHAN *freezes dangerously.* MORTIMER *crosses to* ABBY.) Aunt Abby, I owe you an apology. (*He kisses her on forehead.*) I have very good news for you. Jonathan is leaving. He's taking Dr. Einstein and their cold companion with him. (JONATHAN *rises, but holds his ground.*) Jonathan, you're my brother. You're a Brewster. I'm going to give you a chance to get away and take the evidence with you—you can't ask for more than that. (JONATHAN *doesn't move.*) Very well—in that case I'll have to call the police. (MORTIMER *crosses to phone and picks it up.*)

JONATHAN: Don't reach for that telephone. Are you still giving me orders after seeing what's happened to Mr. Spenalzo?

MARTHA: Spenalzo?

ABBY: I knew he was a foreigner.

JONATHAN: Remember what happened to Mr. Spenalzo can happen to you too.

(*There is a knock on door.* ABBY *crosses and opens it and* OFFICER O'HARA *sticks his head in.*)

O'HARA: Hello, Miss Abby.

ABBY: Oh, Officer O'Hara. Is there something we can do for you?

(MORTIMER *puts phone down and drifts down to* O'HARA. JONATHAN *turns.*)

O'HARA: I saw your lights on and thought there might be
   sickness in the house. (*He sees* MORTIMER.) Oh, you got
   company—I'm sorry I disturbed you.
MORTIMER (*taking* O'HARA *by the arm*): No, no, come in.
ABBY: Yes, come in.
MARTHA (*crossing to door*): Come right in, Officer O'Hara.
   (MORTIMER *leads* O'HARA *in a couple of steps and shuts
   door.*) This is our nephew, Mortimer.
O'HARA: Pleased to meet you.

(JONATHAN *starts toward kitchen.*)

ABBY (*stopping* JONATHAN): And this is another nephew,
   Jonathan.
O'HARA (*crosses below* MORTIMER *and gestures to* JONATHAN
   with his night stick): Pleased to make your acquaintance.
   (JONATHAN *ignores him.* O'HARA *speaks to* AUNTS.) Well,
   it must be nice havin' your nephews visitin' you. Are they
   going to stay with you for a bit?
MORTIMER: I'm staying. My brother Jonathan is just leaving.

(JONATHAN *starts for stairs.* O'HARA *stops him.*)

O'HARA: I've met you here before, haven't I?
ABBY: I'm afraid not. Jonathan hasn't been home for years.
O'HARA: Your face looks familiar to me. Maybe I seen a pic-
   ture of you somewheres.
JONATHAN: I don't think so. (*He hurries upstairs.*)
MORTIMER: Yes, Jonathan, I'd hurry if I were you. Your
   things are all packed anyway, aren't they?
O'HARA: Well, you'll be wanting to say your good-bys. I'll be
   running along.
MORTIMER: What's the rush? I'd like to have you stick around
   until my brother goes.

(JONATHAN *exits through arch.*)

O'HARA: I just dropped in to make sure everything was all
   right.

MORTIMER: We're going to have some coffee in a minute. Won't you join us?

ABBY: Oh, I forgot the coffee. (*She goes out to kitchen.*)

MARTHA (*crossing to kitchen door*): Well, I'd better make some more sandwiches. I ought to know your appetite by this time, Officer O'Hara. (*She goes out to kitchen.*)

O'HARA: Don't bother. I'm due to ring in in a few minutes.

MORTIMER: You can have a cup of coffee with us. My brother will be gone soon. (*He leads* O'HARA *to armchair.*) Sit down.

O'HARA: Say—ain't I seen a photograph of your brother around here someplace?

MORTIMER: I don't think so. (*He sits at table.*)

O'HARA: He certainly reminds me of somebody.

MORTIMER: He looks like somebody you've probably seen in the movies.

O'HARA: I never go to the movies. I hate 'em! My mother says the movies is a bastard art.

MORTIMER: Yes, it's full of them. Your, er, mother said that?

O'HARA: Yeah. My mother was an actress—a stage actress. Perhaps you heard of her—Peaches Latour.

MORTIMER: It sounds like a name I've seen on a program. What did she play?

O'HARA: Well, her big hit was *Mutt and Jeff.* Played it for three years. I was born on tour—the third season.

MORTIMER: You were?

O'HARA: Yep. Sioux City, Iowa. I was born in the dressing room at the end of the second act, and Mother made the finale.

MORTIMER: What a trouper! There must be a good story in your mother—you know, I write about the theatre.

O'HARA: You do? Saay! You're not Mortimer Brewster, the dramatic critic!

MORTIMER: Yes.

O'HARA: Well, I certainly am glad to meet you. (*He moves his hat and stick preparatory to shaking hands with* MORTIMER. *He also picks up the sport shoe which* MARTHA *has left on the table. He looks at it just for a split second and puts it on the end of table.* MORTIMER *sees it and stares at it.*) Say, Mr. Brewster—we're in the same line of business.

MORTIMER (*still intent on shoe*): We are?

O'HARA: Yeah. I'm a playwright. Oh, this being on the police force is just temporary.

MORTIMER: How long have you been on the force?

O'HARA: Twelve years. I'm collecting material for a play.

MORTIMER: I'll bet it's a honey.

O'HARA: Well, it ought to be. With all the drama I see being a cop. Mr. Brewster—you got no idea what goes on in Brooklyn.

MORTIMER: I think I have. (*He puts the shoe under his chair, then looks at his watch, then looks toward balcony.*)

O'HARA: Say, what time you got?

MORTIMER: Ten after one.

O'HARA: Gee, I gotta ring in. (*He starts for door but MORTIMER stops him.*)

MORTIMER: Wait a minute, O'Hara. On that play of yours— I may be able to help you. (*Sits him in chair.*)

O'HARA (*ecstasy*): You would! (*Rises.*) Say, it was fate my walking in here tonight. Look—I'll tell you the plot!

(*At this point* JONATHAN *enters on the balcony followed by* DR. EINSTEIN. *They each have a bag. At the same moment* ABBY *enters from the kitchen. Helpful as the* COP *has been,* MORTIMER *does not want to listen to his plot. As he backs away from him he speaks to* JONATHAN *as they come downstairs.*)

MORTIMER: Oh, you're on your way, eh? Good! You haven't got much time, you know.

ABBY: Well, everything's just about ready. (*Sees* JONATHAN *and* EINSTEIN *at foot of stairs.*) Oh, you leaving now, Jonathan? Good-by. Good-by, Dr. Einstein. (*She sees instrument case above window seat.*) Oh, doesn't this case belong to you?

(*This reminds* MORTIMER *of Mr. Spenalzo, also.*)

MORTIMER: Yes, Jonathan—you can't go without *all* of your things. (*Now to get rid of* O'HARA. *He turns to him.*) Well, O'Hara, it was nice meeting you. I'll see you again and we'll talk about your play.

O'HARA (*refusing to leave*): Oh, I'm not leaving now, Mr. Brewster.

MORTIMER: Why not?

O'HARA: Well, you just offered to help me with my play, didn't you? You and me are going to write my play together.

MORTIMER: I can't do that, O'Hara—I'm not a creative writer.

O'HARA: I'll do the creating. You just put the words to it.

MORTIMER: But, O'Hara—

O'HARA: No, sir, Mr. Brewster. I ain't leaving this house till I tell you the plot. (*He crosses and sits on window seat.*)

JONATHAN (*starting for door*): In that case, Mortimer . . . we'll be running along.

MORTIMER: Don't try that. You can't go yet. You've got to take *everything* with you, you know. (*He turns and sees* O'HARA *on window seat and runs to him.*) Look, O'Hara, you run along now, eh? My brother's just going—

O'HARA: I can wait. I've been waiting twelve years.

(MARTHA *enters from kitchen with a tray of coffee and sandwiches.*)

MARTHA: I'm sorry I was so long.

MORTIMER: Don't bring that in here. O'Hara, would you join us for a bite in the kitchen?

MARTHA: The kitchen?

ABBY (*to* MARTHA): Jonathan's leaving.

MARTHA: Oh. Well, that's nice. Come along, Officer O'Hara. (*She exits to kitchen.*)

(O'HARA *gets to kitchen doorway as* ABBY *speaks.*)

ABBY: Sure you don't mind eating in the kitchen, Mr. O'Hara?

O'HARA: And where else would you eat?

ABBY: Good-by, Jonathan, nice to have seen you again.

(O'HARA *exits to kitchen, followed by* ABBY. MORTIMER
crosses to kitchen doorway and shuts door, then turns to
JONATHAN.)

MORTIMER: I'm glad you came back to Brooklyn, Jonathan,
because it gives me a chance to throw you out—and the
first one out is your boy friend, Mr. Spenalzo.

(*He lifts up window seat. As he does so,* O'HARA, *sandwich
in hand, enters from kitchen.* MORTIMER *drops window
seat.*)

O'HARA: Look, Mr. Brewster, we can talk in here.
MORTIMER (*pushing him into kitchen*): Coming right out.
JONATHAN: I might have known you'd grow up to write a
play with a policeman.
MORTIMER (*from kitchen doorway*): Get going now—all
three of you. (*He exits, shutting door.*)

(JONATHAN *puts bag down and crosses to window seat.*)

JONATHAN: Doctor, this affair between my brother and me
has got to be settled.
EINSTEIN (*crossing to window seat for instrument case and
bringing it back to foot of stairs*): Now, Chonny, we got
trouble enough. Your brother gives us a chance to get
away—what more could you ask?
JONATHAN: You don't understand. (*He lifts window seat.*)
This goes back a good many years.
EINSTEIN (*foot of stairs*): Now, Chonny, let's get going.
JONATHAN (*harshly*): We're not going. We're going to sleep
right here tonight.
EINSTEIN: With a cop in the kitchen and Mr. Spenalzo in the
window seat?
JONATHAN: That's all he's got on us. (*Puts window seat
down.*) We'll take Mr. Spenalzo down and dump him in the
bay, and come right back here. Then if he tries to inter-
fere—

EINSTEIN: Now, Chonny.

JONATHAN: Doctor, you know when I make up my mind—

EINSTEIN: Yeah—when you make up your mind, you lose your head. Brooklyn ain't a good place for you.

JONATHAN (*peremptorily*): Doctor!

EINSTEIN: O.K. We got to stick together. (*He crosses to bags.*) Someday we get stuck together. If we're coming back here do we got to take these with us?

JONATHAN: No. Leave them here. Hide them in the cellar. Move fast! (*He moves to bags as* EINSTEIN *goes down cellar with instrument case.*) Spenalzo can go out the same way he came in! (*He kneels on window seat and looks out. Then as he starts to lift window seat,* EINSTEIN *comes in from the cellar with some excitement.*)

EINSTEIN: Hey, Chonny, come quick!

JONATHAN (*crossing to him*): What's the matter?

EINSTEIN: You know that hole in the cellar?

JONATHAN: Yes.

EINSTEIN: We got an *ace* in the hole. Come on, I show you. (*They both exit into cellar.* JONATHAN *shuts door.*)

(MORTIMER *enters from kitchen, sees their bags still there. He opens window seat and sees Spenalzo. Then he puts his head out window and yells.*)

MORTIMER: Jonathan! Jonathan! (JONATHAN *comes through cellar door unnoticed by* MORTIMER *and crosses to back of him.* EINSTEIN *comes down into center of room.*) Jonathan!

JONATHAN (*quietly*): Yes, Mortimer.

MORTIMER (*leaping backward to table*): Where have you two been? I thought I told you to get—

JONATHAN: We're not going.

MORTIMER: Oh, you're not? You think I'm not serious about this, eh? Do you want O'Hara to know what's in that window seat?

JONATHAN: We're staying here.

MORTIMER (*crossing around table to kitchen door*): All right! You asked for it. This gets me rid of you and Officer

O'Hara at the same time. (*Opens kitchen door, yells out.*)
Officer O'Hara, come in here!

JONATHAN: If you tell O'Hara what's in the window seat, I'll
tell him what's down in the cellar.

(MORTIMER *closes kitchen door quickly.*)

MORTIMER: The cellar?

JONATHAN: There's an elderly gentleman down there who
seems to be very dead.

MORTIMER: What were you doing down in the cellar?

EINSTEIN: What's *he* doing down in the cellar?

(O'HARA'S *voice is heard offstage.*)

O'HARA: No, thanks, ma'am. They were fine. I've had plenty.

JONATHAN: Now what are you going to say to O'Hara?

(O'HARA *walks in kitchen door.*)

O'HARA: Say, Mr. Brewster, your aunts want to hear it too.
Shall I get them in here?

MORTIMER (*pulling him*): No, O'Hara, you can't do that
now. You've got to ring in.

(O'HARA *stops as* MORTIMER *opens the door.*)

O'HARA: The hell with ringing in. I'll get your aunts in here
and tell you the plot. (*He starts for kitchen door.*)

MORTIMER (*grabbing him*): No, O'Hara, not in front of all
these people. We'll get together alone, someplace later.

O'HARA: How about the back room at Kelly's?

MORTIMER: Fine! You go ring in, and I'll meet you at Kelly's.

JONATHAN (*at window seat*): Why don't you two go down
in the cellar?

O'HARA: That's all right with me. (*Starts for cellar door.*)
Is this the cellar?

MORTIMER (*grabbing him again, pushing toward door*):

Nooo! We'll go to Kelly's. But you're going to ring in on the way.

O'HARA (*as he exits*): All right, that'll only take a couple of minutes. (*He's gone.*)

(MORTIMER *takes his hat from hall tree and crosses to open door.*)

MORTIMER: I'll ditch this guy and be back in five minutes. I'll expect to find you gone. (*Changes his mind.*) Wait for me. (*He exits.*)

(EINSTEIN *sits at table.*)

JONATHAN: We'll wait for him, Doctor. I've waited a great many years for a chance like this.

EINSTEIN: We got him right where we want him. Did he look guilty!

JONATHAN (*rising*): Take the bags back up to our room, Doctor.

(EINSTEIN *gets bags and reaches foot of stairs with them.* ABBY *and* MARTHA *enter from kitchen.* ABBY *speaks as she enters.*)

ABBY: Have they gone? (*Sees* JONATHAN *and* EINSTEIN.) Oh —we thought we heard somebody leave.

JONATHAN: Just Mortimer, and he'll be back in a few minutes. Is there any food left in the kitchen? I think Dr. Einstein and I would enjoy a bite.

MARTHA: But you won't have time.

ABBY: No, if you're still here when Mortimer gets back he won't like it.

EINSTEIN: He'll like it. He's gotta like it.

JONATHAN: Get something for us to eat while we bury Mr. Spenalzo in the cellar.

MARTHA (*crossing to below table*): Oh no!

ABBY: He can't stay in our cellar. No, Jonathan, you've got to take him with you.

JONATHAN: There's a friend of Mortimer's downstairs waiting for him.

ABBY: A friend of Mortimer's?

JONATHAN: He and Mr. Spenalzo will get along fine together. They're both dead.

MARTHA: They must mean Mr. Hoskins.

EINSTEIN: Mr. Hoskins?

JONATHAN: You know about what's downstairs?

ABBY: Of course we do, and he's no friend of Mortimer's. He's one of our gentlemen.

EINSTEIN: Your chentlemen?

MARTHA: And we won't have any strangers buried in our cellar.

JONATHAN (*noncomprehending*): But Mr. Hoskins—

MARTHA: Mr. Hoskins isn't a stranger.

ABBY: Besides, there's no room for Mr. Spenalzo. The cellar's crowded already.

JONATHAN: Crowded? With what?

ABBY: There are twelve graves down there now.

(*The two men draw back in amazement.*)

JONATHAN: Twelve graves!

ABBY: That leaves very little room and we're going to need it.

JONATHAN: You mean you and Aunt Martha have murdered—?

ABBY: Murdered! Certainly not. It's one of our charities.

MARTHA (*indignantly*): Why, what we've been doing is a mercy.

ABBY (*gesturing outside*): So you just take your Mr. Spenalzo out of here.

JONATHAN (*still unable to believe*): You've done that—here in this house—(*Points to floor.*) and you've buried them down there!

EINSTEIN: Chonny—we've been chased all over the world— they stay right here in Brooklyn and do just as good as you do.

JONATHAN (*facing him*): What?

EINSTEIN: You've got twelve and they've got twelve.

JONATHAN (*slowly*): I've got thirteen.

EINSTEIN: No, Chonny, twelve.

JONATHAN: Thirteen! (*Counting on fingers.*) There's Mr. Spenalzo. Then the first one in London—two in Johannesburg
—one in Sydney—one in Melbourne—two in San Francisco
—one in Phoenix, Arizona—

EINSTEIN: Phoenix?

JONATHAN: The filling station. The three in Chicago and the
one in South Bend. That makes thirteen!

EINSTEIN: But you can't count the one in South Bend. He died
of pneumonia.

JONATHAN: He wouldn't have got pneumonia if I hadn't shot
him.

EINSTEIN (*adamant*): No, Chonny, he died of pneumonia. He
don't count.

JONATHAN: He counts with me. I say thirteen.

EINSTEIN: No, Chonny. You got twelve and they got twelve.
(*Crossing to aunts.*) The old ladies are just as good as you
are.

(*The two* AUNTS *smile at each other happily.* JONATHAN *turns,
facing the three of them and speaks menacingly.*)

JONATHAN: Oh, they are, are they? Well, that's easily taken
care of. All I need is one more, that's all—just one more.

(MORTIMER *enters hastily, closing door behind him, and turns
to them with a nervous smile.*)

MORTIMER: Well, here I am!

(JONATHAN *turns and looks at him with the widening eyes of
someone who has just solved a problem.*)

ACT III

SCENE 1

SCENE: *The scene is the same. Still later that night. The window seat is open and we see that it's empty. The armchair has been shifted to right of table. The drapes over the windows are closed. All doors except cellar are closed. ABBY's hymnal and black gloves are on sideboard. MARTHA's hymnal and gloves are on table. Otherwise the room is the same. As the curtain rises we hear a row from the cellar, through the open door. The speeches overlap in excitement and anger until the AUNTS appear on the stage, from cellar door.*

MARTHA: You stop doing that!

ABBY: This is our house and this is our cellar and you can't do that.

EINSTEIN: Ladies! Please! Go back upstairs where you belong.

JONATHAN: Abby! Martha! Go upstairs!

MARTHA: There's no use your doing what you're doing because it will just have to be undone.

ABBY: I tell you we won't have it and you'd better stop it right now.

MARTHA (*entering from cellar*): All right! You'll find out. You'll find out whose house this is. (*She crosses to door, opens it and looks out, then closes it.*)

ABBY (*entering*): I'm warning you! You'd better stop it! (*To* MARTHA.) Hasn't Mortimer come back yet?

MARTHA: No.

ABBY: It's a terrible thing to do—to bury a good Methodist with a foreigner. (*She crosses to window seat.*)

MARTHA (*crossing to cellar door*): I will not have our cellar desecrated!

ABBY (*drops window seat*): And we promised Mr. Hoskins a full Christian funeral. Where do you suppose Mortimer went?

76

MARTHA: I don't know, but he must be doing something—because he said to Jonathan, "You just wait, I'll settle this."

ABBY (*walking to sideboard*): Well, he can't very well settle it while he's out of the house. That's all we want settled—what's going on down there.

(MORTIMER *enters, closes door.*)

MORTIMER (*as one who has everything settled*): All right. Now, where's Teddy?

(*The* AUNTS *are very much annoyed with* MORTIMER.)

ABBY: Mortimer, where have you been?

MORTIMER: I've been over to Dr. Gilchrist's. I've got his signature on Teddy's commitment papers.

MARTHA: Mortimer, what is the matter with you?

ABBY: Running around getting papers signed at a time like this!

MARTHA: Do you know what Jonathan's doing?

ABBY: He's putting Mr. Hoskins and Mr. Spenalzo in together.

MORTIMER (*to cellar door*): Oh, he is, is he? Well, let him. (*He shuts cellar door.*) Is Teddy in his room?

MARTHA: Teddy won't be any help.

MORTIMER: When he signs these commitment papers I can tackle Jonathan.

ABBY: What have they got to do with it?

MORTIMER: You had to go and tell Jonathan about those twelve graves. If I can make Teddy responsible for those I can protect you, don't you see?

ABBY: No, I don't see. And we pay taxes to have the police protect us.

MORTIMER (*going upstairs*): I'll be back down in a minute.

ABBY (*takes gloves and hymnal from table*): Come, Martha. We're going for the police.

(MARTHA *gets her gloves and hymnal from sideboard. They both start to door.*)

MORTIMER (*on landing*): All right. (*He turns and rushes downstairs to door before they can reach it.*) The police! You can't go for the police.

MARTHA: Why can't we?

MORTIMER (*near door*): Because if you tell the police about Mr. Spenalzo they'd find Mr. Hoskins too (*Crosses to* MARTHA.) and that might make them curious, and they'd find out about the other twelve gentlemen.

ABBY: Mortimer, we know the police better than you do. I don't think they'd pry into our private affairs if we asked them not to.

MORTIMER: But if they found your twelve gentlemen they'd have to report to headquarters.

MARTHA (*pulling on her gloves*): I'm not so sure they'd bother. They'd have to make out a very long report—and if there's one thing a policeman hates to do, it's to write.

MORTIMER: You can't depend on that. It might leak out! And you couldn't expect a judge and jury to understand.

MARTHA: Oh, Judge Cullman would.

ABBY (*drawing on her gloves*): We know him very well.

MARTHA: He always comes to church to pray—just before election.

ABBY: And he's coming here to tea some day. He promised.

MARTHA: Oh, Abby, we must speak to him again about that. (*To* MORTIMER.) His wife died a few years ago and it's left him very lonely.

ABBY: Well, come along, Martha. (*She starts toward door.* MORTIMER *gets there first.*)

MORTIMER: No! You can't do this. I won't let you. You can't leave this house, and you can't have Judge Cullman to tea.

ABBY: Well, if you're not going to do something about Mr. Spenalzo, we are.

MORTIMER: I am going to do something. We may have to call the police in later, but if we do, I want to be ready for them.

MARTHA: You've got to get Jonathan out of this house!

ABBY: And Mr. Spenalzo, too!

MORTIMER: Will you please let me do this my own way? (*He starts upstairs.*) I've got to see Teddy.

ABBY (*facing* MORTIMER *on stairs*): If they're not out of here by morning, Mortimer, we're going to call the police.

MORTIMER (*on balcony*): They'll be out, I promise you that! Go to bed, will you? And for God's sake get out of those clothes—you look like Judith Anderson. (*He exits into hall, closing door.*)

(*The* AUNTS *watch him off.* MARTHA *turns to* ABBY.)

MARTHA: Well, Abby, that's a relief, isn't it?

ABBY: Yes—if Mortimer's really going to do something at last, it just means Jonathan's going to a lot of unnecessary trouble. We'd better tell him. (ABBY *starts to cellar door as* JONATHAN *comes in. They meet in front of sofa. His clothes are dirty.*) Oh, Jonathan—you might as well stop what you're doing.

JONATHAN: It's all done. Did I hear Mortimer?

ABBY: Well, it will just have to be undone. You're all going to be out of this house by morning. Mortimer's promised.

JONATHAN: Oh, are we? In that case, you and Aunt Martha can go to bed and have a pleasant night's sleep.

MARTHA (*always a little frightened by* JONATHAN, *starts upstairs*): Yes. Come, Abby.

(ABBY *follows* MARTHA *upstairs.*)

JONATHAN: Good night, Aunties.

ABBY: Not good night, Jonathan. Good-by. By the time we get up you'll be out of this house. Mortimer's promised.

MARTHA (*on balcony*): And he has a way of doing it too!

JONATHAN: Then Mortimer is back?

ABBY: Oh, yes, he's up here talking to Teddy.

MARTHA: Good-by, Jonathan.

ABBY: Good-by, Jonathan.

JONATHAN: Perhaps you'd better say good-by to Mortimer.

ABBY: Oh, you'll see Mortimer.

JONATHAN (*sitting on stool*): Yes—I'll see Mortimer.

(ABBY *and* MARTHA *exit.* JONATHAN *sits without moving. There is murder in his thought.* EINSTEIN *enters from cellar. He dusts off his trouser cuffs, lifting his leg, and we see he is wearing Spenalzo's sport shoes.*)

EINSTEIN: Whew! That's all fixed up. Smooth like a lake. No-body'd ever know they were down there. (JONATHAN *still sits without moving.*) That bed feels good already. Forty-eight hours we didn't sleep. (*Crossing to second stair.*) Come on, Chonny, let's go up, yes?

JONATHAN: You're forgetting, Doctor.

EINSTEIN: Vat?

JONATHAN: My brother Mortimer.

EINSTEIN: Chonny—tonight? We do that tomorrow or the next day.

JONATHAN (*just able to control himself*): No, tonight! Now!

EINSTEIN (*down to floor*): Chonny, please—I'm tired—and tomorrow I got to operate.

JONATHAN: Yes, you're operating tomorrow, Doctor. But tonight we take care of Mortimer.

EINSTEIN (*kneeling in front of* JONATHAN, *trying to pacify him*): But, Chonny, not tonight—we go to bed, eh?

JONATHAN (*rising;* EINSTEIN *straightens up too*): Doctor, look at me. You can see it's going to be done, can't you?

EINSTEIN (*retreating*): Ach, Chonny—I can see. I know dat look!

JONATHAN: It's a little too late for us to dissolve our partner-ship.

EINSTEIN: O.K., we do it. But the quick way. The quick twist like in London. (*He gives that London neck another twist with his hands and makes a noise suggesting strangulation.*)

JONATHAN: No, Doctor, I think this calls for something special. (*He walks toward* EINSTEIN, *with the look of beginning to anticipate a rare pleasure.*) I think perhaps the Melbourne method.

EINSTEIN: Chonny—no—not that. Two hours! And when it

was all over, what? The fellow in London was just as dead
as the fellow in Melbourne.

JONATHAN: We had to work too fast in London. There was no
æsthetic satisfaction in it—but Melbourne, ah, there was
something to remember.

EINSTEIN: Remember! (*He shivers.*) I vish I didn't. No,
Chonny—not Melbourne—not me!

JONATHAN: Yes, Doctor. Where are the instruments?

EINSTEIN: I won't do it, Chonny— I won't do it.

JONATHAN (*advancing on him as* EINSTEIN *backs up*): Get
your instruments!

EINSTEIN: No, Chonny!

JONATHAN: Where are they? Oh, yes—you hid them in the
cellar. Where?

EINSTEIN: I won't tell you.

JONATHAN (*going to cellar door*): I'll find them, Doctor. (*He
exits to cellar, closing door.*)

(TEDDY *enters on balcony and lifts his bugle to blow.* MORTI-
MER *dashes out and grabs his arm.* EINSTEIN *has rushed to
cellar door. He stands there as* MORTIMER *and* TEDDY
speak.)

MORTIMER: Don't do that, Mr. President.

TEDDY: I cannot sign any proclamation without consulting my
Cabinet.

MORTIMER: But this must be a secret.

TEDDY: A secret proclamation? How unusual.

MORTIMER: Japan mustn't know until it's signed.

TEDDY: Japan! Those yellow devils. I'll sign it right away.
(*Taking legal paper from* MORTIMER.) You have my word
for it. I can let the Cabinet know later.

MORTIMER: Yes, let's go and sign it.

TEDDY: You wait here. A secret proclamation has to be signed
in secret.

MORTIMER: But at once, Mr. President.

TEDDY: I'll have to put on my signing clothes. (TEDDY *exits.*)

(MORTIMER *comes downstairs.* EINSTEIN *crosses and takes* MORTIMER's *hat off of hall tree and hands it to him.*)

EINSTEIN (*anxious to get* MORTIMER *out of the house*): Ah, you go now, eh?

MORTIMER (*takes hat and puts it on desk*): No, Doctor, I'm waiting for something. Something important.

EINSTEIN: Please—you go now!

MORTIMER: Dr. Einstein, I have nothing against you personally. You seem to be a nice fellow. Take my advice and get out of this house and get just as far away as possible.

EINSTEIN: Trouble, yah! You get out.

MORTIMER: All right, don't say I didn't warn you.

EINSTEIN: I'm warning you—get away quick.

MORTIMER: Things are going to start popping around here any minute.

EINSTEIN: Listen—Chonny's in a bad mood. When he's like dis, he's a madman—things happen—terrible things.

MORTIMER: Jonathan doesn't worry me now.

EINSTEIN: Ach, himmel—don't those plays you see teach you anything?

MORTIMER: About what?

EINSTEIN: Vell, at least people in plays act like they got sense —that's more than you do.

MORTIMER (*interested in this observation*): Oh, you think so, do you? You think people in plays act intelligently. I wish you had to sit through some of the ones I have to sit through. Take the little opus I saw tonight, for instance. In this play, there's a man—he's supposed to be bright (JONATHAN *enters from cellar with instrument case, stands in doorway and listens to* MORTIMER.)—he knows he's in a house with murderers—he ought to know he's in danger —he's even been warned to get out of the house—but does he go? No, he stays there. Now I ask you, Doctor, is that what an intelligent person would do?

EINSTEIN: You're asking me?

MORTIMER: He didn't even have sense enough to be frightened, to be on guard. For instance, the murderer invites him to sit down.

EINSTEIN (*he moves so as to keep* MORTIMER *from seeing* JONATHAN): You mean—"Won't you sit down?"

MORTIMER (*reaches out and pulls armchair toward himself without turning his head from* EINSTEIN): Believe it or not, that one was in there too.

EINSTEIN: And what did he do?

MORTIMER (*sitting in armchair*): He sat down. Now mind you, this fellow's supposed to be bright. There he sits— just waiting to be trussed up. And what do you think they use to tie him with.

EINSTEIN: Vat?

MORTIMER: The curtain cord.

(JONATHAN *spies curtain cords on either side of window in wall. He crosses, stands on window seat and cuts cords with penknife.*)

EINSTEIN: Vell, why not? A good idea. Very convenient.

MORTIMER: A little too convenient. When are playwrights going to use some imagination! The curtain cord!

(JONATHAN *has got the curtain cord and is moving in slowly behind* MORTIMER.)

EINSTEIN: He didn't see him get it?

MORTIMER: See him? He sat there with his back to him. That's the kind of stuff we have to suffer through night after night. And they say the critics are killing the theatre—it's the playwrights who are killing the theatre. So there he sits —the big dope—this fellow who's supposed to be bright— just waiting to be trussed up and gagged.

(JONATHAN *drops loop of curtain cord over* MORTIMER'S *shoulder and draws it taut. At the same time he throws other loop of cord on floor beside* EINSTEIN. *Simultaneously,* EINSTEIN *leaps to* MORTIMER *and gags him with handker-*

chief, then takes his curtain cord and ties MORTIMER's *legs to chair.*)

EINSTEIN (*finishing up the tying*): You're right about dat fella—he vasn't very bright.

JONATHAN: Now, Mortimer, if you don't mind—we'll finish the story. (*He goes to sideboard and brings two candelabras to table and speaks as he lights them.* EINSTEIN *remains kneeling beside* MORTIMER.) Mortimer, I've been away for twenty years, but never once in all that time—my dear brother—were you out of my mind. In Melbourne one night, I dreamed of you—when I landed in San Francisco I felt a strange satisfaction—once more I was in the same country with you. (JONATHAN *has finished lighting candles. He crosses and flips light switch, darkening stage. As he crosses,* EINSTEIN *gets up and crosses to window seat.* JONATHAN *picks up instrument case at cellar doorway and sets it on table between candelabras and opens it, revealing various surgical instruments both in the bottom of case and on the inside of the cover.*) Now, Doctor, we go to work! (*He removes an instrument from the case and fingers it lovingly, as* EINSTEIN *crosses and kneels on chair left of table. He is not too happy about all this.*)

EINSTEIN: Please, Chonny, for me, the quick way!

JONATHAN: Doctor! This must really be an artistic achievement. After all, we're performing before a very distinguished critic.

EINSTEIN: Chonny!

JONATHAN (*flaring*): Doctor!

EINSTEIN (*beaten*): All right. Let's get it over. (*He closes drapes tightly and sits on window seat.* JONATHAN *takes three or four more instruments out of the case and fingers them. At last, having the necessary equipment laid out on the towel, he begins to put on a pair of rubber gloves.*)

JONATHAN: All ready for you, Doctor!

EINSTEIN: I gotta have a drink. I can't do this without a drink.

(*He takes bottle from pocket. Drinks. Finds it's empty. Rises.*)

JONATHAN: Pull yourself together, Doctor.

EINSTEIN: I gotta have a drink. Ven ve valked in here this afternoon there was wine here—remember? Vere did she put that? (*He looks at sideboard and remembers. He goes to it, opens cupboard and brings bottle and two wine glasses to table top.*) Look, Chonny, we got a drink. (*He pours wine into the two glasses, emptying the bottle.* MORTIMER *watches him.*) Dat's all dere is. I split it with you. We both need a drink. (*He hands one glass to* JONATHAN, *then raises his own glass to his lips.* JONATHAN *stops him.*)

JONATHAN: One moment, Doctor—please. Where are your manners? (*He looks at* MORTIMER.) Yes, Mortimer, I realize now it was you who brought me back to Brooklyn. . . . (*He looks at wine, then draws it back and forth under his nose, smelling it. He decides that it's all right apparently, for he raises his glass*—) Doctor—to my dear dead brother—

(*As they get the glasses to their lips,* TEDDY *steps out on the balcony and blows a terrific call on his bugle.* EINSTEIN *and* JONATHAN *drop their glasses, spilling the wine.* TEDDY *turns and exits.*)

EINSTEIN: Ach Gott!

JONATHAN: Damn that idiot! (*He starts for stairs.* EINSTEIN *rushes over and intercepts him.*) He goes next! That's all—he goes next!

EINSTEIN: No, Chonny, not Teddy—that's where I shtop—not Teddy!

JONATHAN: We get to Teddy later!

EINSTEIN: We don't get to him at all.

JONATHAN: Now we've got to work fast! (*He walks back to* MORTIMER, EINSTEIN *in front of* MORTIMER.)

EINSTEIN: Yah, the quick way—eh, Chonny?

JONATHAN: Yes, Doctor, the quick way! (*He pulls a large silk handkerchief from his inside pocket and drops it around* MORTIMER's *neck.*)

(*At this point the door bursts open and* OFFICER O'HARA *comes in, very excited.*)

O'HARA: Hey! The Colonel's gotta quit blowing that horn!

JONATHAN (*he and* EINSTEIN *are standing in front of* MORTIMER, *hiding him from* O'HARA): It's all right, Officer. We're taking the bugle away from him.

O'HARA: There's going to be hell to pay in the morning. We promised the neighbors he wouldn't do that any more.

JONATHAN: It won't happen again, Officer. Good night.

O'HARA: I'd better speak to him myself. Where are the lights? (O'HARA *puts on lights and goes upstairs to landing, when he sees* MORTIMER.) Hey! You stood me up. I waited an hour at Kelly's for you. (*He comes downstairs and over to* MORTIMER *and looks at him, then speaks to* JONATHAN *and* EINSTEIN.) What happened to him?

EINSTEIN (*thinking fast*): He was explaining the play he saw tonight—that's what happened to the fella in the play.

O'HARA: Did they have that in the play you saw tonight? (MORTIMER *nods his head—yes.*) Gee, they practically stole that from the second act of my play—(*He starts to explain.*) Why, in my second act, just before the—(*He turns back to* MORTIMER.) I'd better begin at the beginning. It opens in my mother's dressing room, where I was born—only I ain't born yet—(MORTIMER *rubs his shoes together to attract* O'HARA'S *attention.*) Huh? Oh, yeah. (O'HARA *starts to remove the gag from* MORTIMER'S *mouth and then decides not to.*) No! You've got to hear the plot. (*He gets stool and brings it to right of* MORTIMER *and sits, continuing on with his "plot" as the curtain falls.*) Well, she's sitting there making up, see—when all of a sudden through the door—a man with a black mustache walks in—turns to my mother and says—"Miss Latour, will you marry me?" He doesn't know she's pregnant.

Scene 2

SCENE: *Scene is the same. Early the next morning. Daylight is streaming through the windows. All doors are closed; all drapes are open. MORTIMER is still tied in his chair and seems to be in a semiconscious state. JONATHAN is asleep on sofa. EINSTEIN, pleasantly intoxicated, is seated with his head resting on table top. O'HARA, with his coat off and his collar loosened, is standing over the stool which is between him and MORTIMER. He has progressed to the most exciting scene of his play. There is a bottle of whisky and a water tumbler on the table along with a plate full of cigarette butts.*

O'HARA: —there she is lying unconscious across the table in her lingerie—the chink is standing over her with a hatchet— (*He takes the pose.*) I'm tied up in a chair just like you are—the place is an inferno of flames—it's on fire—when all of a sudden—through the window—in comes Mayor LaGuardia. (EINSTEIN *raises his head and looks out the window. Not seeing anyone he reaches for the bottle and pours himself another drink.* O'HARA *crosses above to him and takes the bottle.*) Hey, remember who paid for that— go easy on it.

EINSTEIN: Vell, I'm listening, ain't I? (*He crosses to* JONATHAN *on the sofa.*)

O'HARA: How do you like it so far?

EINSTEIN: Vell, it put Chonny to sleep.

(O'HARA *has just finished a swig from the bottle.*)

O'HARA: Let him alone. If he ain't got no more interest than that—he don't get a drink. (EINSTEIN *takes his glass and sits on bottom stair. At the same time* O'HARA *crosses, puts stool under desk and whisky bottle on top of desk, then comes back to center and goes on with his play.*) All right.

It's three days later—I been transferred and I'm under charges—that's because somebody stole my badge. (*He pantomimes through following lines.*) All right. I'm walking my beat on Staten Island—Forty-Sixth Precinct—when a guy I'm following, it turns out—is really following me. (*There is a knock on door.* EINSTEIN *goes up and looks out landing window. Leaves glass behind drape.*) Don't let anybody in. So I figure I'll outsmart him. There's a vacant house on the corner. I goes in.

EINSTEIN: It's cops!

O'HARA: I stands there in the dark and I see the door handle turn.

EINSTEIN (*rushing downstairs, shakes* JONATHAN *by the shoulder*): Chonny! It's cops! Cops! (JONATHAN *doesn't move.* EINSTEIN *rushes upstairs and off through the arch.*)

(O'HARA *is going on with his story without a stop.*)

O'HARA: I pulls my guns—braces myself against the wall—and I says—"Come in." (OFFICERS BROPHY *and* KLEIN *walk in, see* O'HARA *with gun pointed at them and raise their hands. Then, recognizing their fellow officer, lower them.*) Hello, boys.

BROPHY: What the hell is going on here?

O'HARA (*goes to* BROPHY): Hey, Pat, whaddya know? This is Mortimer Brewster! He's going to write my play with me. I'm just tellin' him the story.

KLEIN (*crossing to* MORTIMER *and untying him*): Did you have to tie him up to make him listen?

BROPHY: Joe, you better report in at the station. The whole force is out looking for ya.

O'HARA: Did they send you here for me?

KLEIN: We didn't know you was here.

BROPHY: We came to warn the old ladies that there's hell to pay. The Colonel blew that bugle again in the middle of the night.

KLEIN: From the way the neighbors have been calling in

about it you'd think the Germans had dropped a bomb on
Flatbush Avenue.

(*He has finished untying* MORTIMER. *Puts cords on side-board.*)

BROPHY: The Lieutenant's on the warpath. He says the
Colonel's got to be put away someplace.

MORTIMER (*staggers to feet*): Yes! Yes!

O'HARA (*going to* MORTIMER): Gee, Mr. Brewster, I got to
get away, so I'll just run through the third act quick.

MORTIMER (*staggering*): Get away from me.

(BROPHY *gives* KLEIN *a look, goes to phone and dials.*)

KLEIN: Say, do you know what time it is? It's after eight
o'clock in the morning.

O'HARA: It is? (*He follows* MORTIMER *to stairs.*) Gee, Mr.
Brewster, them first two acts run a little long, but I don't
see anything we can leave out.

MORTIMER (*almost to landing*): You can leave it *all* out.

(BROPHY *sees* JONATHAN *on sofa.*)

BROPHY: Who the hell is this guy?

MORTIMER (*hanging on railing, almost to balcony*): That's
my brother.

BROPHY: Oh, the one that ran away? So he came back.

MORTIMER: Yes, he came back!

(JONATHAN *stirs as if to get up.*)

BROPHY (*into phone*): This is Brophy. Get me Mac. (*To*
O'HARA, *sitting on bottom stair.*) I'd better let them know
we found you, Joe. (*Into phone.*) Mac? Tell the Lieutenant
he can call off the big manhunt—we got him. In the
Brewster house. (JONATHAN *hears this and suddenly becomes very much awake, looking up to see* KLEIN *to his left*

and BROPHY *to his right.*) Do you want us to bring him in?
Oh—all right, we'll hold him right here. (*He hangs up.*)
The Lieutenant's on his way over.

JONATHAN (*rising*): So I've been turned in, eh? (BROPHY *and*
KLEIN *look at him with some interest.*) All right, you've got
me! (*Turning to* MORTIMER, *who is on balcony looking
down.*) And I suppose you and that stool-pigeon brother
of mine will split the reward?

KLEIN: Reward?

(*Instinctively* KLEIN *and* BROPHY *both grab* JONATHAN *by an
arm.*)

JONATHAN (*dragging* COPS): Now I'll do some turning in!
You think my aunts are sweet charming old ladies, don't
you? Well, there are thirteen bodies buried in their cellar.

MORTIMER (*as he rushes off to see* TEDDY): Teddy! Teddy!
Teddy!

KLEIN: What the hell are you talking about?

BROPHY: You'd better be careful what you're saying about
your aunts—they happen to be friends of ours.

JONATHAN (*raving as he drags them toward cellar door*): I'll
show you! I'll prove it to you! You come to the cellar with
me!

KLEIN: Wait a minute! Wait a minute!

JONATHAN: Thirteen bodies! I'll show you where they're
buried.

KLEIN (*refusing to be kidded*): Oh, yeah?

JONATHAN: You don't want to see what's down in the cellar?

BROPHY (*releases* JONATHAN'S *arm, then to* KLEIN): Go on
down in the cellar with him, Abe.

KLEIN (*drops* JONATHAN'S *arm, backs away a step and looks at
him*): I'm not so sure I want to be down in the cellar with
him. Look at that puss. He looks like Boris Karloff. (JONA-
THAN, *at mention of Karloff, grabs* KLEIN *by the throat,
starts choking him.*) Hey—what the hell— Hey, Pat! Get
him off me.

(BROPHY *takes out rubber blackjack.*)

BROPHY: Here, what do you think you're doing! (*He socks* JONATHAN *on head.* JONATHAN *falls unconscious, face down.*)

(KLEIN, *throwing* JONATHAN's *weight to floor, backs away, rubbing his throat.*)

KLEIN: Well, what do you know about that?

(*There is a knock on door.*)

O'HARA: Come in.

(LIEUTENANT ROONEY *bursts in, slamming door after him. He is a very tough, driving, dominating officer.*)

ROONEY: What the hell are you men doing here? I told you *I* was going to handle this.

KLEIN: Well, sir, we was just about to— (KLEIN's *eyes go to* JONATHAN *and* ROONEY *sees him.*)

ROONEY: What happened? Did he put up a fight?

BROPHY: This ain't the guy that blows the bugle. This is his brother. He tried to kill Klein.

KLEIN (*feeling his throat*): All I said was he looked like Boris Karloff.

ROONEY (*his face lights up*): Turn him over.

(*The two* COPS *turn* JONATHAN *over on his back.* KLEIN *steps back.* ROONEY *crosses in front of* BROPHY *to take a look at* JONATHAN.)

BROPHY: We kinda think he's wanted somewhere.

ROONEY: Oh, you kinda *think* he's wanted somewhere? If you guys don't look at the circulars we hang up in the station, at least you could read *True Detective.* Certainly he's wanted. In Indiana! Escaped from the prison for the Criminal

Insane! He's a lifer. For God's sake that's how he was
described—he *looked* like Karloff!

KLEIN: Was there a reward mentioned?

ROONEY: Yeah—and *I'm* claiming it.

BROPHY: He was trying to get us down in the cellar.

KLEIN: He said there was thirteen bodies buried down there.

ROONEY (*suspicious*): Thirteen bodies buried in the cellar?
(*Deciding it's ridiculous.*) And that didn't tip you off he
came out of a nuthouse!

O'HARA: I thought all along he talked kinda crazy.

(ROONEY *sees* O'HARA *for the first time. Turns to him.*)

ROONEY: Oh, it's Shakespeare! (*Crossing to him.*) Where have
you been all night? And you needn't bother to tell me.

O'HARA: I've been right here, sir. Writing a play with Mortimer Brewster.

ROONEY: Yeah? Well, you're gonna have plenty of time to
write that play. You're suspended! Now get back and report
in!

(O'HARA *takes his coat, night stick, and cap from top of desk.
Goes to door and opens it, then turns to* ROONEY.)

O'HARA: Can I come over some time and use the station typewriter?

ROONEY: No! Get out of here. (O'HARA *runs out.* ROONEY
closes door and turns to the cops. TEDDY *enters on balcony
and comes downstairs unnoticed and stands at* ROONEY's
back.) Take that guy somewhere else and bring him to.
(*The cops bend down to pick up* JONATHAN.) See what you
can find out about his accomplice. (*The cops stand up
again in a questioning attitude.* ROONEY *explains.*) The guy
that helped him escape. He's wanted too. No wonder Brooklyn's in the shape it's in, with the police force full of flat-
heads like you—falling for that kind of a story—thirteen
bodies in the cellar!

TEDDY: But there are thirteen bodies in the cellar.

ROONEY (*turning on him*): Who are you?
TEDDY: I'm President Roosevelt.
ROONEY: What the hell is this?
BROPHY: He's the fellow that blows the bugle.
KLEIN: Good morning, Colonel.

(*They salute* TEDDY, *who returns it.* ROONEY *finds himself saluting* TEDDY *also. He pulls his hand down in disgust.*)

ROONEY: Well, Colonel, you've blown your last bugle.
TEDDY (*seeing* JONATHAN *on floor*): Dear me—another yellow fever victim?
ROONEY: Whaat?
TEDDY: All the bodies in the cellar are yellow fever victims.

(ROONEY *crosses exasperatedly to door.*)

BROPHY: No, Colonel, this is a spy we caught in the White House.
ROONEY (*pointing to* JONATHAN): Will you get that guy out of here!

(COPS *pick up* JONATHAN *and drag him to kitchen.* TEDDY *follows them.* MORTIMER *enters, comes downstairs.*)

TEDDY (*turning back to* ROONEY): If there's any questioning of spies, that's my department!
ROONEY: You keep out of this!
TEDDY: You're forgetting! As President, I am also head of the Secret Service.

(BROPHY *and* KLEIN *exit with* JONATHAN *into kitchen.* TEDDY *follows them briskly.* MORTIMER *has walked in.*)

MORTIMER: Captain—I'm Mortimer Brewster.
ROONEY: Are you sure?
MORTIMER: I'd like to talk to you about my brother Teddy— the one who blew the bugle.

ROONEY: Mr. Brewster, we ain't going to talk about that—he's got to be put away!

MORTIMER: I quite agree with you. In fact, it's all arranged for. I had these commitment papers signed by Dr. Gilchrist, our family physician. Teddy has signed them himself, you see—and I've signed them as next of kin.

ROONEY: Where's he going?

MORTIMER: Happy Dale.

ROONEY: All right, I don't care where he goes as long as he goes!

MORTIMER: Oh, he's going all right. But I want you to know that everything that's happened around here Teddy's responsible for. Now, those thirteen bodies in the cellar—

ROONEY (*he's had enough of those thirteen*): Yeah—yeah—those thirteen bodies in the cellar! It ain't enough that the neighbors are all afraid of him, and his disturbing the peace with that bugle—but can you imagine what would happen if that cockeyed story about thirteen bodies in the cellar got around? And now he's starting a yellow fever scare. Cute, ain't it?

MORTIMER (*greatly relieved, with an embarrassed laugh*): Thirteen bodies. Do you think anybody would believe that story?

ROONEY: Well, you can't tell. Some people are just dumb enough. You don't know what to believe sometimes. About a year ago a crazy guy starts a murder rumor over in Greenpoint, and I had to dig up a half-acre lot, just to prove that—

(*There is a knock on door.*)

MORTIMER: Will you excuse me? (*He goes to door and admits* ELAINE *and* MR. WITHERSPOON, *an elderly, tight-lipped disciplinarian. He is carrying a briefcase.*)

ELAINE: (*briskly*): Good morning, Mortimer.

MORTIMER (*not knowing what to expect*): Good morning, dear.

ELAINE: This is Mr. Witherspoon. He's come to meet Teddy.

MORTIMER: To meet Teddy?

ELAINE: Mr. Witherspoon's the Superintendent of Happy Dale.

MORTIMER (*eagerly*): Oh, come right in. (*They shake hands. MORTIMER indicates ROONEY.*) This is Captain—

ROONEY: *Lieutenant* Rooney. I'm glad you're here, Super, because you're taking him back with you today!

WITHERSPOON: Today? I didn't know that—

ELAINE (*cutting in*): Not today!

MORTIMER: Look, Elaine, I've got a lot of business to attend to, so you run along home and I'll call you up.

ELAINE: Nuts! (*She crosses to window seat and sits.*)

WITHERSPOON: I had no idea it was this immediate.

ROONEY: The papers are all signed, he goes today!

(TEDDY *backs into room from kitchen, speaking sharply in the direction whence he's come.*)

TEDDY: Complete insubordination! You men will find out I'm no mollycoddle. (*He slams door and comes down to below table.*) When the President of the United States is treated like that—what's this country coming to?

ROONEY: There's your man, Super.

MORTIMER: Just a minute! (*He crosses to TEDDY and speaks to him as to a child.*) Mr. President, I have very good news for you. Your term of office is over.

TEDDY: Is this March the Fourth?

MORTIMER: Practically.

TEDDY (*thinking*): Let's see—OH! Now I go on my hunting trip to Africa! Well, I must get started immediately. (*He starts across the room and almost bumps into WITHERSPOON. He looks at him, then steps back to MORTIMER.*) Is he trying to move into the White House before I've moved out?

MORTIMER: Who, Teddy?

TEDDY (*indicating WITHERSPOON*): Taft!

MORTIMER: This isn't Mr. Taft, Teddy. This is Mr. Witherspoon—he's to be your guide in Africa.

TEDDY (*shakes hands with WITHERSPOON enthusiastically*):

Bully! Bully! I'll bring down my equipment. (*He crosses to stairs.* MARTHA *and* ABBY *have entered on balcony during last speech and are coming downstairs.*) When the safari comes, tell them to wait.

(*As he passes the* AUNTS *on his way to landing, he shakes hands with each, without stopping his walk.*) Good-by, Aunt Abby. Good-by, Aunt Martha. I'm on my way to Africa—isn't it wonderful? (*He has reached the landing.*) CHARGE! (*He charges up the stairs and off.*)

(*The* AUNTS *are at foot of stairs.*)

MORTIMER (*coming to* AUNTS): Good morning, darlings.

MARTHA: Oh, we have visitors.

MORTIMER (*he indicates* ROONEY): This is Lieutenant Rooney.

ABBY (*crossing, shakes hands with him*): How do you do, Lieutenant? My, you don't look like the fussbudget the policemen say you are.

MORTIMER: Why the Lieutenant is here— You know, Teddy blew his bugle again last night.

MARTHA: Yes, we're going to speak to Teddy about that.

ROONEY: It's a little more serious than that, Miss Brewster.

MORTIMER (*easing* AUNTS *to* WITHERSPOON, *who is at table where he has opened his briefcase and extracted some papers*): And you haven't met Mr. Witherspoon. He's the Superintendent of Happy Dale.

ABBY: Oh, Mr. Witherspoon—how do you do?

MARTHA: You've come to meet Teddy.

ROONEY (*somewhat harshly*): He's come to *take* him.

(*The* AUNTS *turn to* ROONEY *questioningly.*)

MORTIMER (*making it as easy as possible*): Aunties—the police want Teddy to go there, today.

ABBY: Oh—no!

MARTHA (*behind* ABBY): Not while we're alive!

ROONEY: I'm sorry, Miss Brewster, but it has to be done. The papers are all signed and he's going along with the Superintendent.

ABBY: We won't permit it. We'll promise to take the bugle away from him.

MARTHA: We won't be separated from Teddy.

ROONEY: I'm sorry, ladies, but the law's the law! He's committed himself and he's going!

ABBY: Well, if he goes, we're going too.

MARTHA: Yes, you'll have to take us with him.

MORTIMER (*has an idea, crosses to* WITHERSPOON): Well, why not?

WITHERSPOON (*to* MORTIMER): Well, that's sweet of them to want to, but it's impossible. You see, we can't take *sane* people at Happy Dale.

MARTHA (*turning to* WITHERSPOON): Mr. Witherspoon, if you'll let us live there with Teddy, we'll see that Happy Dale is in our will—and for a very generous amount.

WITHERSPOON: Well, the Lord knows we could use the money, but—I'm afraid—

ROONEY: Now let's be sensible about this, ladies. For instance, here I am wasting my morning when I've got serious work to do. You know there are still *murders* to be solved in Brooklyn.

MORTIMER: Yes! (*Covering.*) Oh, are there?

ROONEY: It ain't only his bugle blowing and the neighbors all afraid of him, but things would just get worse. Sooner or later we'd be put to the trouble of digging up your cellar.

ABBY: Our cellar?

ROONEY: Yeah. Your nephew's been telling around that there are thirteen bodies in your cellar.

ABBY: But there are thirteen bodies in our cellar.

(ROONEY *looks disgusted.* MORTIMER *drifts quietly to front of cellar door.*)

MARTHA: If that's why you think Teddy has to go away—you come down to the cellar with us and we'll prove it to you.

ABBY: There's one—Mr. Spenalzo—who doesn't belong here

and who will have to leave—but the other twelve are our gentlemen.

MORTIMER: I don't think the Lieutenant wants to go down in the cellar. He was telling me that only last year he had to dig up a half-acre lot—weren't you, Lieutenant?

ROONEY: That's right.

ABBY (to ROONEY): Oh, you wouldn't have to dig here. The graves are all marked. We put flowers on them every Sunday.

ROONEY: Flowers? (*He steps up toward* ABBY, *then turns to* WITHERSPOON, *indicating the* AUNTS *as he speaks.*) Superintendent—don't you think you can find room for these ladies?

WITHERSPOON: Well, I—

ABBY (to ROONEY): You come along with us, and we'll show you the graves.

ROONEY: I'll take your word for it, lady—I'm a busy man. How about it, Super?

WITHERSPOON: Well, they'd have to be committed.

MORTIMER: Teddy committed himself. Can't they commit themselves? Can't they sign the papers?

WITHERSPOON: Why, certainly.

MARTHA (*sits in chair at table as* WITHERSPOON *draws it out for her*): Oh, if we can go with Teddy, we'll sign the papers. Where are they?

ABBY (*sitting at other side of table;* MORTIMER *helps her with chair*): Yes, where are they?

(WITHERSPOON *opens briefcase for more papers.* KLEIN *enters from kitchen.*)

KLEIN: He's coming around, Lieutenant.

ABBY: Good morning, Mr. Klein.

MARTHA: Good morning, Mr. Klein. Are you here too?

KLEIN: Yeah. Brophy and me have got your other nephew out in the kitchen.

ROONEY: Well, sign 'em up, Superintendent. I want to get this all cleaned up. (*He crosses to kitchen door, shaking his head as he exits.*) Thirteen bodies.

(KLEIN *follows him out.* MORTIMER *is beside* ABBY, *fountain pen in hand;* WITHERSPOON *to right of* MARTHA, *also with pen.*)

WITHERSPOON (*handing* MARTHA *pen*): If you'll sign right here. (MARTHA *signs.*)
MORTIMER: And you here, Aunt Abby. (ABBY *signs.*)
ABBY: I'm really looking forward to going—the neighborhood here has changed so.
MARTHA: Just think, a front lawn again.

(EINSTEIN *enters through arch and comes downstairs to door carrying suitcase. He picks hat from hall tree on way down.*)

WITHERSPOON: Oh, we're overlooking something.
MARTHA: What?
WITHERSPOON: Well, we're going to need the signature of a doctor.
MORTIMER: Oh! (*He sees* EINSTEIN *about to disappear through the door.*) Dr. Einstein! Will you come over here— we'd like you to sign some papers.
EINSTEIN: Please, I must—
MORTIMER (*crosses to him*): Just come right over, Doctor. At one time last night, I thought the Doctor was going to operate on me. (EINSTEIN *crosses to table.*) Just sign right here, Doctor.

(*The* DOCTOR *signs* ABBY's *paper and* MARTHA's *paper.* ROONEY *and* KLEIN *enter from kitchen.* ROONEY *crosses to desk and dials phone.* KLEIN *stands near kitchen door.*)

ABBY: Were you leaving, Doctor?
EINSTEIN: I think I must go.
MARTHA: Aren't you going to wait for Jonathan?
EINSTEIN: I don't think we're going to the same place.

(MORTIMER *sees* ELAINE *on window seat and crosses to her.*)

MORTIMER: Hello, Elaine. I'm glad to see you. Stick around, huh?

ELAINE: Don't worry, I'm going to.

(MORTIMER *stands back of* MARTHA'S *chair.* ROONEY *speaks into phone.*)

ROONEY: Hello, Mac. Rooney. We've picked up that guy that's wanted in Indiana. Now there's a description of his accomplice—it's right on the desk there—read it to me. (EINSTEIN *sees* ROONEY *at phone. He starts toward kitchen and sees* KLEIN *standing there. He comes back to table and stands there dejectedly waiting for the pinch.* ROONEY *repeats the description given him over phone, looking blankly at* EINSTEIN *the while.*) Yeah—about fifty-four—five foot six —hundred and forty pounds—blue eyes—talks with a German accent. Poses as a doctor. Thanks, Mac. (*He hangs up as* WITHERSPOON *crosses to him with papers in hand.*)

WITHERSPOON: It's all right, Lieutenant. The Doctor here has just completed the signatures.

(ROONEY *goes to* EINSTEIN *and shakes his hand.*)

ROONEY: Thanks, Doc. You're really doing Brooklyn a service.

(ROONEY *and* KLEIN *exit to kitchen.*)

(EINSTEIN *stands amazed for a moment then grabs up his hat and suitcase and disappears through door. The* AUNTS *rise and cross over, looking out after him.* ABBY *shuts the door and they stand there.*)

WITHERSPOON: Mr. Brewster, you sign now as next of kin.

(*The* AUNTS *whisper to each other as* MORTIMER *signs.*)

MORTIMER: Yes, of course. Right here?

WITHERSPOON: That's fine.

MORTIMER: That makes everything complete—everything legal?

WITHERSPOON: Oh, yes.

MORTIMER (*with relief*): Well, Aunties, now you're safe.

WITHERSPOON (*to* AUNTS): When do you think you'll be ready to start?

ABBY: Well, Mr. Witherspoon, why don't you go upstairs and tell Teddy just what he can take along?

WITHERSPOON: Upstairs?

MORTIMER: I'll show you.

ABBY (*stopping him*): No, Mortimer, you stay here. We want to talk to you. (*To* WITHERSPOON.) Yes, Mr. Witherspoon, just upstairs and turn to the left.

(WITHERSPOON *puts his briefcase on sofa and goes upstairs, the* AUNTS *keeping an eye on him while talking to* MORTIMER.)

MARTHA: Well, Mortimer, now that we're moving, this house really is yours.

ABBY: Yes, dear, we want you to live here now.

MORTIMER: No, Aunt Abby, this house is too full of memories.

MARTHA: But you'll need a home when you and Elaine are married.

MORTIMER: Darlings, that's very indefinite.

ELAINE (*rises and crosses to* MORTIMER): It's nothing of the kind—we're going to be married right away.

(WITHERSPOON *has exited off balcony.*)

ABBY: Mortimer—Mortimer, we're really very worried about something.

MORTIMER: Now, darlings, you're going to love it at Happy Dale.

MARTHA: Oh, yes, we're very happy about the whole thing. That's just it—we don't want anything to go wrong.

ABBY: Will they investigate those signatures?

MORTIMER: Don't worry, they're not going to look up Dr. Einstein.

MARTHA: It's not his signature, dear, it's yours.

ABBY: You see, you signed as next of kin.

MORTIMER: Of course. Why not?

MARTHA: Well, dear, it's something we never wanted to tell you. But now you're a man—and it's something Elaine should know too. You see, dear—you're not really a Brewster.

(MORTIMER *stares, as does* ELAINE.)

ABBY: Your mother came to us as a cook—and you were born about three months afterward. But she was such a sweet woman—and such a good cook we didn't want to lose her—so brother married her.

MORTIMER: I'm—not—really—a—Brewster?

MARTHA: Now, don't feel badly about it, dear.

ABBY: And Elaine, it won't make any difference to you?

MORTIMER (*turning slowly to face* ELAINE, *his voice rising*): Elaine! Did you hear? Do you understand? I'm a bastard!

(ELAINE *leaps into his arms. The two* AUNTS *watch them, then* MARTHA *takes a few steps.*)

MARTHA: Well, now I really must see about breakfast.

ELAINE (*leading* MORTIMER *to door and opening it*): Mortimer's coming over to my house. Father's gone to Philadelphia, and Mortimer and I are going to have breakfast together.

MORTIMER: Yes, I need some coffee—I've had quite a night.

ABBY: In that case I should think you'd want to get to bed.

MORTIMER (*with a sidelong glance at* ELAINE): I do. (*They exit, closing door.*)

(WITHERSPOON *enters on balcony, carrying two canteens. He starts downstairs when* TEDDY *enters carrying large canoe paddle. He is dressed in Panama outfit with pack on his back.*)

TEDDY: One moment, Witherspoon. Take this with you! (*He*

exits off balcony again as WITHERSPOON *comes on down-stairs to sofa. He puts canteens on sofa and leans paddle against wall.*)

(*At the same time* ROONEY *and the two* COPS *with* JONATHAN *between them enter. The cops have twisters around* JONATHAN'S *wrists.*)

ROONEY: We won't need the wagon. My car's out front.

MARTHA: Oh, you leaving now, Jonathan?

ROONEY: Yeah—he's going back to Indiana. There's some people there want to take care of him for the rest of his life. Come on.

(ROONEY *opens door as the two* COPS *and* JONATHAN *go to it.*)

ABBY: Well, Jonathan, it's nice to know you have someplace to go.

MARTHA: We're leaving too.

ABBY: Yes, we're going to Happy Dale.

JONATHAN: Then this house is seeing the last of the Brewsters.

MARTHA: Unless Mortimer wants to live here.

JONATHAN: I have a suggestion to make. Why don't you turn this property over to the church?

ABBY: Well, we never thought of that.

JONATHAN: After all, it *should* be part of the cemetery.

ROONEY: All right, get going, I'm a busy man.

JONATHAN (*holding his ground for his one last word*): Good-by, Aunties. Well, I can't better my record now but neither can you—at least I have that satisfaction. The score stands even, *twelve* to *twelve*. (JONATHAN *and the* COPS *exit as the* AUNTS *look out after them.*)

(WITHERSPOON *crosses above to window seat and stands quietly looking out the window. His back is to the* AUNTS.)

MARTHA (*starting toward door to close it*): Jonathan always was a mean boy. Never could stand to see anyone get ahead of him. (*She closes door.*)

ABBY (*turning slowly around as she speaks*): I wish we could show him he isn't so smart! (*Her eyes fall on* WITHERSPOON. *She studies him.* MARTHA *turns from door and sees* ABBY'S *contemplation.* ABBY *speaks sweetly.*) Mr. Witherspoon? (WITHERSPOON *turns around facing them.*) Does your family live with you at Happy Dale?

WITHERSPOON: I have no family.

ABBY: Oh—

MARTHA (*stepping into room*): Well, I suppose you consider everyone at Happy Dale your family?

WITHERSPOON: I'm afraid you don't quite understand. As head of the institution, I have to keep quite aloof.

ABBY: That must make it very lonely for you.

WITHERSPOON: It does. But my duty is my duty.

ABBY (*turning to* MARTHA): Well, Martha— (MARTHA *takes her cue and goes to sideboard for bottle of wine. Bottle in cupboard is empty. She puts it back and takes out full bottle from other cupboard. She brings bottle and wineglass to table.* ABBY *continues talking.*) If Mr. Witherspoon won't join us for breakfast, I think at least we should offer him a glass of elderberry wine.

WITHERSPOON (*severely*): Elderberry wine?

MARTHA: We make it ourselves.

WITHERSPOON (*melting slightly*): Why, yes . . . (*Severely again.*) Of course, at Happy Dale our relationship will be more formal—but here— (*He sits in chair as* MARTHA *pours wine.* ABBY *is beside* MARTHA.) You don't see much elderberry wine nowadays—I thought I'd had my last glass of it.

ABBY: Oh, no—

MARTHA (*handing him glass of wine*): No, here it is.

(WITHERSPOON *toasts the ladies and lifts glass to his lips, but the curtain falls before he does. . . .*)

Sidney Kingsley was born in New York City on October 22, 1906. Under the aegis of the Group Theatre, founded by Cheryl Crawford, Lee Strasberg and Herbert Biberman as a studio of the Theatre Guild, which also brought Clifford Odets and Irwin Shaw to fame, Kingsley had his first play, *Men in White*, produced while he was still in his twenties. This play won him the Pulitzer Prize for drama.

Two years later he startled New York with *Dead End*, a study of juvenile delinquency that brought to fame the term "dead-end kids," which is still in vogue. He wrote an antiwar play, *Ten Million Ghosts* (1936), which was a poor play and a failure. In 1939 he dramatized Millen Brand's novel, *The Outward Room*, under the title *The World We Make*, a sensitive study of mental illness. His play about the heroes of the American Revolution, *The Patriots*, won him the New York Drama Critics Circle Award for the best American play in 1943.

Then came *Detective Story* in 1949, a dramatic hit that analyzed crime and police detection, followed the next year by an anti-Communist drama, *Darkness at Noon*, adapted from Arthur Koestler's novel of the same name, which was widely produced and acclaimed. *Lunatics and Lovers* in 1954 was a box-office success but actually was a rather tawdry farce-comedy. Ever since he directed the London production of *Men in White* in 1934, he has directed all of his plays and co-produced some of them.

Detective Story is one of the best plays of its kind ever written. Richard Watts, Jr., in the New York *Post* for March 24, 1949, stated: "One of Sidney Kingsley's outstanding virtues as a playwright is that he is a brilliant reporter, and his new play, *Detective Story*, which had a rousing opening at the Hudson Theatre last night, is filled with pungent and fascinating detail about the activities of a police station in

New York." Ward Morehouse in the New York *Sun* of March 24, 1949, wrote: "Sidney Kingsley's *Detective Story*, which brought a multitudinous cast to the stage of the Hudson last night, is an exciting and jangling melodrama, sharply written and played."

Further Reading

Clark, Barrett H., and Freedley, George. *A History of Modern Drama*. New York: Appleton-Century, 1947, p. 724.

Flexner, Eleanor. *American Playwrights, 1918–1938*. New York: Simon and Schuster, 1938, pp. 22, 306.

———. "Ten Million Ghosts: An Interview with Sidney Kingsley." *New Theatre*, Vol. 3 (October, 1936), p. 7.

Freedley, George, and Reeves, John Adams. *A History of the Theatre*, rev. ed. New York: Holt, 1955, pp. 596, 684, 686, 687.

Gassner, John. *The Theatre in Our Times*. New York: Crown, 1954, pp. 16, 79, 305, 450, 514.

——— (ed.). *Twenty Best Plays of the Modern American Theatre*. New York: Crown, 1939, pp. 681–738.

———. *Best Plays of the Modern American Theatre, 2nd Series, 1939–1946*. New York: Crown, 1947, pp. 683–724.

Hartnoll, Phyllis. (ed.). *Oxford Companion to the Theatre*, rev. ed. London: Oxford, 1957, p. 440.

Lader, Lawrence. "Sock and Buskin Soldier." *Players Magazine*, Vol. 20 (April, 1944), p. 8.

Mantle, Burns. (ed.). *The Best Plays of 1933–1934*. New York: Dodd, Mead, 1934, pp. 76–114.

———. *The Best Plays of 1935–1936*. New York: Dodd, Mead, 1936, pp. 239–276.

———. *The Best Plays of 1939–1940*. New York: Dodd, Mead, 1940, pp. 110–141.

———. *The Best Plays of 1942–1943*. New York: Dodd, Mead, 1943, pp. 29–67.

"Sidney Kingsley, Playwright." *Theatre Arts Monthly*, Vol. 22 (July, 1938), p. 526.

Detective Story

ACT I

SCENE: *The entire action of the play takes place in the detective squad room of a New York precinct police station.* NICHOLAS DAKIS *is seated at a typewriter, making out a form and interrogating a woman who has been picked up for shoplifting. At the center desk his partner,* GALLAGHER, *is writing up some "squeals."*
It is a day in August, 5:30 P.M.

DAKIS: Eyes? (*Squints at* SHOPLIFTER'S *eyes.*)

SHOPLIFTER (*seated in chair near* DAKIS' *desk*): Brown.

DAKIS (*typing*): Hair?

SHOPLIFTER: Titian.

DAKIS: Red. (*Phone buzzer sounds.*)

GALLAGHER (*into phone*): Twenty-first Squad Detectives, Gallagher. Yes, madam? What is your name, please? Address? (*He reaches for pad, glances at clock, writes.*) Phone number? Plaza 9-1855. . . .

DAKIS (*typing*): Weight?

GALLAGHER: One second, please. (*Another buzzer sounds.*

Picks up other receiver, balancing first on his shoulder.)
Twenty-first Squad Detectives, Gallagher.

SHOPLIFTER: One hundred nine, I think.

DAKIS (*typing*): One hundred nine will do. Height?

SHOPLIFTER: I don't know. About . . . (*Shrugs shoulders.*)

DAKIS: Stand up against the wall! Over there. (*Waves her to
    height chart on wall near fingerprint shelf.*) Five one, all
    right, come back.

GALLAGHER (*on phone*): Hello, Loot. No, nothing. A shop-
    lifter. Macy's. A pocketbook. (*To* DAKIS.) Hey, Nick, what
    was the price on that purse she lifted?

SHOPLIFTER: Six dollars.

GALLAGHER (*on phone*): Six bucks.

DAKIS: Age?

SHOPLIFTER: Twenty-six—(*Corrects herself, quickly.*) Twen-
    ty-two.

DAKIS (*squinting at her, types*): Twenty-six.

GALLAGHER: Right, Loot. It came in too late. Night court.
    Right, Chief. (*Hangs up, takes other receiver.*) Sorry,
    Mrs. . . . (*Glances at his pad.*) Andrews? Yes. Have you a
    list of just what's missing? It would help. Any cash? You
    do? One of the servants? All right. I'll be there. Yes, madam.
    (*Hangs up, makes notes on scratch pad.*)

SHOPLIFTER: My God, the times I spent twice as much for a
    pocketbook!

DAKIS: Well, you took it.

SHOPLIFTER: I don't know why. It was crazy.

DAKIS: It's your first offense. You'll get off on probation.

SHOPLIFTER: I didn't need it. I didn't even like it. Crazy!
    (*A burst of song from offstage, an operatic aria.* SHOP-
    LIFTER, *puzzled, looks about; looks at detectives inquisi-
    tively, but they're absorbed in their work.* PATROLMAN
    KEOGH *enters from hall singing.*)

KEOGH (*crossing to* GALLAGHER's *desk*): Got any 61's?

GALLAGHER: You're off key today, Gus. (*Hands him several
    slips.* KEOGH *studies them, exits singing.*)

DAKIS (*rises, crosses to fingerprint board, rolls ink on pad*):
    Come here! (SHOPLIFTER *walks over to* DAKIS. *He takes her*

hand. She stiffens.) Take it easy, girlie. Let me do the
work. You just supply the finger.

SHOPLIFTER: Ooh! !

DAKIS: This finger. Relax, now. I'm not going to hurt you.
Just r . . r . . roll it. (*Presses her finger down on sheet.*)

GALLAGHER (*rising, glancing toward door leading into hall-
way*): Uh-uh! Here comes trouble. Look at the calendar.

DAKIS: Full moon tonight.

GALLAGHER: It never fails.

MRS. FARRAGUT: Officer, Officer!

GALLAGHER (*returning to his desk*): Come in, Mrs. Farragut.
Are those people still bothering you?

MRS. FARRAGUT (*entering*): Worse than ever, Officer. If I
hadn't wakened last night and smelled that gas coming
through the walls . . . I'd be gone—we'd all be gone.

GALLAGHER: Have a chair.

MRS. FARRAGUT: Why haven't you given me protection? I
demand protection.

GALLAGHER: I got twelve men on duty day and night guarding you.

MRS. FARRAGUT: But whose side are they really on? Are you
sure you can trust them?

GALLAGHER: One of them is my own brother, Mrs. Farragut.

MRS. FARRAGUT (*sitting in a nearby chair*): Oh, I'm sorry! I
didn't mean to offend you. Only it's so important. You see,
they know I know all about it—atom bombs. They're making them—these foreigners next door. They blow this
atomic vapor through the wall at me. And they have a man
watching me from the top of the Empire State Building . . .
with radar. . . .

GALLAGHER: We got that man covered.

MRS. FARRAGUT: You have?

GALLAGHER: Day and night.

MRS. FARRAGUT: Does the President know about this?

GALLAGHER: I talked to him only an hour ago.

MRS. FARRAGUT: Oh, that's very important. Very important.
You see these foreigners know I have electronic vision. I
can see everything around us vibrating with electricity . . .

billions of atoms . . . stars in the universe . . . turning . . .
turning . . . vibrating . . . vibrating . . . with electricity.
Every human being is a dynamo. Out there in the street . . .
ten million living dynamos—coming, going . . . crosscur-
rents. (Joe Feinson *enters from hall.*) And those great tall
skyscrapers draw up all this human electricity to the top of
the Empire State Building, where that man sits, and he
turns it back and shoots it down on us . . . it's a terrifying
situation . . . terrifying.

Gallagher (*rising, crosses to her*): Mrs. Farragut, I'm watching it . . . every second, every second. (*Takes her up to
gate.*) I've got it all under control. I'm going to double the
men I've got guarding you. Twenty-five men day and
night. How's that?

Mrs. Farragut: Oh, much better. Much better. Thank you.
Thank you. (*Exits into hall.*)

Gallagher (*at gate of rail*): Get out the butterfly net.

Joe: You sure do a good hand job.

Gallagher (*crossing to his desk and sitting*): This job is
ninety per cent salesmanship!

Dakis (*finishes fingerprinting*): O. K., girlie, wash your
hands. In there! (*Points to washroom door and sits at his
desk.*)

Joe (*crossing to Gallagher's desk*): What's new?

Gallagher: It's quiet. (*Knocks wood.*)

Joe: The town's dead as Kelcey's. (*Saunters over to Gallagher's desk, sits.*)

Shoplifter: There isn't any lock on the door. (*Opens washroom door, frowning.*)

Dakis: Just wash your hands.

Shoplifter: Fine thing! (*Slams door.*)

Joe: Story for me?

Gallagher: No. Shoplifter.

Joe: She anybody?

Gallagher: Nobody at all.

Joe: Any angles?

Gallagher: Nah! Just a slob. (*Two Detectives enter from
hall, both youngish men. One of them, Callahan, is very*

*exuberant and high-spirited, Tenth Avenue in his speech
and dressed in a flashy yellow shirt and baggy trousers
which do not match his wrinkled jacket. The other, DE-
TECTIVE O'BRIEN, is an older man, neatly dressed, soft-
spoken.)*

CALLAHAN (*offstage*): Come on, Johnny, my feet are killing
me. (*Enters.*) Hi, Tom, Nick, Joel Gee, it's hot out. Sweat
your kolonjas off!

JOE: What the hell are you dressed up for? Must be Hal-
loween?

CALLAHAN: Wonder what he means?

O'BRIEN: Saks Fifth Avenue pays Mike to advertise their
clothes.

CALLAHAN: Boy, were we given the runaround! We tailed a
guy for two hours, from Fifty-thoid to Ninety-first and
back. Looked like a good man, didn't he? (*Crosses to files.*)

O'BRIEN: Sure did.

CALLAHAN: Then the jerko took a bus. (*Looks at his sched-
ule.*) Moider! Sunday again! What the hell am I? A Sunday
detective? My kids'll grow up and they won't even know
me. (*Crosses to* JOE.) Say, Joe, there's a big story on
Thoid Avenue. You get it? The brewery truck?

JOE: No, what about it?

CALLAHAN: A brewery truck backed up into the sidewalk
and a barrel of beer fell right into a baby carriage.

JOE: Was the baby in it?

CALLAHAN: Yeah.

JOE: Was it killed?

CALLAHAN: No, it was light beer! Ha! Ha! Ha! (*Crosses to
gate.*)

JOE (*groans*): You're a cute kid. What's your name, Berle?
(SHOPLIFTER *comes from washroom and crosses to desk.*)

DAKIS: Sit down.

O'BRIEN (*crossing down to the other desk*): Busy day?

GALLAGHER: Quiet.

O'BRIEN: Good. (*Knocks wood.*)

GALLAGHER: Too quiet.

O'BRIEN: We're due. We're ripe for a homicide.

GALLAGHER: Ssh! Wait till I get out of here. (*Desk phone rings; GALLAGHER groans.*) Can't you keep your big mouth shut? (O'BRIEN *crosses to table. Picks up receiver.*) Twenty-first Squad Detectives, Gallagher. Yes, madam. What is it you lost?

JOE: Her virginity.

GALLAGHER: In a taxicab?

JOE: Hell of a place!

GALLAGHER: Did you get his number? Can you describe it?

JOE: This is going to be very educational.

GALLAGHER: What's your name? Address? Yes, madam. I'll check that for you. Not at all.

JOE (*simultaneously with GALLAGHER's last speech*): I got a squeal for you. I lost something. My manhood.

CALLAHAN (*crossing to file, files card, then to table*): We don't take cases *that* old, Joe. (JOE *crosses to* CALLAHAN.)

GALLAGHER (*hanging up*): Outlawed by the statute of limitations. (DETECTIVE LOU BRODY *enters with several containers of coffee and a bag of sandwiches.*)

BRODY: Here you are, Nick!

DAKIS: Thanks, Lou, I appreciate that.

BRODY: My pleasure. Here you are, Miss.

SHOPLIFTER: With Russian dressing? (*Standing up, searching in purse.*)

BRODY (*enters* LIEUTENANT's *office, hangs hat and coat on rack*): They ran out.

SHOPLIFTER: How much do I owe you?

DAKIS: It's on the house.

SHOPLIFTER: You're all awful decent. You know, really, awful decent.

DAKIS: Well, you didn't kill anyone. (*A middle-aged man,* SIMS, *enters from hall, well-dressed, carrying a briefcase. He appears at railing.*)

GALLAGHER: Yes, sir? (SIMS *fishes a card out of his wallet and presents it.*)

SIMS: My name is Sims, Endicott Sims. I'm an attorney.

GALLAGHER: What can we do for you, Counsellor?

SIMS (*crossing to* GALLAGHER's *desk*): I represent Mr. Kurt Schneider. Your office has a warrant out for him?

DAKIS: Hey, Lou! This is Jim's squeal, ain't it? Kurt Schneider.

BRODY: Yeah. I'll take it. (*Crosses to* SIMS.) This is my partner's case. What about Schneider, Counsellor? Where is he?

SIMS: He's ready to surrender himself into your custody.

BRODY: Fine, bring him in.

SIMS: First, however, I have here some photographs. . . . (*Takes photos from his briefcase, hands them to* BRODY.) He had these taken half an hour ago.

BRODY: Naked? Ugly, ain't he?

SIMS: He's no Mr. America.

BRODY: No, that he ain't.

SIMS: The purpose is not esthetic. I don't want any rubber hoses used on him.

BRODY: Counsellor, how long have you been practicing law? We don't assault our prisoners.

SIMS: Who's handling this case here?

BRODY: My partner.

SIMS: A man named James McLeod?

BRODY: Yeah.

SIMS: I've heard a good deal about him. A law unto himself. You will please tell him for me. . . . (McLEOD *is heard off-stage.* CALLAHAN *goes into* LIEUTENANT's *office.*)

BRODY: Wait a minute. Tell him for yourself. Here he is. (JAMES MCLEOD *comes from hall into the room, leading by the arm* ARTHUR KINDRED, *a young man with a sensitive face.*) Oh, Jim, this is your squeal. (*To* SIMS.) Detective McLeod . . . Mr. Sims.

MCLEOD: How do you do, sir?

SIMS: How do you do?

BRODY: Mr. Sims is an attorney.

MCLEOD: And very clever. I've seen him in court.

SIMS: Thank you.

BRODY: He's here for Kurt Schneider.

MCLEOD: Oh, yes. (*To* SIMS.) I had the pleasure of arresting your client a year ago.

SIMS: So I am informed.

MCLEOD: He's changed his lawyer since, if not his business.

SIMS: Kurt Schneider is a successful truck farmer from New Jersey.

MCLEOD: With a little abortion mill in New York for a sideline. Nothing fancy, just a quick ice-tong job. (*Throws hat on table.*) I've a yen for your client.

SIMS: I'm aware of that. (*Takes pictures from* BRODY *and hands them to* MCLEOD.) Take a look at these pictures.

MCLEOD (*looks at pictures, grimaces*): There's no doubt the process of evolution is now reversing itself.

SIMS: You understand, Officer, that my client has certain rights. I don't want to be antagonistic, but I am here to defend my client.

MCLEOD: One second, Counsellor. I'll be right with you. Have a chair. (O'BRIEN *moves one of chairs.* SIMS *sits.* MCLEOD *guides Kindred into the squad room toward bench.*)

GALLAGHER: Jim, call your wife!

MCLEOD: Thanks, Tom. When'd she phone? (*Phone buzzer sounds.*)

GALLAGHER: Twenty minutes ago.

MCLEOD: All right, Buster. Sit down over there. (ARTHUR *sits.*)

GALLAGHER (*answering phone*): Twenty-first Squad Detectives, Gallagher. Yes, sir. Oh, Jim, the Lieutenant. (*Hands phone to* MCLEOD.)

MCLEOD (*takes phone; it is evident from the faces he makes that he has no great love for his lieutenant. Sits on* GALLAGHER'S *desk.*) Yes, Lieutenant, I just got back.

JOE (*crosses floor, pulls chair with him, and sits on chair next to* MCLEOD): Hi'ya, Seamus.

MCLEOD (*smothers mouthpiece of phone*): Oh, Yussel, Yussel! You're supposed to be an intelligent reporter.

JOE: What's the matter, Seamus?

MCLEOD: That Langdon story!

JOE: Didn't I spell your name right?

MCLEOD: It's the only thing you did get right. (*On phone.*)

Yes, Lieutenant. I just brought him in. (*To* ARTHUR) Arthur, were you arrested before?

ARTHUR: I told you.

McLEOD: Tell me again.

ARTHUR: No.

McLEOD (*to phone*): Says no. We'll check his prints. Yes, sir. Yes, sir. (*Covers mouthpiece.*) You're degenerating into a real sob sister, Yussel. Grrrim grray prrrison walls! Wish you'd have seen Langdon in the bullpen. "Hi'ya, Jack! Hi'ya, Charley!" Smiling. He was happy! He was home again! (*On phone.*) Yes, Lieutenant. Yes, sir.

JOE: The mortal God—McLeod! Captain Ahab pursuing the great gray Leviathan! A fox with rabies bit him in the ass when he was two years old, and neither of them recovered. Don't throw water on McLeod. He goes rabid!

McLEOD (*hangs up*): You apple-headed member of the fourth estate—to look natural, you should have a knife and fork sticking out of the top of your head. City College is going to be proud of you yet! (*Rises, starts towards* LIEUTENANT'*s door. Turns back to* JOE, *talks Jewish.*) Mir daft ihr dihagginun!

JOE (*still seated—pushing chair toward* GALLAGHER'*s desk*): Is this story worth a picture?

McLEOD: Later, Joe! . . . Later. (*To* ARTHUR.) Don't try running for it, Buster. You'd just about reach that door and suddenly you'd put on weight. Bullets are supersonic.

ARTHUR: Don't worry. (BRODY *walks over to* ARTHUR.)

McLEOD: I won't. Either way. (BRODY *comes over, scrutinizes* ARTHUR'*s face.*) Know him?

BRODY: No. . . . No . . . I . . . (*Shakes head.*)

McLEOD (*calls across the room to* SIMS): One second, Counsellor. (*Crosses to* LIEUTENANT'*s office, comes face to face with* CALLAHAN. *Pauses to survey* CALLAHAN'*s attire. Shakes his head.*) Strictly Pier 6!

CALLAHAN: I ain't no friggin' barber-college detective with a Brooks Brothers coat. (*Crosses to files, takes out card.*)

McLEOD: No, you *ain't*. . . . (*Goes into* LIEUTENANT'*s office, dials a number on* LIEUTENANT'*s phone.*)

CALLAHAN (*miffed*): Remind me to get that college graduate a bicycle pump for Christmas to blow up that big head of his.

O'BRIEN: He needling you again?

CALLAHAN: Yeah! Big needle-man from sew-and-sew. (*Laughs at his own joke.* JOE *rises—joins* CALLAHAN *at table.*)

McLEOD (*sits on* LIEUTENANT's *desk*): Hello! Hello, darling. (*His voice at once takes on warmth and tenderness, his eyes, his smile, his whole being seem to undergo a metamorphosis.*) What did the doctor say? Yeah! Good! Good! Mm. Nothing organic? Sure? Sure, now, Mary. How does he explain those palpitations? Psychosomatic? Mm! And how does he explain that? Yeah! What tensions? (*Laughs.*) What'd he prescribe . . . short of a new world? Mm, h'm! Phenobarbital and vitamin B-1. The history of our times. (*Laughs.*) Oh, Mary! You're wonderful. I love you. . . . I'll call you later, darling. Good-by. (*In squad room,* ARTHUR *goes a greenish color, clutches his stomach and bites his lip.* BRODY, *who has been studying him, walks over to him.*)

BRODY: What's the matter, sonny?

ARTHUR: Nothing.

BRODY: Would you like a drink of whisky?

ARTHUR: No, thanks.

BRODY: In there. (BRODY *points to washroom.* ARTHUR *goes in. Desk phone rings;* GALLAGHER *reaches for it.*) O. K., Tom. I'll take over now. Go on home. (*Picks up phone.*)

GALLAGHER: Home? I got a squeal. (GALLAGHER *takes coat from back of chair and exits.*)

BRODY (*on phone, sitting at* GALLAGHER's *desk*): Twenty-first Squad. Detective Brody. Yeah? Get his license number? . . . (*Glances at clock, scribbles data on pad.*)

McLEOD (*enters squad room from* LIEUTENANT's *office, crosses to* SIMS): Now, Counsellor?

SIMS (*rises; presents him with the photos again*): You will observe there are no scars or lacerations of any kind! (*Points to photos.*) This is the way I'm delivering my client to you, and this is the way I want him back.

McLEOD: I should think that any change whatsoever would be an improvement, Counsellor.

SIMS: I want you to know I'm not going to allow you to violate his constitutional rights. You're not going to abuse him physically or degrade his dignity as a human being—understand?

McLEOD (*bites this off*): Counsellor, I never met a criminal yet who didn't wrap himself in the Constitution from head to toe—or a hoodlum that wasn't filled to the nostrils with habeas corpus and the rights of human dignity. Did you ever see the girl your client operated on last year—in the morgue—on a marble slab? Wasn't much human left of her, Counsellor—and very little dignity—

SIMS: My client was innocent of that charge. The court acquitted him.

McLEOD: He was guilty.

SIMS: Are you setting yourself above the courts of the land?

McLEOD: There's a higher court, Counsellor. . . .

SIMS: I'm sure there is, Officer. Are you qualified to speak for it? I'm not. I'm not one of the elite. God doesn't come down and whisper in my ear, but it comes to the man-made law on terra firma; I know it; I obey it; and I respect it.

McLEOD: What do you want to do? Try the case here? This isn't a court of law. Save it for the judge. Now . . . Counsellor—we're busy here. You'll excuse me, I'm certain. Your client will be treated with as much delicacy as he is entitled to. So bring him in—or get off the pot. (*Crosses to* GALLAGHER'S *desk.*)

SIMS: I've heard about you. You're quite an anomaly, McLeod. Quite an anomaly. . . . It's going to be a real pleasure to examine you on the witness stand.

McLEOD: Anything to give you a thrill, Counsellor. (*Throws photos on desk.*)

SIMS: We may have a thriller or two in store for you.

McLEOD: Meaning?

SIMS: For over a year you have been personally making my client's life a living hell. Why?

McLeod: I beg your pardon.

Sims: Why?

McLeod (*crossing to* Sims. Arthur *exits from washroom and stands by file cabinet.*) Because I'm annoyed by criminals that get away with murder. They upset me.

Sims: You're easily upset.

McLeod: I'm very sensitive. To me your client is just another criminal. (*Turns away, dismissing* Sims.) O. K., Arthur. In there. (*Pointing to* Lieutenant's *office.* Arthur *enters* Lieutenant's *office.*)

Sims: That's your story. At considerable expense we have investigated and discovered otherwise. (*Exits into hall.*)

Brody: What the hell's he driving at?

McLeod: A fishing expedition. That's a shrewd mouthpiece. I've seen him operate. (*Goes into* Lieutenant's *office. Speaks to* Arthur.) Take everything out of your pockets and put them on the desk. (Arthur *takes contents out of his pockets with* McLeod's *help and places them on desk.*) That all?

Arthur: Yes.

McLeod: Turn your pockets inside out. (Arthur *obeys.*) Sit down over there. What'd you do with the money?

Arthur (*sitting in chair*): I spent it.

McLeod (*examines articles one by one, very carefully*): All of it?

Arthur: Yes.

McLeod (*picks up book of Stork Club matches*): When were you at the Stork Club?

Arthur: Wednesday night.

McLeod: Been doing the hot spots?

Arthur: Some.

McLeod: Any of the money left?

Arthur: How far can you go with four hundred dollars?

McLeod: Four hundred and eighty.

Arthur: Was it four-eighty?

McLeod: So your employer claims.

Arthur: He ought to know.

McLeod: Arthur, why'd you take the money?

Arthur: What's the difference? I took it, I admit it, I took it!

McLeod: Where'd you spend last night?

Arthur: In my room.

McLeod: I was there. Where were you? Under the bed?

Arthur: I sat in the park.

McLeod (*walking over to* Arthur): All night?

Arthur: Yes.

McLeod (*moving across floor*): It rained.

Arthur: Drizzled.

McLeod: You sat in the drizzle?

Arthur: Yes.

McLeod: What were you doing?

Arthur: Just dreaming.

McLeod: In the park at night? Dreaming?

Arthur: Night is a time for dreams.

McLeod (*crossing to desk*): And *thieves!* (McLeod *examines the articles. Phone buzzer in squad room sounds.* Brody *answers.*)

Brody: Twenty-first Squad. Detective Brody. Callahan, for you.

Callahan (*crosses, lays parking ticket on desk*): A kiss from Judge Bromfield. (*Into phone.*) Callahan!

Joe (*crossing to desk; examines ticket*): You get a parking ticket?

Dakis (*morosely*): I got one, too. In front of the Criminal Court Building. You're such a big shot, Joe. Why don't you do something about it?

Joe (*to* Brody): Mind if I use the phone?

Brody: Go ahead. The outside one. (Joe *takes up phone at corner desk and dials a number.*)

O'Brien (*crossing to behind* Joe *to gate*): Some of these judges haven't the brains God gave them. They refrigerate them in law school.

Dakis: It isn't enough we use our own cars to take our prisoners to court. We got to use our own gas. We can't even deduct it from our income tax. How do you like that!

JOE (*into phone*): Hello, Jerry—this is Joe Feinson. (*Screaming.*) Who the hell does that Judge Bromfield think he is? He's persecutin' cops, that's what. Parkin' tickets on duty. Yeah! I'm going to stir up a hornet's nest. All right! All right! (*Calmly.*) Yeah. Fine. Sure. I got one here. All right. Yeah. Fine. (*Hangs up, takes tickets.*) O. K. Forget it. It's fixed. (*Crosses to get* DAKIS' *ticket on desk.*)

O'BRIEN: You frighten him?

JOE: I frightened myself. Look at my hand shaking. (DAKIS *laughs heartily.*)

CALLAHAN: A cop's got to get a reporter to fix a ticket for him! Now I've seen everything.

JOE (*crossing to* CALLAHAN): That's the way it should be. A free press is the tocsin of a free people. The law keeps you in line, we keep the law in line, the people keep *us* in line, you keep the people in line. Everybody kicks everybody else in the ass! That way nobody gets too big for his britches. That's democracy! (*Crosses to gate.*)

DAKIS: You have the gall to call that yellow, monopolistic sheet—a free press? Ha! Ha! You kill me. (JOE *exits through door, waving ticket.*)

SHOPLIFTER (*rises*): So?

DAKIS: So . . . what?

SHOPLIFTER: So what happens to me now?

DAKIS: We wait here till night court opens. Nine o'clock. Then the magistrate will probably set bail for you.

O'BRIEN (*crossing to* SHOPLIFTER): Have you got a lawyer? You might save the bail bond.

SHOPLIFTER: My brother-in-law's a lawyer.

DAKIS (*belches*): Excuse me! Call him up. . . .

SHOPLIFTER: Gee, I hate to. He's kind of a new brother-in-law. If my sister finds out . . . Oh, God! She'll die . . . and she's in the fourth month, too.

O'BRIEN (*crossing to files*): It's up to you.

DAKIS: Suit yourself. . . . The court'll appoint you one.

SHOPLIFTER (*sits*): Gee, I don't know what to do. . . .

McLEOD (*in* LIEUTENANT's *office*): Ever been arrested before, Arthur?

ARTHUR: I told you no.

McLEOD: You sure?

ARTHUR: Yes.

McLEOD: It would help your case if you returned the money.

ARTHUR: I know. But I can't. I told you it's gone. (BRODY *rises from squad room desk, enters* LIEUTENANT'S *office and listens to interrogation. Leans against door jamb.*)

McLEOD: What's this pawn ticket for?

ARTHUR: Textbooks.

McLEOD: Where did you get them?

ARTHUR: College.

McLEOD: Graduate?

ARTHUR: No.

McLEOD: What stopped you?

ARTHUR: World War Two, the first time.

McLEOD: And the second time?

ARTHUR: World War Three.

McLEOD: Foolish question, foolish answer. (*Examining contents of* ARTHUR'S *pockets.*) Have you any identifying marks on you, Arthur? Any scars? . . . Roll up your sleeves. . . . (ARTHUR *obeys. On his left wrist is a tattoo mark.*) A tattoo mark. A heart. And what's the name? J—O—Y! Who's Joy?

ARTHUR: A girl.

McLEOD: Your girl?

ARTHUR: No.

McLEOD (*sits in swivel chair*): Whose girl?

ARTHUR: What's the difference?

McLEOD: What branch of the service were you in?

ARTHUR: Navy.

McLEOD: How long?

ARTHUR: Five years.

McLEOD: What rank?

ARTHUR: Chief Petty Officer.

McLEOD: You married?

ARTHUR: No.

McLEOD: How old are you?

ARTHUR: Twenty-seven.

McLEOD: How long you been in New York?

ARTHUR: A year.

McLEOD: Where you from?

ARTHUR: Ann Arbor, Michigan. (BRODY *crosses to back of desk.*)

McLEOD: What's your father's business?

ARTHUR: My father's dead.

McLEOD: What *was* his business?

ARTHUR: He was a teacher. Music. History of music.

McLEOD: History of music? Where's your mother?

ARTHUR: She's dead.

McLEOD (*looking through* ARTHUR'S *address book*): Ah! Here's Joy again—Joy Carmichael. Maybe I better give her a ring?

ARTHUR: What for? Why drag her into this? She doesn't know anything about it.

McLEOD (*mockingly*): You wouldn't lie to me, would you, Arthur?

ARTHUR: Why should I lie?

McLEOD: I don't know. Why should you steal? Maybe it's because you're just no damn good, hm, Arthur? The judge asks me, I'm going to throw the book at you— Tattoo that on your arm! (McLEOD *rises.*)

BRODY: Admission?

McLEOD: Yes.

BRODY: Got the money?

McLEOD: No. He doesn't milk easily. A superman. I've got an angle. (*Crosses into the squad room, sits at* GAL-LAGHER'S *desk, dials phone.*)

BRODY (*crossing to* ARTHUR): Sonny, you look like a nice boy. How'd you get into this mess?

ARTHUR (*rises*): What is this? Are you going to give me a lecture?

BRODY: Don't get funny with me, son. I'll knock you right through the floor! Sit down! (ARTHUR *sits.*) How'd you get into this mess, son? (BRODY *sits in chair left of desk.*)

ARTHUR: I don't know. You get trapped.

BRODY: Where's the money?

ARTHUR (*shakes head*): Gone! It's gone.

BRODY: What did you do with it?

ARTHUR: Spent it.

BRODY (*pauses, takes out cigarette, offers* ARTHUR *one, lights both*): You went to college? What did you study?

ARTHUR: Majored in History.

BRODY: History? What for?

ARTHUR: To teach. I wanted to be a teacher.

BRODY: Much of a career in that?

ARTHUR: I used to think so.

BRODY: You're a long way from home?

ARTHUR: Yes.

BRODY: Why didn't you finish?

ARTHUR: No time. There's no time. You can't start from scratch at twenty-five. (*Loud voices offstage.*)

CALLAHAN (*rises from chair at table in squad room*): Uh-uh! Here comes trouble! A couple of customers. (PATROLMAN BARNES, *Negro, enters with two* BURGLARS, LEWIS *and* CHARLIE, *handcuffed to each other . . . followed by a hysterical* MRS. BAGATELLE *and* JANITOR. BRODY, *hearing the noise, crosses back into squad room.*)

McLEOD (*rises, calls from other office*): What have you got there?

PATROLMAN BARNES: Burglars. Caught 'em red-handed. Forcible entry.

MRS. BAGATELLE (*in French accent*): I come up to my apartment. The door was open. The lock was burst wide open. The jamb was broken down. They were inside. I started to run. This one grabbed me and choked me.

CHARLIE: It's a lie! It's a pack of lies! I don't know what she's talking about. . . .

BARNES: I was right across the street when I heard her scream. They come running down the stairs. I collared them. . . . This one put up a struggle.

CHARLIE (*screaming across desk at* McLEOD): I was walkin' down the stairs mindin' my own business—the cop jumps on me and starts beatin' the crap outa me.

McLeod (*crossing around back of desk to* Lewis; *gruffly*):
All right! We'll come to you.

Charlie: Think I'm crazy to do a thing like this?

Brody (*crossing to chair and moving it over for* Charlie):
You'll get your turn to talk. Sit down.

Barnes: On this one I found a jimmy, and this. . . . (*Takes
out revolver from his own pocket, hands it to* McLeod.)

Brody: Twenty-two?

McLeod: Yeah, loaded.

Brody (*to* Charlie): What's your name? Stand up! (*Searches
him more thoroughly.*)

Charlie: Gennini. Charles Gennini. And I don't know
nothin'. I don't even know this guy. (*To* Lewis.) Ask him!
Do I know you? No!

Brody: Take it easy, Charlie. Sit down! (Charlie *sits. Crosses
to* Lewis.) What's your name?

Lewis: Lewis Abbott.

Brody (*brandishes revolver and jimmy*): Were you carrying these, Lewis?

Lewis (*matter-of-factly*): Ya.

Mrs. Bagatelle (*begins to cry*): By the throat he grabbed
me! How can this happen in New York?

McLeod (*gently. Places chair at right of desk for her*): Take
it easy, madam. You're all right, now. Sit down. I'll get
you a nice cold glass of water. (*She sits.*)

Mrs. Bagatelle: Oh, please, please! (McLeod *crosses into
washroom.*)

Brody: You're a bad boy, Lewis, and what's more, you're a
bad thief. Don't you know a good thief never carries a
loaded pistol? It means five years added to your sentence,
Lewis.

Lewis: I'd never use it.

Brody: That's what you think, Lewis. But it'd happen.
You're lucky you were picked up. Probably saved you from
a murder rap. Just once you'd walk in—a woman, she'd
scream, resist, you'd get scared . . .

Callahan (*crossing to right of desk*): Boom! Boom! (*Sings
a funeral dirge.*) Ta-da-de-da-da-de-da-de-da-de-dum. . . .

BRODY: You like the smell of burning flesh? Your own?

LEWIS: Na. (McLEOD *returns from washroom with glass of water; gives it to* MRS. BAGATELLE.)

BRODY: Getting dropped today was the luckiest thing ever happened to you. (*Turns to* CHARLIE. *Pulls him to his feet.*) Now, you! (CHARLIE *rises*. BRODY *searches him more carefully.*)

CHARLIE: I got nothing to do with this, I swear. You think I got rocks in my head?

BRODY (*producing a large wad of bills from* CHARLIE's *pockets*): Look at this!

McLEOD (*takes roll from* BRODY): Quite a bundle! How much is here, Charlie?

CHARLIE: Fourteen hundred bucks.

McLEOD (*crosses to* CHARLIE; *digs into his own pocket, takes out tiny roll of bills*): Eleven! Why is it every time one of you bums comes in, you've got fourteen hundred dollars in your kick, and I've got eleven in mine?

BRODY: You don't live right.

McLEOD: No, evidently not. (*To* CHARLIE.) Where'd you get this?

CHARLIE: I saved it. I worked.

McLEOD: Where?

CHARLIE: I was a bricklayer.

McLEOD (*hands money to* BARNES, *who crosses to desk, counts money*): Count this. This goes to the custodian. (*To* CHARLIE.) Let's see your hands! (*He feels them.*) The only thing you ever laid, Charlie, was a two-dollar floozy. (DAKIS *sits at desk. Gives* BARNES *envelope for money.*)

CALLAHAN (*to* CHARLIE): Do you always carry so much money around?

CHARLIE: Yeah.

McLEOD: What's the matter, Charlie . . . don't you trust the banks?

BRODY (*crosses to back of chair*): When were you in stir last, Charlie?

CHARLIE: Me? In jail? Never. I swear to God on a stack of Bibles.

McLeod: What's your B number?

Charlie: I ain't got none.

McLeod: You sure?

Charlie: On my mother's gravel I ain't got no B card.

Callahan: You're stupid.

McLeod: You just gave yourself away, Charlie. . . . How do
you know what a B card is . . . if you never had one?

Charlie: I . . . I . . . heard . . . I been around.

McLeod: I'll bet you have. You've been working this precinct
for the last three months.

Charlie: No. I swear . . .

McLeod (*laughs in his face*): Who the hell do you think
you're kidding? (Charlie *glares at him.*) I know that face.
This is a good man. He's been in jail before.

Charlie: Never. So help me, God! What are you tryin' to do?
Hang me? I wanta call my lawyer. (*Tries to reach for phone
on desk, but is stopped by* Brody *and* Callahan *standing
back of him.*)

McLeod: Shut up! Print him. You'll find he's got a sheet as
long as your arm.

Charlie: I don't know what you're talkin' about. I swear to
God! I get down on my knees. . . . (*Falls to his knees,
crying.*) What do you want me to . . . ?

McLeod: Get up! Get up! I can smell you. He's a cat burglar.
A real murderer!

Callahan: How many women you raped? (Callahan *stands
nearby, his back to prisoner, his revolver sticking out of
holster.* Charlie *looks at it. He moves fast to bench, sits.*)

McLeod (*to* Callahan): Watch the roscoe! (Callahan
takes his revolver out of his holster, puts it in his pocket.)

Mrs. Bagatelle: Isn't anybody going to take care of me?

McLeod (*crossing to woman*): Look, madam! You're very
upset. We don't need you here. Why don't you go home
and rest up?

Mrs. Bagatelle: No, no, no! I am afraid to go back there
now. I'm afraid even to go out in the street.

McLeod (*laughs*): Now come on: You've got nothing to be

afraid of. Suppose I send a policeman with you? What time do you expect your husband back?

MRS. BAGATELLE: Seven o'clock.

McLEOD: I'll send a policeman home with you to keep you company. A nice handsome Irish cop. How's that?

MRS. BAGATELLE (*thinks it over, giggles at him, nods*): That would be fine. Thank you very much!

McLEOD (*turns her over to* KEOGH): Gus, see that this lady gets home safely. (PATROLMAN KEOGH *takes her in tow. Exit* KEOGH *and* MRS. BAGATELLE, *giggling.* McLEOD *calls* O'BRIEN *and crosses to* LEWIS, *who sits.*)

BRODY: Now, Lewis, sit down. You're in trouble. (*Placing chair left of desk.*)

SHOPLIFTER (*sitting*): I think I better call my brother-in-law.

DAKIS: What's the number?

SHOPLIFTER: Jerome 7-2577. (DAKIS *crosses to phone on* GALLAGHER's *desk and dials number.*)

McLEOD: You help us, we'll help you. We'll ask the D.A. to give you a break.

BRODY: Tell us the truth. How many burglaries you committed here? (LEWIS *is silent.*)

CALLAHAN: Be a man! You got dropped! Face it!

O'BRIEN: Why not get the agony over with?

CALLAHAN: If you don't—we gonna get the D.A. to throw away the key. (McLEOD *and* BRODY *go to* LIEUTENANT's *office files.* CALLAHAN *sits on end of desk and* O'BRIEN *at window ledge.*)

DAKIS (*to* SHOPLIFTER): All right. Here you are, girlie. Come and get it. (*Hands her phone.*)

SHOPLIFTER (*stands at end of desk*): Oh, God! What'll I tell her? What should I say? (*Crosses to phone, takes it and assumes casual voice.*) Oh, hello, Milly. Yeah. . . . Nothin'! I just didn't have any change. How are you? . . . Fine. . . . How was the party? You went to Brooklyn? In your delicate condition? Milly! Yeah. . . . Yeah. (*Laughs feebly.*) Oh! What do you know? Say, Millie . . . is . . . er . . . is . . . Jack there by any chance? Could I talk to him? Oh, nothin'! Some friend of mine wants some advice . . . on somethin'! . . .

I don't know. . . . (*Puts hand over mouthpiece.*) He's there
. . . what should I tell him? I don't know what to tell him.
. . . (SIMS *appears with* KURT SCHNEIDER *at gate, and talks
with* BARNES *at rail.*)

DAKIS: Tell him to meet you at night court, 101 Center
Street. . . .

SHOPLIFTER: Shall I tell him to bring hard cash?

DAKIS: He'll know better than we . . .

SHOPLIFTER (*her voice changes*): Hello, Jack? Listen—can
Milly hear me? I don't want her to know, but I'm in a
jam. I need your help. So don't let on. Make out like it's
nothing. I can't give you all the details. I'm at the police
station. Yeah. . . . I took a bag. . . . Best's. I had to admit
it, Jack. . . . It was on my arm. Thanks, Jack. 101 Center
Street. If Milly asks, tell her . . . Gee, Jack . . . you're a
. . . prince with a capital P. (*Hangs up slowly, sighs with
relief to detective.*) Boy! Am I relieved!

DAKIS: Sit down there. (*He and* SHOPLIFTER *cross to table.
She sits in chair.* MCLEOD *comes out of* LIEUTENANT'S *office.
Crosses to desk and takes container of coffee and empty
container. Turns and sees* KURT *and* SIMS *standing by gate.*)

MCLEOD: Hello, Kurt! Come on in. (*Crosses to* SIMS.)

SIMS (*to* MCLEOD): I have advised my client of his legal
rights. He will answer no questions other than his name
and address. Remember, Kurt! Name and address, that's
all. Is that understood?

MCLEOD: As you say, Counsellor.

SIMS: When are you going to book him?

MCLEOD: In a couple of hours, when we get around to it.

SIMS: I want to arrange his bail bond.

MCLEOD: You'll have to get Judge Carter to stand bail for
him.

SIMS: Suppose you tend to your business and I'll tend to mine!

MCLEOD: I'll be glad to, if you'll get the hell out of here and
let me.

SIMS: Remember, Kurt! Name and address, that's all. (*Exits.*)

MCLEOD: Sit down, Kurt. Over here! How you been? (*Crosses
with* KURT *to desk, and sets chair for him.*)

KURT: So-so.

MCLEOD: You look good, Kurt. That farm life agrees with you. Some coffee?

KURT: You got enough?

MCLEOD: Sure. There's plenty. (*Pours coffee into empty container.*) Here you are! Sandwich?

KURT: I just ate.

MCLEOD: Cruller?

KURT: I'm full—

MCLEOD: Be right with you. (*Hands him newspaper, crosses to table.*)

BRODY: Steve! Take Charlie in there. (*Pointing to washroom.*)

BARNES: Come on, Charlie, in here! (*Takes CHARLIE into washroom. Goes in with him, closes door. DAKIS enters LIEUTENANT's office, gets list from files.*)

BRODY (*crossing to LEWIS*): Charlie let you carry the gun and the jimmy. . . . You're the one that's going to burn. Don't you see how he's crossed you?

CALLAHAN (*crossing floor, sits at desk*): You ever hear of the guy who sold his buddy up the river for thirty pieces of silver? (*O'BRIEN crosses back of LEWIS. MCLEOD crosses back of LEWIS.*)

LEWIS: Ya.

O'BRIEN: Well? Think!

BRODY: When were you in jail last? (*Silence.*)

MCLEOD: Look, Lewis, we're gonna fingerprint you—in half an hour we'll know your whole record, anyway.

BRODY: Make it easy for yourself. How many burglaries have you committed in New York, Lewis?

LEWIS: What'll I get?

CALLAHAN: Were you in jail before? (*DAKIS returns from LIEUTENANT's office with list.*)

LEWIS: Yeah. Elmira. I got out in March.

BRODY: How long were you in?

LEWIS: Three and a half years.

BRODY: What for?

LEWIS: Burglary.

BRODY: Well—I'd say—seven and a half to ten, maybe less
—if you co-operate—if not—fifteen to twenty.

LEWIS: What do you want to know?

BRODY: How many burglaries have you committed in New
York?

LEWIS: Nine or ten. . . .

CALLAHAN: That's better.

BRODY: What'd you do with the stuff?

LEWIS: Gave it to Charlie.

CALLAHAN: He was in on it, then?

LEWIS: Yes.

BRODY: He sell it?

LEWIS: Yeah.

BRODY: Where?

LEWIS: In Boston . . . I think.

BRODY: You think? Didn't he tell you?

LEWIS: No.

CALLAHAN: You're a bit of a shmuck, ain't you, Lewis?

BRODY: No, Lewis is all right. He's co-operating. How much
did Charlie give you altogether?

LEWIS: Half. . . . Four hundred dollars.

CALLAHAN: Wha . . . a . . . t?

BRODY: This stuff was worth thirty to forty thousand dollars.

LEWIS: It was? Charlie said it was mostly fake.

BRODY (*takes list from* DAKIS): Look! Here's the list! See for
yourself! (LEWIS *looks at it, his face drops.*)

McLEOD: Lewis, you've been robbed. (LEWIS *nods.*)

BRODY: Where does Charlie live?

LEWIS: One Hundred and Twenty-ninth Street, west. I know
the house. I don't know the number. . . . I can show it to
you. (LIEUTENANT MONOGHAN *enters.*)

BRODY: Fine. (DAKIS *crosses to washroom, opens door, nods
to* BARNES, *who brings* CHARLIE *back into room to bench.*)

CALLAHAN: That's using your . . . (*Taps his head.*) tokas,
Lewis.

O'BRIEN: Hello, Chief!

BRODY (*moving*): Hi, Lieutenant!

LIEUTENANT (*crossing to* LEWIS, *looking around*): Busy house!

O'BRIEN: Yes, sir, we're bouncin', all of a sudden.

CALLAHAN: John! Got your car here? (O'BRIEN *nods*.) Run us over? We're gonna hit this bum's flat, Chief.

LIEUTENANT (*squints at* LEWIS): What's your name?

LEWIS: Lewis Abbott.

CALLAHAN (*shows* LIEUTENANT *the jimmy*): Look at this . . . (*Shows him gun.*) and this.

LIEUTENANT: Loaded?

CALLAHAN: Yeah.

BRODY (*indicating* CHARLIE): The other burglar.

LIEUTENANT (*crossing to* CHARLIE *on bench*): What's your name?

CHARLIE (*as* BARNES *prods him to his feet*): Gennini. I don't know nothing about this, Lieutenant. I was . . .

LIEUTENANT: Print him!

CALLAHAN: Yes, sir.

LIEUTENANT: Who made the collar?

BRODY: Uniform arrest. Patrolman Barnes.

LIEUTENANT (*to* BARNES): Nice goin'!

McLEOD (*indicating* KURT *to* LIEUTENANT): Kurt Schneider. Turned himself in.

LIEUTENANT: Mm! That mouthpiece of his got hold of me downstairs, chewed my ear off. I wanna have a talk with you. (*Beckons* McLEOD *into his office.*)

DAKIS: Charlie, on your feet! Let's go. (*Leads* CHARLIE *over to fingerprint board and "prints" him.*)

McLEOD (*in* LIEUTENANT's *office, indicates* ARTHUR): Kindred. The Pritchett complaint.

LIEUTENANT: Admission?

McLEOD: Yes.

LIEUTENANT: Step inside, lad. In there. (*Indicates anteroom off right.* ARTHUR *exits. To* McLEOD.) Shut the door. (*McLEOD shuts door to squad room.* LIEUTENANT *takes off his hat and jacket, tosses them onto rack.*) On Schneider—what's your personal angle?

McLEOD (*subtly mimics* LIEUTENANT's *speech*): Personal angle! None. Why?

LIEUTENANT (*looks up sharply*): His mouthpiece hinted at something or other.

McLEOD: Fishing expedition.

LIEUTENANT: You sure?

McLEOD: Sure, I'm sure. What did Mr. Sims imply?

LIEUTENANT (*takes off his shoulder holster, hangs it on rack, transferring revolver to his hip pocket*): Just vague hints.

McLEOD: You can write those on the air!

LIEUTENANT: What have you got? (*Takes off his shirt, hangs it up.*)

McLEOD: Girl—Miss Harris in the hospital. Critical. I called the D.A.'s office. I'm taking Schneider over to the hospital for a positive identification. I got a corroborating witness. I phoned her. She's on her way over here. And I want to get a signed statement from Schneider.

LIEUTENANT: How?

McLEOD: Persuasion.

LIEUTENANT: Keep your big mitts off. That's an order.

McLEOD: Were you ever in those railroad flats of his? Did you ever see that kitchen table—covered by a filthy blood-stained oilcloth on which Kurt Schneider performs his delicate operations?

LIEUTENANT (*crosses to desk, opens drawer, takes out shaving articles and towel; crosses back to McLEOD*): This is an impersonal business! Your moral indignation is beginning to give me a quick pain in the butt. You got a Messianic complex. You want to be the judge and the jury, too. Well, you can't do it. It says so in the book. I don't like lawyers coming in here with photos. It marks my squad lousy. I don't like it—and I won't have it. You understand?

McLEOD: Yes, sir.

LIEUTENANT: Can't you say "Yes, sir," without making it sound like an insult?

McLEOD: Yes, sir.

LIEUTENANT: You're too damn superior. That's your trouble. For the record, I don't like you any more'n you like me; but you got a value here and I need you on my squad.

That's the only reason you're not wearing a white badge again.

McLEOD (*reaches in his pocket for his shield*): You wouldn't want it back now, would you?

LIEUTENANT: When I do, I'll ask for it.

McLEOD: Because you can have it—with instructions.

LIEUTENANT: Get what you can out of Schneider, but no roughhouse! You know the policy of this administration.

McLEOD: I don't hold with it.

LIEUTENANT: What the hell ice does that cut?

McLEOD: I don't believe in coddling criminals.

LIEUTENANT: Who tells you to?

McLEOD: You do. The whole damn system does.

LIEUTENANT: Sometimes, McLeod, you talk like a maniac.

McLEOD (*starts to speak*): May I . . . ?

LIEUTENANT: No. You got your orders. That's all.

McLEOD: May I have the keys to the files, *sir?*

LIEUTENANT: You got to have the last word, don't you? (*Throws keys on desk, exits.* JOE *enters and crosses to table.*)

DAKIS (*finishes fingerprinting* CHARLIE, *waves him to washroom*): Charlie, wash up! In there! (CHARLIE *crosses to washroom, starts to close door.* BARNES *stops it.*)

JOE (*to* BRODY): How many burglaries?

BRODY: Nine or ten. (*A handsome young girl,* SUSAN, *enters, stands at gate, looking about for help.*)

JOE: Any important names? Any good addresses?

BRODY (*moans*): We don't know yet. You'll get it. Don't rush us, will you, Joey? (*Exits.*)

CALLAHAN (*crosses up to gate*): Yes, Miss?

SUSAN: May I see Detective McLeod?

CALLAHAN: He's busy. Anything I can do for you? (*He scrutinizes her.*) I seen your face before?

SUSAN: No.

CALLAHAN: I never forget a face. (JOE *looks at her, then wanders into* LIEUTENANT'S *office.*)

SUSAN: You probably saw my sister.

CALLAHAN: Who's your sister?

SUSAN: Please tell him Miss Susan Carmichael is here.

CALLAHAN: Yes, Miss. Just a minute. (*Puts cards away in his files.*)

MCLEOD (*in* LIEUTENANT'S *office, examining burglary sheets, still fuming at* LIEUTENANT): Ignorant, gross ward-heeler! Why don't you print the truth for once, Yussel?

JOE: Which truth? Yours, his, theirs, mine?

MCLEOD: *The* truth.

JOE: Oh, that one? Who would know it? If it came up and blew in your ear, who would know it?

CALLAHAN (*pokes head into doorway of* LIEUTENANT'S *office*): Kid outside for you!

JOE: A nice tall kid. (*Watching* MCLEOD, *who is going through files.*) I love these kids today. I got a nephew, seventeen, six-foot-three, blond hair, blue eyes. Science tells us the turn of the century all the kids are going to be seven foot tall. Seven foot . . . that's for me.

MCLEOD: No time for a philosophic discussion today, Yussel. (*Starts for outer office through door to squad room.*)

JOE (*following*): Don't throw water on McLeod. He goes rabid.

BARNES (*to* CHARLIE, *as he comes out of washroom*): O. K., Charlie. Come with me. (*They exit through gate.* CALLAHAN *takes* LEWIS *out, followed by* CHARLIE *and* BARNES.)

MCLEOD (*to* O'BRIEN, *who is following* CHARLIE *out*): Hey, John, I need eight or ten fellas up here for a line-up. Ask a couple of the men downstairs to get into civvies!

O'BRIEN: Line-up? Sure. (*Exits.* JOE *sits at table in front of windows.*)

MCLEOD (*coming down to desk, addresses* SUSAN *at gate*): Miss Carmichael?

SUSAN: Yes. I'm Susan Carmichael.

MCLEOD: Come in, please!

SUSAN (*enters through gate, crosses down to desk, facing* MCLEOD): Are you the officer who phoned?

MCLEOD: Yes. I'm Detective McLeod.

SUSAN (*frantic*): Where's Arthur? What happened to him? What's this about?

McLeod: Did you contact your sister?

Susan (*hesitating*): N . . . no!

McLeod: Why not?

Susan: I couldn't reach her.

McLeod: Where is she?

Susan: Visiting some friends in Connecticut. I don't know the address. Where's Arthur? Is he all right?

McLeod: Yes. He's inside. How well do you know Arthur Kindred?

Susan: Very. All my life. We lived next door to each other in Ann Arbor.

McLeod: Kind of a wild boy, wasn't he? (Brody *enters, crosses to rail—listens.*)

Susan: Arthur? Not at all. He was always very serious. Why?

McLeod: Did he give your sister any money?

Susan: My sister earns twenty-five dollars an hour. She's a very successful model. She averages three to four hundred dollars a week for herself. Will you please tell me what this is about?

McLeod: Let me ask the questions. Do you mind?

Susan: Sorry!

McLeod: Arthur was in the Navy?

Susan: Five years.

McLeod: He got a dishonorable discharge.

Susan: What are you talking about? (Brody *becomes interested, edges over, listening.*)

McLeod: That's a question.

Susan: You didn't punctuate it.

McLeod: Correction. (*Smiles.*) Did he?

Susan: Arthur was cited four times. He got the silver star. He carried a sailor up three decks of a burning ship. He had two ships sunk under him. He floated around once in the Pacific Ocean for seventeen hours with sharks all around him. When they picked him up, he was out of his head, trying to climb onto a concrete platform that wasn't there. He was in the hospital for ten weeks after that. Any more questions?

McLeod: What is his relationship to your sister?

SUSAN: I told you, we all grew up together.

McLEOD: Is he in love with her?

SUSAN: My sister is one of the most beautiful girls in New York. A lot of men are in love with her. May I talk to Arthur now, please?

McLEOD: He didn't give her any money, then?

SUSAN: No.

McLEOD: Did he give it to you?

SUSAN: Are you kidding?

McLEOD: I'm afraid not. Your sister's boy friend is in trouble.

SUSAN: What trouble?

McLEOD: He's a thief.

SUSAN: Who says so?

McLEOD: He does.

SUSAN: I don't believe you.

McLEOD: Sit down. (*Calls through door of* LIEUTENANT's *office to room off right.* SUSAN *sits in chair near desk.*) Arthur! (ARTHUR *comes through* LIEUTENANT's *office into squad room, sees* SUSAN.)

SUSAN (*rises*): Jiggs! What happened?

ARTHUR (*goes to her*): Suzy! (*Glares indignantly at* Mc-LEOD.) Did you have to drag children into this?

McLEOD: Now, Jiggs!

ARTHUR: Susan, you shouldn't have come here.

SUSAN: What happened?

ARTHUR: I took some money.

SUSAN: Who from?

ARTHUR: The man I worked for.

SUSAN: But why, Jiggs, why?

ARTHUR: None of your business.

BRODY: Say, Jim!

McLEOD: Yes? (*Steps up to desk for a moment, talks to* BRODY *sotto voce.* ARTHUR *whispers hoarsely, urgently.*)

ARTHUR (*to* SUSAN): Suzy, go home—quick—go home—get out of here. And don't say anything to anyone.

SUSAN (*whispering*): Jiggs, what happened? Have you got a lawyer?

ARTHUR: No!

SUSAN: I'll phone Joy and tell her.

ARTHUR: Do you want to get her involved? You want to ruin her career?

SUSAN (*whispering*): But, Jiggs—

ARTHUR (*whispering*): Get out of here, will you? (MCLEOD *returns*.)

MCLEOD: Well, young lady—satisfied?

SUSAN: How much did he take?

MCLEOD: Four hundred and eighty dollars.

ARTHUR: What's the difference? Will you please tell her to go home, Officer? She's only a kid.

SUSAN: I'm not. I wish you'd . . .

ARTHUR: She shouldn't be here. She's got nothing to do with this.

MCLEOD: All right, young lady. I'm sorry to have bothered you. Have your sister get in touch with me as soon as you hear from her.

ARTHUR: What for? Don't you do it, Suzy—you don't have to. (*To* MCLEOD.) You're not going to get her involved in this.

MCLEOD: You shut up! (*To* SUSAN.) O. K. (*Motions* SUSAN *to go. She bites her lip to keep from crying, and goes out.*)

BRODY (*to* ARTHUR): Is it true that you carried a wounded sailor on your shoulders up three decks of a burning ship? (MCLEOD *gets coffee from table.*)

ARTHUR: Yes.

BRODY: Pretty good.

ARTHUR: Could I have that drink now? Please!

BRODY: Yeah. (ARTHUR *sits at bench.* BRODY *crosses over to his files, takes out bottle of whisky, pours a drink.* MC-LEOD *crosses over to* KURT, *sipping coffee from container.*)

MCLEOD: You're looking well, Kurt. (DAKIS *sits at table.*)

KURT: Could be better.

MCLEOD (*sits at typewriter desk, inserts sheet of paper*): How's the farm?

KURT: All right!

MCLEOD: Wasn't there a drought in Jersey this year? (*Starts to type statement.*)

KURT: I irrigate my crops. I've got plenty of water.

McLEOD: What do you raise?

KURT: Cabbage . . . lettuce . . . kale! Truck stuff!

McLEOD (*typing*): That's the life. Picturesque country, North Jersey. Nice hills, unexpected!

KURT: Yes. How're things with you?

McLEOD: This is one business never has a depression.

BRODY (*comes down, hands drink to* ARTHUR): Here you are, son!

McLEOD (*drinks—surveys his container*): They make pretty good cup of coffee across the street.

KURT: So-so.

McLEOD (*types*): When I retire I'm going to buy myself a little farm like yours, settle down. Does it really pay for itself?

KURT: If you work it.

McLEOD: How much can a man average a year?

KURT: Varies. Two thousand a good year.

McLEOD: Clear? That's pretty good.

KURT: Sometimes you lose a crop.

McLEOD: How long you had that farm, Kurt? (*Stops typing.*)

KURT: Eleven years.

McLEOD: And you average two thousand a year? (*Silence.*) Then how'd you manage to accumulate fifty-six thousand bucks in the bank, Kurt? H'm? (*Silence.*) H'm, Kurt? How?

KURT: Who says I have?

McLEOD: I do. I checked. Fifty-six thousand. That's a lot of kale. (*Takes notebook from his pocket.*) You got it in four banks. Passaic—Oakdale—two in Newark. Here are the figures. How'd you get that money, Kurt?

KURT: I got it honestly.

McLEOD: How? How?

KURT: I don't have to tell you that.

McLEOD: Oh, come on, Kurt. How? (KURT *shakes head.*) Make it easy for yourself. You still running that abortion mill, aren't you?

KURT: My name is Kurt Schneider—I live in Oakdale, New Jersey. That's all I have to answer.

MCLEOD (*rises*): You operated on Miss Harris, didn't you?

KURT: No, I did not!

MCLEOD: She identified your picture. (KURT *shrugs shoulders.* MCLEOD *hands him paper he has typed.*) Sign that, Kurt!

KURT: What is it?

MCLEOD: An admission.

KURT: You think I'm crazy?

MCLEOD: We've got you dead to rights. Make it easy for yourself.

KURT: I'm not saying anything more, on advice of counsel!

MCLEOD: I'm getting impatient! You better talk, Kurt.

KURT: I'm standing on my constitutional rights!

MCLEOD (*rising, moving over to* KURT): Hold your hats, boys, here we go again. (*Looking down on* KURT *from behind him.*) You know you're lucky, Kurt. You've gotten away with it once before. But the postman rings twice. And this time we've got you, Kurt. Why don't you cop a plea? While you can. . . . Miss Harris is waiting for you. We're going to visit her in the hospital. She's anxious to see you. And what you don't know is . . . there was a corroborating witness, and she's downstairs ready to identify you right now. . . . You're getting pale, Kurt. (KURT *laughs softly to himself.*) What are you laughing at?

KURT: Nothing.

MCLEOD: That's right! That's just what you've got to laugh about—nothing. You're on the bottom of this joke.

KURT: Maybe I am. Maybe I'm not. Maybe somebody else is.

MCLEOD: What's that mean?

KURT: I know why you're out to get me.

MCLEOD: Why? . . .

KURT (*shakes head*): You know why.

MCLEOD: Why? Why, Kurt? This is your last chance. Do you want to talk?

KURT: My name is Kurt Schneider—I live in Oakdale, New Jersey. That's all I'm obliged to say by law.

MCLEOD: You should have been a lawyer, Kurt. A Philadelphia lawyer. (*Crosses to rail, shouts downstairs.*) Gus, O. K. on the line-up.

GUS (*offstage, shouts up*): O. K., Jim, be right with you. (*Starts to sing.*)

MCLEOD (*to DAKIS*): Nick, put on your hat and coat for a line-up. (*DAKIS goes for coat. BRODY crosses down to ARTHUR, again seated at bench. ARTHUR hands him the glass.*)

ARTHUR: Thanks. (*BRODY looks at ARTHUR with sweet compassion.*)

BRODY: My boy was in the Navy, too. *The Juneau.* Know her?

ARTHUR: She was a cruiser.

BRODY: Yeah.

ARTHUR: Didn't she go down with all hands? In the Pacific?

BRODY: There were only ten survivors. He wasn't one of them.

ARTHUR: Too bad.

BRODY: Yeah! He was my only boy. It's something you never get over. You never believe it. You keep waiting for a bell to ring. Phone, door. Sometimes I hear a voice on the street, or see a young fellow from the back, the set of his shoulders —like you—for a minute it's him. Your whole life becomes like a dream . . . a walking dream.

ARTHUR: Maybe he was one of the lucky ones.

BRODY: Don't say that. (*Entrance of line-up from hall. KEOGH, KURT, O'BRIEN, and CALLAHAN enter and stand from left to right. GALLAGHER stands at center, BRODY following him. DAKIS enters and stands in front of desk.*)

ARTHUR: Why not?

BRODY: Because it wouldn't make sense then.

ARTHUR: Does it?

BRODY: Yes. (*Fiercely.*) Goddamn it! Yes. (*GALLAGHER enters from LIEUTENANT's anteroom and crosses into squad room.*)

MCLEOD: Say, Lou! Will you put on your hat and coat for a line-up? (*The men in the line-up are in civilian clothes, they are laughing and kidding. BRODY gets hat and coat from LIEUTENANT's rack.*) O. K., Kurt. Put on your hat.

Pick your spot. End? Middle? Any place. No alibis later.

CALLAHAN: Say, Gus, you look almost human in civvies.

GUS: Wish I could say the same for you.

CALLAHAN: You could if you were as big a liar as I am. (DAKIS *and others laugh.*)

MCLEOD (*calling to offstage hall*): All right! Come in, please. (MISS HATCH *enters, wearing a new fur stole.*) How do you do, Miss Hatch?

MISS HATCH: I'm fine, thank you. (*Goes over to* MCLEOD. MCLEOD *scrutinizes her, frowns.*) What'sa . . . ?

MCLEOD (*indicating furpiece*): Rushing the season, aren't you?

MISS HATCH (*laughs nervously*): Oh!

MCLEOD: New?

MISS HATCH: Yes.

MCLEOD: Mink?

MISS HATCH: Uh-uh! Dyed squirrel! Looks real, though, doesn't it?

MCLEOD: It was nice of you to come down and help us. We appreciate that.

MISS HATCH: Don't mention it. Let's just get it over with, huh? I got an engagement. What do I— (*She looks about for ashtray for her cigarette.*)

MCLEOD: Throw it on the floor. (*She does so. He steps on it.*) You have your instructions?

MISS HATCH: Yeah. I look at them all, then touch the one on the shoulder. (*He nods. She walks slowly down line from right to left, nervously scrutinizing the faces a little too quickly to be convincing. Turns to* MCLEOD.) He isn't here.

MCLEOD: You haven't looked.

MISS HATCH: I looked. Of course I did.

CALLAHAN: It's the new look.

MCLEOD: Just look, will you? Not at me. Over there.

MISS HATCH: I don't recognize anyone. I never saw any of these guys in my life before.

MCLEOD (*steps toward her*): You identified a picture of one of these men. . . .

MISS HATCH (*steps toward him*): What are you trying to do

. . . make me give you a wrong identification? Well, I ain't
gonna do it.

McLEOD (*rubs his thumb and forefinger*): Do you know what
this means?

MISS HATCH: Yeah. That's your cut on the side.

McLEOD: You're fresh. (*Phone rings at* GALLAGHER's *desk.*
BRODY *answers it.*)

BRODY: Twenty-first Squad. Brody. (*Conversation sotto voce.*)

McLEOD: I've a good mind to prefer charges against you.

MISS HATCH (*screams at him*): That's what I get for coming
all the way downtown to help you! The cops are all the
same. Give you a badge and you think you can push the
world around.

McLEOD: You identified one of these men . . . now, goddamn
it, point him out or I'm going to throw you into the clink!

MISS HATCH: You'll do what? (BRODY *hangs up phone, calls*
McLEOD *to one side.*)

BRODY: Jim!

McLEOD (*crossing to* BRODY): Yes?

BRODY (*in subdued tones*): That was the D.A.'s office. The
Harris girl died.

McLEOD: When?

BRODY: A couple of hours ago.

McLEOD: Why weren't we informed?

BRODY: I don't know.

McLEOD: There goes the case.

BRODY: The D.A. says just go through the motions. He can't
get an indictment now. Just book him and forget it, he says.

McLEOD: Yes. Forget it. Let him go. Let him fill the morgues.
(*Crosses to* KURT.) Congratulations, Kurt. The girl died.
Sit down. All right, Miss Hatch. You've earned your fur-
piece. I hope you'll enjoy it.

MISS HATCH (*crosses to* McLEOD): You can't talk to me that
way. I'm no tramp that you can talk to me that way. Who
the hell do you think you are anyway?

McLEOD: Get out! Take a couple of drop-dead pills. Get lost.

MISS HATCH: You big cheese! I'm going to see my lawyer
about you.

McLeod: All right, men, thank you. (*They go, as they came in, except* Dakis.)

Gus: I was waiting for her to put the finger on you, boy.

Dakis (*exits into washroom*): Me? Do I look like an ice-tong man?

O'Brien: Regular Sarah Heartburn.

Callahan: One minute more we'd have gotten the witches' scene from *Macbeth*. Come on. We've got to hit this bum's flat. (Willy, *the janitor, has entered with men from the line-up.*)

Willy (*sweeping vigorously, muttering all the while*): Now look at this joint, will you? You filthy slobs. You live in a stable. (*To* Shoplifter.) Come on, get up. (*She rises. He sweeps right through her.*) Wouldn't think I swept it out an hour ago. Boy, I'd like to see the homes you bums live in. Pigpens, I bet. (*Exits.*)

McLeod (*goes to duty chart, takes it off wall, and walks to desk with it, murmuring for* Joe's *benefit; sits*): Why am I wasting my life here? I could make more driving a hack. I like books. I like music. I've got a wonderful, wonderful wife—I could get a dozen jobs would give me more time to enjoy the good things of life. I should have my head examined. All this work. These hours! What for? It's a phoney. (*He removes letters spelling out* G-A-L-L-A-G-H-E-R *and* D-A-K-I-S, *places them in drawer, takes out other letters, inserts his name and* Brody's.)

Joe (*comes down*): Was she reached, you think?

McLeod: What do *you* think?

Joe: I don't know.

McLeod (*groans*): Oh, Yussel.

Joe: I don't know.

McLeod: This is a phoney. The thieves and murderers could have written the penal code themselves. Your democracy, Yussel, is a Rube Goldberg contraption. An elaborate machine a block long—you set it all in motion, three thousand wheels turn, it goes ping. (*He crosses up again, replaces chart on wall.*)

Joe: That's what's great about it. That's what I love. It's so

confused, it's wonderful. (*Goes to* McLeod.) After all,
Seamus, guilt and innocence! The epistemological question!
Just the knowing . . . the mere knowing . . . the ability to
ken. Maybe he didn't do it. Maybe she can't identify him.
How do you know? (Brody *enters squad room from files
in* Lieutenant's *office, sits at desk.*)

McLeod: How do you know anything? You got a nose you
can smell, you've got taste buds you can taste, you've got
nerve endings you can feel, and, theoretically, you've got in-
telligence . . . you can judge.

Joe: Ah-ha! That's where it breaks down!

McLeod (*to* Brody): Got an aspirin? (Brody *hands him box
of aspirin,* McLeod *crosses over into* Lieutenant's *office,*
Joe *follows him.*)

Joe: That's where it breaks down. I was talking to Judge
Mendez today. He just got on the bench last year, you
know. Twenty-nine years a successful lawyer. He thought
this would be a cinch. He's lost forty pounds. He's nervous
as a cat. His wife thinks he has a mistress. He has. The
law. Said to me today: "Joe, I've got to sentence a man
to death tomorrow. How can I do it? Who am I to judge?
It takes a God to know! To really know!"

McLeod (*in* Lieutenant's *office, gets glass of water from
cooler, tosses aspirin into his mouth*): Bunk!

Joe: I'm quoting Judge Mendez.

McLeod: Then he's a corrupt man himself. All lawyers are,
anyway. I say hang all the lawyers, and let justice triumph.
(*Washes down aspirin with a drink, sits in swivel chair,
takes off tie, rolls up sleeve, slowly reflecting.*) Evil has a
stench of its own. A child can spot it. I know . . . I know,
Yussel. My own father was one of them. No good he was
. . . possessed. Every day and every night of my childhood
I saw and heard him abuse and torment my mother. I saw
that sadistic son-of-a-bitch of a father of mine with that
criminal mind of his drive my mother straight into a lunatic
asylum. She died in a lunatic asylum. . . . Yes, I know it
when I smell it. I learned it early and deep. I was fourteen
and alone in the world. I made war on it. Every time I

look at one of the babies, I see my father's face! (*Phone rings in outer office.* BRODY *answers.*)

BRODY: Twenty-first Squad. Brody. (*Pause.*) Lock the door. Don't let him out! I'll be right over. (*Rushing to* LIEUTENANT'S *office for his hat and coat.*) Say, Jim, there's a guy at O'Donovan's bar with a badge and gun, arresting a woman. Claims he's a cop. Might be, might be a shakedown. I'll be right back. Catch the phone for me! (*Takes his gun out of drawer desk and runs off.* DAKIS *comes out of washroom, sits and reads newspaper.*)

JOE (*runs after him*): Might be shooting. Wait for me, baby! (*Exits.* MCLEOD *comes out of* LIEUTENANT'S *office.*)

MCLEOD (*to* KURT): You're a lucky man, Kurt. Kissed in your cradle by a vulture. So the girl died, Kurt.

KURT: That's too bad.

MCLEOD (*crossing to* KURT): What have you got, Kurt, in place of a conscience? (KURT *starts to speak.*) Don't answer! I know—a lawyer. I ought to fall on you like the sword of God.

KURT: The sword's got two edges. You could cut your own throat.

MCLEOD (*crossing room, takes out cigarette, turns away to light it*): Look! The gate's open! While I'm lighting my cigarette—why don't you run for it? One second, you'll be out in the street.

KURT: I'll go free, anyway. Why should I run?

MCLEOD: Give me the little pleasure—of putting a hole in the back of your head.

KURT: You wouldn't do that. Talk!

MCLEOD: Is it?

KURT: You're an intelligent man. You're not foolish.

MCLEOD: Try me, Kurt. Why don't you? Go ahead, dance down that hall!

KURT (*smiles, shakes his head*): Soon as you book me, I'm out on bail. When I go to trial, they couldn't convict me in a million years. You know that. Even if I were guilty, which I'm not. . . . The girl is dead. There are no witnesses. That's the law.

McLeod: You've been well briefed. You know your catechism.

Kurt: Sure, I know more than my catechism!

McLeod: What, for example? (*Crosses back to* Kurt.) What, Kurt? What goes on under that monkey skull of yours, I wonder! (Kurt *is silent.*) On your feet! (Kurt *looks up at* McLeod's *face, is frightened by its almost mad intensity.* McLeod *roars at him.*) Get up!! (Kurt *rises.*) Go in there! (*Points to* Lieutenant's *office.* Kurt *goes in;* McLeod *follows him, shuts door.*) Sit down, Kurt. (Kurt *sits.*) I'm going to give you a piece of advice. When the courts and the juries and the judges let you free this time, get out of New York. Go to Georgia. They won't extradite criminals to us. So, you see, Kurt—take my advice, go to Georgia, or go to hell, you murdering son-of-a-bitch, but you butcher one more girl in this city—and law or no law, I'll find you and I'll put a bullet in the back of your head, and I'll drop your body in the East River, and I'll go home and I'll sleep sweetly.

Kurt: You have to answer to the law the same as I. You don't frighten me. Now, I'll give you some advice. I've got plenty on you, too. . . . I know why you're so vindictive. And you watch your step! Because I happen to have friends, too, downtown . . . with pull . . . lots of pull. . . .

McLeod: Have you? What do you know? Aren't you the big shot! Pull! Have you got any friends with *push!* Like *that!* . . . for example! (*Kicks him—*Kurt *goes over, chair and all.*)

Kurt: Cut that out! You let me alone now. . . . (McLeod *grabs him by the lapels, pulls him to his feet.*) You let me go! Let me go!

McLeod: No, Kurt! Everybody else is going to let you go. You got it all figured . . . exactly. The courts—the juries—the judges— (*Slaps him.*) Everybody except me. . . . (Kurt *starts to resist,* McLeod *hits him in the belly.* Kurt *crumples to the floor.*) Why didn't you obey your lawyer and keep your mouth shut? All right! Get up, Kurt! Come on! Get up!

Kurt (*moaning and writhing*): I can't . . . I can't. . . .

Something inside . . . broke! (*He calls feebly.*) Help! (*Very loud.*) HELP!

MCLEOD: Get up! You're all right. Get up! (LIEUTENANT MONOGHAN *enters through one door and* GALLAGHER *enters through another door.*)

LIEUTENANT: What's going on? (*He sees* KURT, *goes to him, bends down.*)

KURT: Inside! It broke. He hurt me. . . . (DAKIS *rushes in from squad room.*)

LIEUTENANT: Take it easy, son, you'll be all right.

KURT: I feel terrible.

LIEUTENANT: Nick! Quick! Get an ambulance.

DAKIS: Yes, sir. (*Goes to phone; puts in a call.*)

LIEUTENANT: Did he resist you?

MCLEOD: No.

LIEUTENANT: No? You lunatic! Didn't I just get through warning you to lay off? (*To* KURT, *who is on floor, moaning in agony.*)

KURT (*gasping for breath*): He tried to kill me!

LIEUTENANT: Why should he do that?

KURT: Tami Giacoppetti! . . . Same thing! . . . She got him after me, too. . . . Tami Giacoppetti. . . .

LIEUTENANT (*leans over* KURT): What? Tami Giacoppetti? Who's he? What about him? (*Puts ear to* KURT'S *mouth.*) A little louder! Just try and talk a little louder, lad. (KURT'S *eyes close, his head falls back. He is unconscious. To* GALLAGHER.) Wet some towels! (GALLAGHER *rushes to washroom.* DAKIS *loosens* KURT'S *collar, tries to bring him to.* LIEUTENANT *rises, confronts* MCLEOD, *glaring at him.*) Who's Tami Giacoppetti?

MCLEOD: I've no idea.

LIEUTENANT: What's the pitch here, McLeod?

MCLEOD: He needled me. He got fresh. He begged for it, and I let him have it. That's all. (GALLAGHER *returns with wet towels.* DAKIS *takes them from him, applies them to* KURT'S *head.*)

LIEUTENANT: Don't con me! That ain't all. Come on! Let's have it! What about this Tami Giacoppetti?

MCLEOD: I never heard of him.

GALLAGHER: Giacoppetti? I know him. A black market guy. Runs a creep joint in the village.

LIEUTENANT: This could be a very hot potato. If this man's hurt, the big brass'll be down here throwin' questions at me. And I'm going to have the answers. What plays between you two guys? What's he got on you? What's the clout?

MCLEOD: Nothing.

LIEUTENANT: Then what was his mouthpiece yellin' and screamin' about?

MCLEOD: Red herring. Red, red herring!

LIEUTENANT (*stands*): Then I'm gonna goddamn well find out for myself. There's something kinky about this. McLeod, if you're concealing something from me, I'll have your head on a plate. (*To* GALLAGHER.) This Giacoppetti! Find him and bring him in!

GALLAGHER: Yes, sir. (*Goes out through squad room.*)

LIEUTENANT (*calls after him*): My car's downstairs. Use it.

GALLAGHER: Yes, sir. (*Exits.* LIEUTENANT *bends down to* KURT. MCLEOD, *grim-faced, lights another cigarette.*)

ACT II

SCENE: *The scene is the same: it is 7:30 P.M. The lawyer,* ENDICOTT SIMS, *is closeted in the* LIEUTENANT's *office, scolding* LIEUTENANT *and* MCLEOD. SHOPLIFTER *is reading the comics outside.* ARTHUR *is seated on bench, quietly, his head bowed in thought.* DAKIS, *the* JANITOR *and* GUS *are in a huddle, whispering, glancing over toward* LIEUTENANT's *door.* BRODY *is talking sotto voce to an excited man and woman,* MR. *and* MRS. FEENEY, *who are glaring at a tough-looking specimen.*

SIMS: How dare you take the law in your own hands? Who are you to constitute yourself a court of last appeal? (*Phone bell.*)

LIEUTENANT (*trying to appease*): Now, Counsellor . . .
(BRODY *goes to answer phone.*)

BRODY: Twenty-first Squad, Detective Brody. . . . Yeah. . . . Yeah.

SIMS: No. Lieutenant! This is a felony. I'm going to press a felony assault here. So help me, I'm going to see you in jail!

McLEOD: On which side of the bars, Counsellor?

SIMS: Be careful. I'm an attorney and an officer of the court, and I don't like that talk.

McLEOD: I'm an officer of the peace and I don't like collusion.

SIMS (*a step toward* McLEOD): What do you mean by that?

McLEOD: By that I mean collusion. Subornation of witnesses, Counsellor.

SIMS: What the devil are you talking about?

McLEOD: Subornation. I'm charging you with subornation.

SIMS: Your lips are blistering with lies.

McLEOD: Praise from an expert! I had a witness here today against your client whom you bought off, Counsellor.

SIMS: That's so absurd I'm not even going to answer it.

McLEOD: I'll prove it.

LIEUTENANT: All right! Cut it! Cut it out. Enough's enough.

SIMS: I intend to carry this to the Commissioner.

LIEUTENANT (*pushes phone over*): Call him now. That's your privilege.

SIMS: And don't think you're entirely free of blame in this, Lieutenant.

LIEUTENANT: Me? What have I——?

SIMS: I warned you that personal motives are involved in this case, and I was afraid this was going to happen. You should have taken the necessary steps to prevent it. Luckily, I came armed with photos and affidavits.

LIEUTENANT: Mystery! Mystery! What motives?

McLEOD: Yes. Why don't you tell us? I'd like to hear. Let's get it out in the open. What are these motives?

SIMS: It is not to my client's interests to reveal them at this moment.

McLEOD (*to* LIEUTENANT): Legal bull!

LIEUTENANT: I'm beginning to think so.

SIMS: Sure. One hand washes the other. (BRODY *knocks at door of* LIEUTENANT's *office.*)

LIEUTENANT: Come in!

BRODY: Phone, Lieutenant.

LIEUTENANT (*picks up phone*): Twenty-first Squad, Lieutenant Monoghan. . . . Yeah. . . . Yeah. . . .

SIMS: On what evidence do you make these serious charges?

MCLEOD: The evidence of my intelligent observation.

SIMS: Insufficient, incompetent and irrelevant.

LIEUTENANT: Sh! Sh!

SIMS: You're pretty cagey, McLeod, but your tactics don't fool me for a second. You are not going to duck out of this so easily. You are in a position of responsibility here and you have got to answer for your actions. You can't use your badge for personal vengeance. That doesn't go. The public isn't your servant. You're theirs. You're going to be broken for this.

MCLEOD: Go ahead! Break me! You're worse than the criminals you represent, Counsellor. (*Rises, faces* SIMS.) You're so damn respectable. Yet look at you! The clothes you wear, your car downstairs, your house in Westchester, all bought with stolen money, tainted with blood.

LIEUTENANT: Shut up! I got the hospital.

SIMS: How is he?

LIEUTENANT (*as they listen attentively*): Yes. Yes. I see. Will you keep in touch with me? Let me know right away. (*Hangs up.*) See, Counsellor, it always pays to await events. There are no external lacerations on your client that would warrant a felony assault. They are now making X-ray and other tests to see if there are any internal injuries. So far you haven't got a leg to stand on.

MCLEOD: No! Let him bring charges. (*To* SIMS.) Bring your felony charge. It'll give me a chance to get your client on the stand and really tear his clothes off. And yours, too, Counsellor.

LIEUTENANT: McLeod! Step outside! (MCLEOD *comes out of* LIEUTENANT's *office.*)

BRODY: What's the score?

McLEOD: Tempest in a teapot.

SIMS (*walks across floor*): What kind of officer is that?

LIEUTENANT: Detectives are like fingerprints. No two alike. He has his quoiks.

SIMS: The understatement of the year.

LIEUTENANT: We all got 'em. He has a value here. He's honest. He ain't on the take. I stand up for him on that. Got no tin boxes.

SIMS: I wasn't saying he had.

LIEUTENANT: I thought you was, maybe.

SIMS: No . . .

LIEUTENANT: Then what was you saying? I guess I fumbled it.

SIMS: I can't discuss it with you.

LIEUTENANT: I'd love to discuss it with someone. Who do you suggest?

SIMS: McLeod.

LIEUTENANT: Counsellor!

SIMS: Or his wife!

LIEUTENANT (*looks up sharply*): His wife? What do you mean by that?

SIMS: Never mind! Skip it!

LIEUTENANT: No. You mentioned his wife. What do you mean by that? Look! I got to get it clear up here. A little co-operation would go a long way.

SIMS: When it serves my client's interests . . . not before.

LIEUTENANT: Four years ago I threw my radio set the hell outa the window. You know why? Because, goddamn it, I hate mysteries!

SIMS (*smiles*): I'm not free to discuss this, Lieutenant. (*Looks at his watch.*) Gouverneur Hospital?

LIEUTENANT: Yeah.

SIMS: I want to see my client. Will I be allowed in?

LIEUTENANT: Yeah.

SIMS: I'll be back. (*Leaves* LIEUTENANT'S *office. In squad room he pauses to confront* McLEOD.) I'll be back. I'm not through with you.

McLEOD: I can't wait. (SIMS *exits.*)

BRODY (*to* McLEOD, *indicating the tough, surly-looking* CRUMB-BUM): This creep was impersonating an officer.

WOMAN: I didn't know. I thought he might be a policeman. His badge looked real.

BRODY: A shake-down. After he took you outside he probably would have taken all your money and let you go. You see, that's how we get a bad reputation. Now you will appear in court at ten o'clock tomorrow morning, won't you?

WOMAN: Oh, yes.

MAN: W-e-l-l . . . tomorrow morning? But I've got a job.

WOMAN: You'll explain to your boss. You'll just take off, that's all.

MAN: But, Isabel . . .

WOMAN: He'll be there. Don't you worry. Thank you. Thank you. (*They exit.*)

BRODY: I'm going down to book this crumb-bum.

CRUMB-BUM: What did you call me?

BRODY: Crumb-bum. Come on.

LIEUTENANT (*squints at his cigar a moment, rises, bellows*): McLeod!

McLEOD: Yes, sir? (*Crosses to* LIEUTENANT'S *door, opens it.*)

LIEUTENANT: What the hell is this about? What's he driving at? I want the truth.

McLEOD: Lieutenant, I give you my solemn word of honor . . .

LIEUTENANT (*studies him, waves him away*): Shut the door! (McLEOD *shuts door to office. A sad-looking* GALLANTZ *appears at gate.*)

McLEOD: Yes, sir? What can I do for you?

GALLANTZ: I want to report, someone picked my pocket.

McLEOD: Come in!

GALLANTZ (*exposes his backside, revealing a patch cut out of his trousers*): Look! They cut it right out.

McLEOD: They work that way. With a razor blade. Sit down! Did you see the man?

GALLANTZ: No. First I knew I was in a restaurant. I ate a big meal, reached in my pocket to pay the check. Boy, I almost dropped dead. I'm lucky I'm not here under arrest myself.

McLEOD: Yeah! (*Smiles.*) What's your name?

GALLANTZ: Gallantz, D. David.

WILLY (*to* GALLANTZ): Get up.

McLEOD: Address? (WILLY *empties basket under desk into his pail.*)

GALLANTZ (*rises, staring at* WILLY): Four-one-nine West Eightieth Street.

WILLY (*muttering indignantly, paying no attention to anyone as he goes off*): Look at this room, will you? Wouldn't think I cleaned up an hour ago! Detectives! The brains of the department! Couldn't find a Chinaman on Mott Street.

McLEOD: What did you lose?

GALLANTZ: My wallet.

McLEOD: Can you describe the wallet?

GALLANTZ: Black leather.

McLEOD (*on phone*): Lost Property.

SHOPLIFTER (*reading paper*): Have you got one of them two-way radio wristwatches like Dick Tracy?

DAKIS: No.

SHOPLIFTER: Behind the times, ain't you?

DAKIS: Yeah, behind the behind.

SHOPLIFTER (*feels her pulse*): Gee, I think I'm getting a reaction. Emotions are bad for me. I got diabetes. I'm not supposed to get emotions.

DAKIS (*belches*): Excuse me. I got ulcers. I'm not supposed to eat sandwiches. A hot meal was waiting for me at home. Do me a favor. Next time get yourself arrested before four o'clock, let a fellow eat a home-cooked meal.

SHOPLIFTER: I'm sorry.

DAKIS: Do you realize this is on my own time? Look at all these forms I had to type up. And when we get to court, what'll happen? The judge'll probably let you off. I won't even get a conviction. You cause me all this work for nothin'.

SHOPLIFTER: I'm sorry . . .

DAKIS: That's a big help.

SHOPLIFTER: I'm sorry . . . (LIEUTENANT *takes address book out of his desk drawer, thumbs through it for a number, reaches for phone, dials.*)

McLeod (*hangs up; to* Gallantz): Sorry. Nothing yet. We'll follow it up. If we hear anything, we'll let you know.

Gallantz: Thanks! My best pants, too. (*He exits.*)

Lieutenant (*on phone*): Hello. Mrs. McLeod? This is Lieutenant Monoghan at the Twenty-first. No, no! He's all right. Nothing like that! (*The rest of his conversation is drowned out by entrance of* Callahan *with* Barnes *and* Brody *and* Charlie, *all talking at once.* Callahan *and* Policeman *are carrying two suitcases and several pillowcases filled with "loot" from* Charlie's *apartment.* Brody *completes the parade, carrying in more loot.* Callahan *knocks at* Lieutenant's *door.*) Come in!

Dakis: How'd you do with Charlie?

Callahan (*opens* Lieutenant's *door, holds up "loot"*): Look what we found, boss. And by a strange coincidence—in Charlie's apartment.

Barnes (*unlocks* Charlie's *handcuffs*): Sit down! There! (Charlie *sits in designated chair.*)

Callahan: O'Brien is taking Lewis around to identify the houses.

Lieutenant: Good! (*Waves him out to squad room.*) Shut the door! (Callahan, *in squad room, aided by* McLeod, Brody *and* Dakis, *starts dumping stolen goods on table.* Willy *enters with suits on hangers, puts them on same table.*)

Callahan (*holding up some loot*): Look at this! These jockeys sure get around! . . . (Lieutenant *picks up his phone and continues conversation, which is drowned out by the racket in squad room as men proceed to help unload stolen goods.* Callahan *holds up an expensive clock, shakes it.*) This worth anything?

McLeod (*examines it*): Very good piece. Tiffany. . . . Where'd you get this, Charlie?

Charlie: I bought it.

McLeod: Where?

Charlie: Outside the jewelry exchange. On the street.

BRODY: Who from?

CHARLIE: Some guy—

McLEOD: What's his name? (LIEUTENANT *leaves office*.)

CHARLIE: I don't know. I never saw him again.

McLEOD: Or before?

CHARLIE (*nods*): Yeah.

McLEOD: Or at all. The little man that wasn't there.

SHOPLIFTER (*stands*): Yeah! I'm getting a reaction. Emotions are bad for me.

DAKIS (*checking stolen article against list*): Girls with diabetes shouldn't steal pink panties.

SHOPLIFTER: It wasn't pink pants.

DAKIS (*sighs*): I know.

SHOPLIFTER: It was a bag.

DAKIS (*closes eyes, sighs*): I know.

SHOPLIFTER: Alligator.

DAKIS: I know.

SHOPLIFTER: Imitation alligator.

DAKIS (*sorry he started it all*): I know.

McLEOD: Wait! Here's something! Monogrammed: J. G. (*Checks with list.*) Sure. This is some of the Gordon stuff. Where'd you get this, Charlie?

CHARLIE: What's the use of talking? You won't believe me, anyway.

BRODY: Where?

CALLAHAN: Where'd you get it, Charlie? (*Takes out blackjack.*) Know what this is? A persuader. (*Bangs it on a desk. WILLY enters; stands by gate.*)

CHARLIE: Go ahead! Beat me! Beat me unconscious. Go ahead.

CALLAHAN (*laughs, puts "persuader" away*): You're too eager, Charlie. Some-a them creeps like it, you know. Gives 'em a thrill. Look at that kisser! I'm a son-of-a-bitch, I'm right!

BRODY (*holding up piece of silver*): Where'd you get this, Charlie? (*CHARLIE hangs his head.*)

DAKIS: Why don't you be professional, Charlie? He's talking to you. . . . What's the matter? What are you hanging your head for? What are you ashamed of? Nobody made you be

a burglar. You wanted to be a burglar. So you're a burglar.
So be a good one! Be proud of your chosen profession! Hold
your head up. (DAKIS *lifts* CHARLIE's *head up by the chin.*)
That's better. You're a good thief, Charlie. You're no bum.
They wear sweaters. Not you! You got a hundred-dollar
suit on. You . . . Wait a minute! (*Opens* CHARLIE's *coat,
looks at label.*) Take it off, you bum. Stolen! The name's
still in it. Where'd you get it?

CHARLIE (*takes off coat, talking fast*): You mean it's stolen?
O. K., O. K. I'll tell you . . . the whole story . . . may I drop
dead on this spot! (DAKIS *hands coat to* BRODY.)

CALLAHAN: On this one? Be careful, Charlie.

CHARLIE: Honest—the truth! But don't tell Lewis! He'll kill
me. He makes out like he's a dummy, don't he? He ain't.
He's smart. Ooh, he's as smart as they come. Look . . . I just
been in New York two weeks. I came here from Pittsburgh
two weeks ago. So help me. I lose my valise in the station.
I meet this guy, Lewis, in a poolroom.

CALLAHAN: Where? What poolroom?

CHARLIE: Fourteenth Street, corner of Seventh Avenue. . . .
Look it up! Check it! I'm telling you the truth, so help me!
I shoot a game of pool with him. He says to me, "You got a
place to stay?" I says, "No." He says, "Share my flat." I say
"O. K." My suit's all dirty. He lends me this one. Says it
belongs to his brother, who's in Florida. (*Looks up at the
unbelieving faces circling him.*) So help me!

CALLAHAN: I could tell you a story would bring tears to your
eyes. Get in there and take off your pants! (CHARLIE *goes
to washroom.*)

BRODY: Willy! Got an old pair of pants?

WILLY: Yeah, I got some, somewhere. (*Exits.*)

BRODY (*to* CHARLIE): You're not even smart enough to take
out the label. The name's still in it. Jerome Armstrong.

CALLAHAN (*examining his list*): Wait! I got that squeal right
here. I think there was a rape connected with this one.

BRODY: I wouldn't be surprised.

LIEUTENANT (*calls*): Dakis! (DAKIS *hurries to* LIEUTENANT's
door, opens it.)

DAKIS: Yes, sir?

LIEUTENANT: Wait downstairs for Mrs. McLeod. When she gets here, let me know foist.

DAKIS: Right, Chief.

LIEUTENANT: And . . . a . . . Nick! (*Touches his lips.*) Button 'em up.

DAKIS: Yes, sir. (*He goes out, shutting door behind him. As he crosses to gates he glances at* McLEOD, *his forehead furrows. Exits.* LIEUTENANT *studies his cigar, frowns, goes off. Through the little window we see* CHARLIE *throw up washroom shade, try iron grillwork.* McLEOD *crosses to washroom door, calls in.*)

McLEOD: The only way you can get out of there, Charlie, is to jump down the toilet and pull the chain. (JOE FEINSON *enters; comes over to* BRODY.)

JOE: Lot of loot! They do the Zaza robbery?

BRODY (*to* CHARLIE): You robbed that Zaza dame's flat, Charlie?

CHARLIE: I don't know nuttin'!

BRODY: He don't know from nuttin'!

CALLAHAN: He's ignorant and he's proud of it.

JOE: Any good names?

BRODY: Don't know yet—

JOE: Any good addresses?

BRODY: They're taking the other bum around. He's identifying the houses. We'll crack this case in an hour. (WILLY *enters with old pants. Gives them to* BRODY, *who throws them to* CHARLIE *in washroom.*)

JOE (*saunters over to* McLEOD): What's with Schneider?

McLEOD: No story.

JOE: He left here twenty-five minutes ago in an ambulance. What happened? He trip?

McLEOD: Yes.

JOE: Over his schnozzola?

McLEOD: Could have. It's long enough.

JOE: No story?

McLEOD: No.

JOE: His lawyer's sore as a boil. What happened?

McLeod: You tell me. You always have the story in your pocket.

Joe: Look, Seamus! There are angles here I don't feel happy about.

McLeod: What angles?

Joe: I don't know . . . yet. Come! Give! Off the record.

McLeod: You can print it if you want to. Kurt Schneider was a butcher who murdered two girls and got away with it. High time somebody put the fear of God in him. The law wouldn't, so I did. Print it, Yussel. Go ahead. You don't like the cops. Here's your chance.

Joe: I don't like cops? For a smart guy, Seamus, you can be an awful schmoo. If I got fired tomorrow, you'd still find me here, hanging around, running errands for you guys, happy as a bird dog! I'm a buff way back. I found a home. You know that.

McLeod: Sentimental slop, Yussel. (CHARLIE *throws pants out from washroom. They drape on* BARNES' *neck.* MR. PRITCHETT *enters.*)

Joe: My sixth sense is still bothering me.

McLeod: Have a doctor examine it. (*Turning, seeing* PRITCHETT *at gate.*) Yes, sir? (*Recognizes him.*) Oh! Come in, Mr. Pritchett. We've been waiting for you. (JOE *pushes chair to desk.*)

MR. PRITCHETT: Did you get my money back?

McLeod: I'm afraid not.

MR. PRITCHETT: What'd he do with it?

McLeod: Women and plush saloons . . . cabarets.

MR. PRITCHETT: Cabarets? I wouldn't have thought it. He seemed such an honest boy. I don't make many mistakes. I'm a pretty good student of human nature! Usually.

McLeod: You'll be in court tomorrow morning?

MR. PRITCHETT: Oh, yes.

McLeod: We can count on you?

MR. PRITCHETT: When I make my mind up, I'm like iron.

McLeod: Fine! Thank you, Mr. Pritchett.

MR. PRITCHETT: Iron.

McLEOD: Arthur, on your feet! (ARTHUR *rises*.) Is this the boy?

MR. PRITCHETT: I'm afraid it is.

McLEOD: Arthur, over here. (*Indicating chair below desk. ARTHUR crosses over. A phone rings*.) Twenty-first Squad! McLeod!

BARNES: All right, Charlie. (*Leads CHARLIE back into squad room. CHARLIE is wearing an ill-fitting, ancient pair of trousers and is disgusted with them. CHARLIE sits at bench*.)

MR. PRITCHETT (*sits*): Well, Arthur, is this your journey's end?

ARTHUR: I guess so.

MR. PRITCHETT: Did I treat you badly?

ARTHUR: No, Mr. Pritchett.

MR. PRITCHETT: Did I pay you a decent salary?

ARTHUR: Yes.

MR. PRITCHETT: Then why did you do this to me? (SUSAN *appears at gate*.)

SUSAN (*catches McLEOD's eyes*): May I? (*He nods. She comes in, walks across to ARTHUR and MR. PRITCHETT*.)

MR. PRITCHETT (*to ARTHUR*): You spent my money on fast women?

ARTHUR: Now, just a second . . . !

MR. PRITCHETT: No! I didn't grow my money on trees. I built up my business from a hole in the wall where I sold neckties, two for a quarter. Thirty years I built it. By the sweat of my brow. I worked darn hard for it. I want my money back.

SUSAN: And you'll get it back. I promise you. (*She takes money out of her purse*.) The bank was closed. All I could scrape together tonight was one hundred and twenty dollars. (*She hands money to MR. PRITCHETT*.) I'll have the rest for you tomorrow.

ARTHUR: Susan! Put that back!

SUSAN: Let me alone! Don't interfere, Jiggs!

MR. PRITCHETT (*rises*): Who is this? Who are you, Miss?

SUSAN: I'm an old friend of Mr. Kindred's family. And I'd like to straighten this out with you. What is your name?

MR. PRITCHETT: Pritchett, Albert J. Pritchett.

SUSAN: Mr. Pritchett. How do you do? I'm Susan Carmichael.

MR. PRITCHETT: How do you do? You say you're prepared to
return the rest of my money, young lady?

SUSAN: Yes, I'll sign a promissory note. Or, whatever you suggest.

MCLEOD (*into phone*): One second! (*To* SUSAN.) Where'd
you get that cash, Miss Carmichael?

SUSAN (*crossing to* MCLEOD): I had some. And I pawned
jewelry. Here are the tickets. Do you want to see them?

MCLEOD: If you don't mind. (*Takes them, examines them.*)
Anything of your sister's here?

SUSAN: Nothing. Not a bobby pin.

MR. PRITCHETT: Is this the young lady who . . . ?

ARTHUR: No. She doesn't know anything about it.

SUSAN: I know all there is to know. (*To* MR. PRITCHETT.) Mr.
Pritchett, this whole mess you can blame on my sister.

ARTHUR: What's the matter with you, Suzy? What are you
dragging Joy into this for? She's got nothing to do with it.

SUSAN (*crossing to him*): Hasn't she?

ARTHUR: No.

SUSAN: I've got news for you. I just spoke to her on the
phone. . . .

ARTHUR: You didn't tell her?

SUSAN: Of course I did.

ARTHUR: What'd she say?

SUSAN: She was upset.

ARTHUR: Naturally, she would be. You shouldn't have . . .

SUSAN: Naturally? My blue-eyed sister was in a tizzy because
she didn't want to get involved in your troubles. You know
where I called her? At Walter Forbes' in Connecticut. She's
afraid this might crimp her chances to be the next Mrs.
Forbes. . . . Big deal!

ARTHUR: I know, Suzy. That's not news to me. I know.

SUSAN: Till ten minutes ago I thought my sister was the
cherubim of the world. There wasn't anything I wouldn't
have done for her. But if she can do this to you—to you,

Jiggs—then I don't want any part of her. And I mean that. I'm through with her. I loathe her.

ARTHUR: Suzy! Take it easy.

SUSAN: All my life everything I wanted Joy got. All right! I didn't mind. I felt she was so special. She was entitled to be queen. But now I'm through.

ARTHUR: Suzy, maybe you don't understand? Like everybody else, Joy is frightened. She wants to grab a little security. Don't blame her for it. I don't.

SUSAN: Security? You've seen Walter Forbes. He's had four wives. He gets falling-down drunk every single night of his life. Some security!

ARTHUR (*crossing to chair and sitting*): He's very rich. You can't have everything.

SUSAN: Jiggs! Don't! Don't you be disgusting too. (*To* MR. PRITCHETT.) Should I make out a note for the rest?

MCLEOD: Wait a minute. (*Hangs up phone, crosses to* MR. PRITCHETT, *takes money from him, hands it back to* SUSAN.) We don't run a collection agency here! This man is a thief. We're here to prosecute criminals, not collect money. (DAKIS *comes in and goes into* LIEUTENANT'S *office, pantomimes to* LIEUTENANT *that* MRS. MCLEOD *is downstairs. Exits.*)

SUSAN: He's not a criminal.

MCLEOD: Miss Carmichael, you seem like a very nice young lady. I'm going to give you some advice. I've seen a thousand like him. *He's no good!* Take your money and run.

LIEUTENANT (*comes out of office*): McLeod!

MCLEOD (*crosses toward him*): Yes, sir!

LIEUTENANT: Get me the old files on the Cottsworth squeal!

MCLEOD (*thinks*): 1938?

LIEUTENANT: Yeah.

MCLEOD: March twelfth . . . (LIEUTENANT *nods.*) That'll be buried under a pile inside. I'll have to dig them up.

LIEUTENANT: Dig 'em up! Do it now!

MCLEOD: Yes, sir. (*As he crosses off.*) He spells one thing for you—*misery* the rest of your life. He's no good. Believe me, I know! (*Exits.*)

SUSAN (*indignantly*): That isn't true! (*To* MR. PRITCHETT.) That isn't true. I've known Arthur all my life. He never did a thing before in his life that was dishonorable. He was the most respected boy in Ann Arbor. (BRODY *crosses down to listen to* SUSAN *and* MR. PRITCHETT.)

MR. PRITCHETT: Little lady, once I saw a picture, *Less Miserables*. A dandy! That was before your time. This Gene Valjeane—his sister's nine children are starving. He steals a loaf of bread. He goes to jail for—I don't know—twenty years. I'm on Gene Valjeane's side there. Impressed me very much. I gave a little talk on it at my lodge. . . . But this? I don't go along with. He wasn't starving. He had a good job. He went cabareting . . . With my money? Heck, I don't go to them myself!

BRODY: Mr. Pritchett, maybe once a year we get someone in here steals because he's actually hungry. And we're all on his side. I'd do the same, wouldn't you?

MR. PRITCHETT: Absolutely. I always say self-preservation is the first law of nature.

BRODY: But that's one in a thousand cases.

MR. PRITCHETT: Exactly my point! And what did *he* do it for?

ARTHUR (*softly*): I did it because I was hungry.

MR. PRITCHETT: What?

ARTHUR: Hungry. You can be hungry for other things besides bread. You've been decent to me, Mr. Pritchett. You trusted me, and I let you down. I'm sorry. It's hard to explain, even to myself. I'd been separated from my girl for five years—five long, bloody years! The one human being in the world I loved. She's very beautiful, Mr. Pritchett. Tall, a silvery blond girl . . . Warm, understanding.

SUSAN: Jiggs, don't!

ARTHUR: At least she was. She was, Susan. We all change. When I came back from the war, I tried going back to school, but I couldn't get myself settled. I came to New York just to be near her. She'd moved on into a new world. She was out of my reach. I should have accepted that. I couldn't. To take her out to dinner and hold her hand cost a month's salary. I hung on, anyway. Last Wednesday I had to face it. I was going to lose my girl. She told me she wanted to marry someone else. I made a final grandstand play for her. Late collections had come in. Your money was in my pocket. I blew the works on her. I didn't give a damn about anything except holding on to her. It was my last chance. I lost, anyway. . . .

BRODY: You admit you did wrong?

ARTHUR: Yes, God, yes!

BRODY: You're willing to make restitution?

ARTHUR: If I get the chance.

SUSAN: Tomorrow morning. I promise you!

BRODY: That's in his favor. How do you feel, Mr. Pritchett?

MR. PRITCHETT: Well . . .

BRODY: This kid has a fine war record, too, remember.

MR. PRITCHETT: I know.

BRODY: He took a lot of chances for us, maybe we ought to take one for him. You see, these kids got problems nobody ever had. We don't even understand them. New blood. We're varicosed. I guess if a new world is gonna be made, looks like they're the ones gotta do it.

MR. PRITCHETT: It's funny you should say that. I was talking to my brother-in-law only the other night about my nephew and I made exactly that point. I was saying to him . . .

BRODY: Mr. Pritchett, do you mind stepping over here a minute?

MR. PRITCHETT: Not at all! (*Rises, follows him to files.*)

BRODY: You, too, Miss!

CHARLIE: Give me another cigarette.

BARNES: What do you do? Eat these things?

CHARLIE: Give me a cigarette! (BARNES *gives him another cigarette.* DAKIS *enters with* MARY MCLEOD, *leads her to* LIEUTENANT'S *office.*)

JOE: How do you do, Mrs. McLeod! Remember me? I'm Joe Feinson, the reporter.

MARY (*studies him for a split second, then recalls him*): Oh, yes, of course. I met you with my husband. What's happened to Jim?

JOE: Nothing. He's all right. He's in there.

MARY: Mr. Feinson, please tell me!

JOE: I am.

DAKIS (*holds door open*): This way, please. . . . (*She follows him into* LIEUTENANT'*s office.* DAKIS *sits at desk,* JOE *exits, and* CALLAHAN *crosses and sits at the other desk.*)

LIEUTENANT: How do you do, Mrs. McLeod?

MARY: Lieutenant Monoghan?

LIEUTENANT: Yes, ma'am.

MARY: What is this about, Lieutenant?

LIEUTENANT: Have a seat?

MARY: Where's my husband?

LIEUTENANT: He'll be back in a few minutes.

MARY: He hasn't been *shot*?

LIEUTENANT: No-o-o!

MARY: I had a terrible feeling that he . . .

LIEUTENANT: Nothing like that. He's all right.

MARY: You're sure? You're not trying to break it easy?

LIEUTENANT: Nothing like that! I give you my word. You'll see him in a few minutes.

MARY: Then what is it? What's wrong?

LIEUTENANT: A certain situation has come up, and you might be able to help us out.

MARY: Me? . . . I'm all at sea, Lieutenant!

LIEUTENANT: Mrs. McLeod, your husband and I never got along too well, I want you to know that right now. I'm sticking my neck out a mile to save him. I'm not doing it because I like him—I don't. I'm doing it because he has a value here and I need him on the squad. So, like I say, I'm going to help him, if you help me.

MARY: What kind of trouble is Jim in?

LIEUTENANT (*crossing around desk, sits*): A prisoner here was assaulted, maybe injured by your husband.

MARY: Jim wouldn't do that.

LIEUTENANT: He did. You'll have to take my word for it.

MARY: Then there must have been a reason. A very good reason.

LIEUTENANT: That's what I have to find out.

MARY: Jim is kind and gentle.

LIEUTENANT: That's one side of him.

MARY: It's the only side I know. I've never seen any other.

LIEUTENANT: Please sit down!

MARY: Is this man badly hurt?

LIEUTENANT: I don't know yet. This could become serious, Mrs. McLeod. This might cost your husband his job. He could even wind up in jail.

MARY (*sinks into chair*): How can I help?

LIEUTENANT: By answering some questions. By telling me the truth. Are you willing to go along?

MARY: Yes, of course.

LIEUTENANT: Did you ever run into a man named Kurt Schneider?

MARY (*hoarsely*): No. (*Coughs.*)

LIEUTENANT: My cigar bothering you?

MARY: No. I love the smell of a cigar. My father always smoked them.

LIEUTENANT: Did you ever hear your husband mention that name?

MARY: What name?

LIEUTENANT: This prisoner's name? Kurt Schneider.

MARY (*shakes head*): Jim made it a rule never to discuss his work with me.

LIEUTENANT: It's a good rule. We don't like to bring this sordid stuff into our homes.

MARY: I'm well trained now. I don't ask.

LIEUTENANT: How long you been married?

MARY: Three years.

LIEUTENANT: It took me ten years to train my wife. It's a tough life—being married to a cop.

MARY: I don't think so. I'm happy.

LIEUTENANT: You love your husband?

MARY: Very much.

LIEUTENANT: Where did you live before you were married? (*Phone in squad room rings.*)

DAKIS (*answers phone*): Twenty-first Squad, Detective Dakis.

MARY: New York.

LIEUTENANT: You don't sound like a native. Where you from? Upstate?

MARY: Highland Falls. You've got a good ear.

LIEUTENANT: It's my business.

DAKIS (*knocks on* LIEUTENANT'*s door*): Captain on the phone, Lieutenant. (*Returns to desk.*)

LIEUTENANT: Excuse me! . . . (*Picks up phone. In squad room* SHOPLIFTER *rises and stretches.*)

SHOPLIFTER (*to* CALLAHAN, *who is at a desk typing*): You don't look like a detective.

CALLAHAN: No? What does a detective look like?

SHOPLIFTER: They wear derbies. (*She giggles.*) You're a nice-looking fellow.

CALLAHAN: Thanks.

SHOPLIFTER: Are you married?

CALLAHAN: Yes.

SHOPLIFTER (*disgusted—the story of her life*): Ya-a-a! (*Sits down again above desk.*)

LIEUTENANT: Thanks, Captain! (*Hangs up, turns to* MRS. MCLEOD.) When'd you leave Highland Falls?

MARY: The spring of 1941. I got a job in a defense plant.

LIEUTENANT: Where?

MARY: In Newark.

LIEUTENANT (*rises*): This doctor was practicing in Newark about that time.

MARY: Doctor?

LIEUTENANT: Schneider.

MARY: Oh, he's a doctor?

LIEUTENANT: Yes. You never met him? Around Newark, maybe?

MARY: No. I don't know him.

LIEUTENANT (*sits on desk*): He knows you.

MARY: What makes you think that?

LIEUTENANT: He said so.

MARY: I'm afraid he's mistaken.

LIEUTENANT: He was positive. . . . Kurt Schneider! Ring any bells?

MARY: No. I'm afraid not.

LIEUTENANT: You averted my gaze then. Why?

MARY: Did I? I wasn't conscious of it.

LIEUTENANT: Are you sure a Dr. Schneider never treated you?

MARY (*indignantly*): Certainly not. I just told you, "No."

LIEUTENANT: Why are you so indignant? I didn't say what he treated you for.

MARY: Did this man tell my husband he treated me?

LIEUTENANT (*sits at desk*): If you'll tell the truth, Mrs. McLeod, you'll help your husband. You'll save me time and trouble. But that's all. In the end, I'll get the correct answers. We got a hundred ways of finding out the truth.

MARY: I don't know what you're talking about, Lieutenant. I'm not lying. (GALLAGHER *arrives with* TAMI GIACOPPETTI, *a handsome, swarthy man, very expensively dressed.*)

GALLAGHER: One second, Tami.

GIACOPPETTI: Can I use the phone, Champ?

GALLAGHER: Not yet, Tami. (*Knocks at* LIEUTENANT'*s door.*)

GIACOPPETTI (*stands*): O. K., Champ.

LIEUTENANT: Yeah! (GALLAGHER *hands note to* LIEUTENANT, *who glances at it, pockets it.*) Mrs. McLeod, I'm going to ask you a very personal question. Don't get angry. I would never dream of asking any woman this type of question unless I had to. You must regard me as the impersonal voice of the law. Mrs. McLeod, did Dr. Schneider ever perform an abortion on you?

MARY (*rising*): You've no right to ask me that!

LIEUTENANT: I have to do my job—and my job is to find out the truth. Let's not waste any more time! Please answer that question!

MARY: It seems to me I have some rights to privacy. My past life concerns nobody but me.

LIEUTENANT: You have the right to tell the truth. Did he?

MARY: No, Lieutenant Monoghan, he did not.

LIEUTENANT: Does this name mean anything to you? Tami Giacoppetti?

MARY: No.

LIEUTENANT (*opens door to squad room, and calls*): Mr.

Giacoppetti! (TAMI *enters* LIEUTENANT's *office, sees* MARY, *crosses down to her.*)

GIACOPPETTI (*very softly*): Hello, Mary. (*She withers, all evasion gone; her head droops as she avoids their glance.*)

LIEUTENANT (*to* MARY): Would you mind stepping in here a minute! (*Indicating room off right. They exit.* TAMI *sits, whistling a tune.* O'BRIEN *returns with* LEWIS *and* KEOGH.)

BARNES: Here's your boyfriend, Charlie!

DAKIS (*rises*): How'd you do?

O'BRIEN: We got the addresses and most of the names.

DAKIS: How many?

O'BRIEN: Nine. (*To* LEWIS.) Sit down! Over here! Lewis has been very co-operative. (LEWIS *sits.*)

CALLAHAN: Whither to, Charlie?

CHARLIE: I got to go.

CALLAHAN: Again? This makes the sixth time.

CHARLIE: Well, I'm noivous.

BARNES: Sit down, Charlie! (CHARLIE *sits at bench.*)

CALLAHAN: He's noivous, poor kid.

O'BRIEN: He needs a vacation.

DAKIS: He's gonna get one. A long one. At the state's expense.

CALLAHAN: Nuttin's too good for Charlie. (*Dialing; then on phone.*) Hello, Mrs. Lundstrom? This is Detective Callahan of the Twenty-foist Squad. We got that property was burglarized from your apartment. Will you please come down and identify it? Yeah! Yeah! We got 'em. Right. Yes, ma'am. (*Hangs up, looks at squeal card, dials another number.*)

O'BRIEN (*on phone at another desk, simultaneously*): Hello, Mr. Donatello, please. Mr. Donatello? This is Detective O'Brien of the Twenty-first Squad. Yes, sir. I think we've caught them. Yes, I have some articles here. Not all. Would you mind coming down to the station house and identifying them? Right. (*Hangs up.*)

CALLAHAN (*on phone*): Hello! Mrs. Demetrios? This is De-tective Callahan. Remember me? Twenty-foist Squad. Yeah. I'm still roarin'! How are you, Toots? (*Laughs.*) Return match? Where's your husband tonight? Okay. (McLEOD

*enters from door with bundle of records wrapped in a
sheet of dusty paper, tied with twine.*) I'll be off duty
after midnight. Oh, by the way, we got that stuff was
burglarized from your apartment. Come down and identify
it. O. K., yuh barracuda! (*Hangs up.*) A man-eater.

O'BRIEN: You watch it!

CALLAHAN: What I don't do for the good of the soivice! I
should be getting foist-grade money.

McLEOD (*undoing package*): You'll be getting a "foist" grade
knock on the head.

CALLAHAN (*disdainfully*): Brain trust. (*Walks away.*)

BRODY (*to* McLEOD): Say, Jim. I had a long talk with Mr.
Pritchett and he's willing to drop the charges.

McLEOD: He is? (*Crosses over to them.*) What's this about,
Mr. Pritchett?

MR. PRITCHETT: I decided not to bring charges against . . .
(*Nods to* ARTHUR.)

McLEOD: I thought you were going to go through with this?

MR. PRITCHETT: I'd like to give the boy another chance.

McLEOD: To steal from someone else?

MR. PRITCHETT: I wouldn't want this on my conscience.

McLEOD: Supposing he commits a worse crime. What about
your conscience then, Mr. Pritchett?

MR. PRITCHETT: I'll gamble—I'm a gambler. I bet on horses.
This once I'll bet on a human being.

McLEOD: Stick to horses—the percentage is better.

BRODY: Wait a minute, Jim. I advised Mr. Pritchett to do
this. I thought . . .

McLEOD (*harshly*): You had no right to do that, Lou. This
is my case. You know better.

BRODY: I didn't think you'd mind.

McLEOD: Well, I do.

BRODY (*angrily*): Well, I'm sorry! (KEOGH *enters.*)

SUSAN: But I'm going to return the money. And if he's satisfied, what difference does it make to you?

McLEOD: It isn't as easy as that. This isn't a civil action. This
is a *criminal* action.

GUS (*enters with sheet in his hand*): Jim! Look at this sheet on Charlie! As long as your arm. (McLEOD *takes it, studies it.* Gus *to* BARNES.) You better keep your eye on that son-of-a-bitch! (McLEOD *still studying sheet, exits with* O'BRIEN *through gate.*)

MR. PRITCHETT (*to* BRODY): But you said . . . ?

BRODY: I'm sorry. I made a mistake. It's his case. The disposition of it is up to him.

SUSAN: But if everybody concerned is . . .

BRODY: I'm sorry, girlie. You gotta leave me outa this. I got no right to interfere. Take it up with him. (*Walks away, out door, leaving* SUSAN *and* PRITCHETT *suspended in midair.* SUSAN *sinks into chair, waits for* McLEOD's *return, glancing off despairingly in his direction.* LIEUTENANT *returns to his office from anteroom.*)

GIACOPPETTI (*rises*): What's this about, Champ?

LIEUTENANT: Sit down, Tami! (*Picks up* TAMI's *hat, which is on the desk; looks at label in it.*) Dobbs Beaver? (*Impressed.*) A twenty-buck hat. You must be rolling.

GIACOPPETTI (*sits*): Forty bucks. I'm comfortable. No complaints. What's on your mind, Champ?

LIEUTENANT (*sits in swivel chair*): The woman you just said hello to.

GIACOPPETTI: Mary! What kind of trouble could she be in?

LIEUTENANT: I'd just like a little information.

GIACOPPETTI (*frowns*): That girl's a hundred per cent. I wouldn't say a word against her.

LIEUTENANT: You don't have to. She ain't in no trouble.

GIACOPPETTI: No? That's good. What do you want from me, Champ?

LIEUTENANT: Mr. Giacoppetti, all this is off the record.

GIACOPPETTI: When I talk, it's always for the record, Champ. I only say something when I got something to say, Champ.

LIEUTENANT: Look, Giacoppetti, I'm Lieutenant Monoghan. I'm in charge here. Keep your tongue in your mouth, and we'll get along.

GIACOPPETTI: Mind if I phone my lawyer?

LIEUTENANT: It ain't necessary.

GIACOPPETTI: My lawyer gets mad.

LIEUTENANT: Nothing you say here will be held against you, understand? I give you my woid.

GIACOPPETTI: I won't hurt that girl.

LIEUTENANT: I don't want you to. She's only a witness. It's someone else.

GIACOPPETTI: O. K. Shoot!

LIEUTENANT: Married?

GIACOPPETTI: Yeah.

LIEUTENANT: How long?

GIACOPPETTI: Fifteen years. What a racket that is!

LIEUTENANT: You're an expert, ain't you?

GIACOPPETTI: On what? Marriage?

LIEUTENANT: Rackets.

GIACOPPETTI: I'm a legitimate business man. Take it up with my attorney.

LIEUTENANT: Look, Mr. Giacoppetti. We've got a sheet on you. We know you're in black market up to your neck. But we don't operate in the State of New Jersey. And what went on there ain't none of our business. Unless you make it so. Kapish?

GIACOPPETTI: Yeah, I kapish.

LIEUTENANT: Got any kids?

GIACOPPETTI: No.

LIEUTENANT: I got five. You don't know what you're missing, Tami.

GIACOPPETTI (*rises, furious*): Don't rub salt in! I know. I got a wife as big as the Sahara Desert—and twice as sterile. I got nine brothers, four sisters . . . all on my payroll. None of 'em worth anything. They got kids—like rabbits they got 'em—nephews, nieces all over the lot. But a guy like me, I should become a nation, and I got no kids. Not one. So don't rub salt in, eh?

LIEUTENANT (*laughs*): O. K. I guess I know how you feel.

GIACOPPETTI (*controls himself, smiles sheepishly*): You're a sharpshooter, Champ. You hit me right on my spot.

LIEUTENANT: When did you know this girl?

GIACOPPETTI: Seven years ago.

LIEUTENANT: You like her?

GIACOPPETTI: I was crazy about her. She was my girl once.
I'd married her if I could have gotten a divorce.

LIEUTENANT: What broke it up?

GIACOPPETTI: I don't know.

LIEUTENANT: What do you think?

GIACOPPETTI: I think maybe I better call my lawyer.

LIEUTENANT: Come on, Giacoppetti. What the hell! You've
gone this far. It's off the record. Gave you my woid.

GIACOPPETTI: Aah, she gave me the air! She got caught . . .
and that soured her on me. Dames! Who can understand
them?

LIEUTENANT: Send her to a doctor?

GIACOPPETTI: To a doctor? Me? I wanted that kid. I told her,
"Give me a son—anything goes." Anything she wants. The
moon out of the sky . . . I'd get it for her. Dames! Who can
understand them? She goes off. That's the last I see of her.
Next thing I know I hear she went to some doctor. I went
looking for her. If I'da found her, I'da broken her neck. I
found him, though. I personally beat the hell out of him.
Sent him to a hospital.

LIEUTENANT: What was his name?

GIACOPPETTI: A Dutchman. Schneider . . . something.

LIEUTENANT: Kurt Schneider.

GIACOPPETTI: That's it. (LIEUTENANT *goes toward door,
beckons* MARY *in.*)

LIEUTENANT: Thank you, Tami!

GIACOPPETTI: That all?

LIEUTENANT: Almost.

GIACOPPETTI: Now will you tell me what this is about,
Champ?

LIEUTENANT: Just a minute. (MARY *enters.*) Mrs. McLeod,
Mr. Giacoppetti has told me everything.

MARY: He has?

GIACOPPETTI: In a case like this, they find out, anyway. It's
better to. (MARY *folds up, begins to weep.*)

LIEUTENANT: I'm sorry, Mrs. McLeod. (*To* GIACOPPETTI.)
Mr. Giacoppetti! (*Beckons him, both exit.*)

MCLEOD (*as it is getting dark in squad room,* MCLEOD *re-*

enters, CHARLIE's *sheet in his hand*): So you didn't done it, Charlie. (*Switches on lights.*)

CHARLIE (*weeping*): No! No! On my mother's grave!

MCLEOD: And you never been in jail?

CHARLIE (*wailing*): May I drop dead on this spot! What do you guys want from me?

MCLEOD (*to* MR. PRITCHETT): Heartbreaking, isn't it? (*Crosses to* CHARLIE.) These are your fingerprints, Charlie. They never lie. (*Reads sheet. Crosses to* CHARLIE *on bench.*) Burglary, eight arrests. Five assaults. Seven muggings. Three rapes. Six extortions. Three jail sentences. One prison break! Twenty-seven arrests. Nice little sheet, Charlie. This bum is a four-time loser. You have a club. If he makes one false move—you know what to do with it—hit him over the head.

BARNES: Don't worry, I will.

MCLEOD: Book him! Book this bum, too! (*Nods in* LEWIS' *direction.* LEWIS *rises.*)

CHARLIE (*looks at* MCLEOD): Hey, got a cigarette?

MCLEOD: What do you want—room service?

CHARLIE: It's the green-light hotel, ain't it?

MCLEOD (*growls*): Take him away!

BARNES: O. K. Charlie, come on. (*Exit* BARNES *and* CHARLIE, *laughing his head off at* MCLEOD.)

MCLEOD (*turns to* MR. PRITCHETT): Don't invest these criminals with your nervous system, Mr. Pritchett. Sure! They laugh, they cry. But don't think it's your laughter or your tears. It isn't. They're a different species, a different breed. Believe me, I know. I know it from my childhood. (JOE FEINSON *enters, stands at gate.*)

SUSAN: My God—didn't you ever make a mistake?

MCLEOD: Yes. When I was new on this job we brought in two boys who were caught stealing from a car. They looked like babies. They cried. I let them go. Two nights later— two nights later—one of them held up a butcher in Harlem. Shot him through the head an' killed him. Yes, I made a mistake, and I'm not going to do it again.

SUSAN: But, Officer, you . . .

McLEOD (*harshly*): Young lady, I don't want to discuss this
with you. Now don't interrupt me again.

ARTHUR (*rises*): Don't talk to her like that. She has a right
to speak.

McLEOD (*roars at* ARTHUR): Shut up! Sit down! (ARTHUR
sits. McLEOD *controls himself, lights cigarette.*) When
you're dealing with the criminal mind, Mr. Pritchett, softness is dangerous.

MR. PRITCHETT: But if it's a first offense?

McLEOD: It's never a first offense! It's just the first time they
get caught.

SUSAN: Why are you so vicious?

McLEOD: I'm not vicious, young lady. I didn't steal this
man's money. (*Extinguishes match, hurls it in* ARTHUR'S
direction.) He did. (*To* MR. PRITCHETT.) This is a war,
Mr. Pritchett. We know it; they know it; but you don't.
We're your army. We're here to protect you. But you've
got to co-operate. I'm sick and tired of massaging the complainant into doing his simple duty. You civilians are too
lazy or too selfish or too scared or just too indifferent to
even want to appear in court and see the charges through
that you, yourselves, bring. That makes us—street-clean-
ers. They have a stick, sweep out the street; we have a
stick—sweep out the human garbage; they pile it in
wagons, dump it in the East River; we pile it in wagons,
dump it in the Tombs. And what happens? The next day
. . . all back again.

MR. PRITCHETT: But if I get paid . . .

McLEOD: I don't care about that. This is a criminal action.
Are you? Or aren't you? Because I'm not going to let this
go.

MR. PRITCHETT: If I don't bring charges?

McLEOD: Then I'm going to book him, anyway, and sub-
poena you into court.

MR. PRITCHETT: Well . . . I . . . I . . .

McLEOD: It's my duty to protect you in spite of yourself.

MR. PRITCHETT: I guess I've got to leave it up to you, Officer.
Whatever you say.

McLEOD (*crossing to* MR. PRITCHETT): I say prosecute.

MR. PRITCHETT: All right! You know best. (*To* SUSAN.) I'm sorry. But he had no right to rob me . . . in the first place . . . that was a terrible thing to do.

McLEOD (*takes him by arm, leads him toward gate*): We won't take up any more of your time. In court tomorrow morning at ten. (MR. PRITCHETT *exits.*)

SUSAN: Mr. Pritchett . . . (*Runs after him and off.*)

McLEOD: There goes John Q. Public. "A man of iron!"

JOE: Humble yourself, sweetheart! Humble yourself!

McLEOD: What?

JOE: Seamus, Seamus, why must you always make everything so black and white? Remember, we're all of us falling down all the time. Don't be so intolerant.

McLEOD: You're out of line.

JOE: Listen to me, Seamus. Listen! I love you, and I'm trying to warn you.

McLEOD: What about? What's on your mind?

JOE: You're digging your own grave. It's right there in front of you. One more step and you're in. Now humble yourself, sweetheart, humble yourself!

McLEOD: You're very Delphic today, Yussel. What's the oracle of C.C.N.Y. trying to tell me?

JOE: Nothing. Forget it. (*He goes.*)

LIEUTENANT (*returns to his office, followed by* GIACOPPETTI. MARY *rises.*) You feel better?

MARY: Yes. Thank you.

LIEUTENANT: Are you ready to tell me the truth?

MARY: Yes.

LIEUTENANT: Your husband's been after Schneider a long time because of this?

MARY: No.

LIEUTENANT: Schneider's attorney says so.

MARY: I don't care what he says. Jim never knew. He never knew. I'm sure of that.

LIEUTENANT: Careful now! Weigh your words. This is very important. Any minute that phone'll ring. If Schneider is critically hurt, it's out of my hands. The next second this case'll be with the homicide squad. The Commissioner'll be here, the District Attorney. If that happens, I gotta have all the facts.

MARY: Jim didn't know.

LIEUTENANT: That's the question I gotta be sure of . . . now. McLeod!

McLEOD: Yes, sir? (McLEOD *enters* LIEUTENANT's *office, sees* MARY, *stops short.*) Mary! What are you doing here? What's this, Lieutenant? What's my wife . . . ?

LIEUTENANT: I sent for her.

McLEOD: Why?

LIEUTENANT: This is Mr. Giacoppetti.

GIACOPPETTI: Hi, Champ!

McLEOD: What's this about, Lieutenant?

LIEUTENANT: Schneider! Why'd you lie to me?

McLEOD: I didn't lie to you.

MARY: May I . . . may I . . . please?

LIEUTENANT: Yes. Go ahead. (*Watching* McLEOD.)

MARY: Jim, the Lieutenant won't believe me that you knew nothing about this . . . I . . .

McLEOD: About what, Mary?

MARY: Dr. Schneider.

McLEOD: What's he got to do with you?

MARY: This man you struck, this Dr. Schneider . . .

McLEOD: Don't keep saying that, Mary. He's no doctor.

MARY: He isn't? I thought he was. I . . . had occasion to see him once. I went to him once when I needed help.

McLEOD: You what?

MARY: A long time ago, Jim. (*To* LIEUTENANT.) I told you he didn't . . .

McLEOD: Wait a minute! What's he got to do with this?

MARY: We were going together.

McLEOD: I see.

MARY: I . . .

McLEOD: O. K. Diagrams aren't necessary. I get the picture.

GIACOPPETTI: I beat the hell out of this Schneider myself.

(*Touches* McLeod *on arm.* McLeod, *with a roar, slaps his hand.*) Geezel (*Holds his hand in agony.*)

LIEUTENANT: Cut that out!

GIACOPPETTI: I don't have to take that from you, Champ!

McLEOD: Touch me again and I'll tear your arm out of the socket.

LIEUTENANT (*to* McLEOD): You cut that out! In one second I'm going to flatten you myself.

McLEOD: Do you mind if I talk to my wife . . . alone? (LIEUTENANT *looks at* MARY.)

MARY: Please!

LIEUTENANT: All right, Tami. You can go. (GIACOPPETTI *goes off through squad room;* LIEUTENANT *walks into his anteroom and slams door.*)

MARY: I'm terribly sorry, Jim. Please forgive me. (*She touches him. He moves away to avoid her touch.*) Is this man badly hurt?

McLEOD: No.

MARY: Then you're not in serious trouble, Jim?

McLEOD: He's only acting. Nothing will come of it.

MARY: You're sure?

McLEOD: Yes.

MARY: Thank God for that.

McLEOD: My immaculate wife!

MARY: I never said I was.

McLEOD: You never said you weren't! Why didn't you tell me?

MARY: I loved you and I was afraid of losing you.

McLEOD: How long did you go with him?

MARY: A few months.

McLEOD: How many?

MARY: About four.

McLEOD: Four isn't a few.

MARY: No, I suppose not.

McLEOD: Did he give you money?

MARY: No.

McLEOD: But he did give you presents?

MARY: Yes. He gave me some presents, of course.

McLEOD: Expensive ones?

MARY: I don't know.

McLEOD: What do you mean you don't know?

MARY: I don't know. What difference does it make?

McLEOD: This difference. I'd just as soon Schneider died. I'd sooner go to jail for twenty years—than find out this way that my wife was a whore.

MARY: Don't say that, Jim.

McLEOD: That's the word. I didn't invent it. That's what they call it.

MARY: I don't care what anybody says. I only care about you, Jim, and it isn't true. You know it isn't true.

McLEOD: Why didn't you tell me?

MARY: I wanted to, but I didn't dare. I would have lost you.

McLEOD: I thought I knew you. I thought you were everything good and pure. . . . And with a pig like that! Live dirt!

MARY: Jim, don't judge me. Try and understand. Right and wrong aren't always as simple as they seem to you. I was on my own for the first time in a large city. The war was on. Everything was feverish! I'd only been out with kids my own age until I met this man. He paid me a lot of attention. I was flattered. I'd never met anyone like him before in my whole life. I thought he was romantic and glamorous. I thought I was in love with him. (*Phone rings on desk in squad room.*)

McLEOD: Are you trying to justify yourself in those terms?

MARY: Not justify! Just explain. It was wrong. I know it. I discovered that for myself.

McLEOD: When? Just now?

MARY: Jim, I'm trying to make my life everything you want it to be. If I could make my past life over I'd do that, too, gladly. But I can't. No one can. I made a mistake. I admit it. I've paid for it . . . plenty. Isn't that enough?

DAKIS (*crosses to* LIEUTENANT's *office, opens door, looks in*): Where's the Lieutenant?

McLeod: Inside.

Dakis (*shouting*): Lieutenant! Hospital's on the phone.

Lieutenant (*enters, picks up phone on desk*): Lieutenant Monoghan—Twenty-first. . . . Yeah! . . . Put him on! . . . Yeah? You're sure? O. K., Doc. Thank you. (*Hangs up.*) The devil takes care of his own! . . . It looks like Schneider is all right. They can't find anything wrong with him.

Mary: May I go now?

Lieutenant: Yes, Mrs. McLeod. (*Exit Lieutenant.*)

Mary: Jim, I beg you! Please understand.

McLeod: What's there to understand? . . . You got undressed before him.

Mary: Jim!

McLeod: You went to bed with him.

Mary: Jim! I can't take much more of this.

McLeod: You carried his child awhile inside you . . . and then you killed it.

Mary: Yes. That's true.

McLeod: Everything I hate . . . even murder. . . . What the hell's left to understand! (Mary *backs up to door of* Lieutenant's *office, opens it, turns, flees.*)

ACT III

SCENE: *The scene is the same. The time is 8:35 p.m.* McLeod *is seated at typewriter;* Arthur *in a chair near desk;* Susan *stands behind* Arthur's *chair;* Shoplifter *sits in chair above desk.* Brody *is left of fingerprint board, with* Lewis *at right of it.* Mr. and Mrs. Bagatelle *are behind rail;* Callahan *is at gate talking with them as they leave. They do so soon after curtain has risen.* Lady *and* Gentleman *are talking with* Keogh; Dakis *is at upstage edge of desk.* Joe *has his foot on chair as he watches* Lady *and* Gentleman. Photographer *squats down,* Charlie *is seated at*

downstage end of bench. BARNES *is standing at upstage
end of same bench.*

PHOTOGRAPHER (*to chic* LADY, *who holds stolen silver tu-
reen*): Hold up the loot! Little higher, please! (*She holds
it higher. There is a flash.*)

McLEOD (*at desk, to* ARTHUR): Hair?

ARTHUR: Brown.

McLEOD: Eyes?

ARTHUR: Eyes? I don't know . . . greenish?

McLEOD (*peering at* ARTHUR): Look brown.

SUSAN: Hazel. Brown and green flecked with gold.

McLEOD: Hazel. (*Types.*)

PHOTOGRAPHER: Thank you! (*Reloads his camera.*)

DAKIS (*to* GENTLEMAN): Sign here. (*He signs.*)

PHOTOGRAPHER (*to* JOE): Did you get the name?

JOE (*writing story in notebook*): I got it.

PHOTOGRAPHER (*going to* JOE): Park Avenue?

JOE: Spell it backwards.

PHOTOGRAPHER: K-R-A-P.

JOE: *You* got it. (PHOTOGRAPHER *chortles. They go to rail.*)

DAKIS (*to* GENTLEMAN): That's all. We'll notify you when to
come down to pick up the rest of your property.

GENTLEMAN (*plucks out some tickets from his wallet, hands
them to* DAKIS): Excellent work, Officer, excellent. (*Exits
with* LADY.)

DAKIS (*examines tickets with a slow, mounting burn. To*
CALLAHAN): How do you like that jerk? Two tickets for the
flower show! There are two kinds of people in this precinct
—the crumbs and the elite; and the elite are crumbs. (CAL-
LAHAN, *seated at a desk, laughs through his nose.* DAKIS
sits down and checks through his "squeals.")

McLEOD (*typing*): You might as well go home now, young
lady: soon as we finish this we're through.

SUSAN: A few minutes more . . . ? Please!

McLEOD (*sighs; to* ARTHUR): Weight?

ARTHUR: A hundred and fifty-two.

McLEOD: Height?

ARTHUR: Five eleven.

McLEOD: Identifying marks? Scars? Come here! (*Pulls
ARTHUR's face around.*) Scar on the left cheek. (*Types.*)
And a tattoo. Which arm was that on? (ARTHUR *raises left
hand.*) Left? A heart and the name "Joy." (*Phone rings.
CALLAHAN answers it.*)

CALLAHAN: Twenty-first Squad, Detectives, Callahan. Yeah?
A jumper? Fifty-thoid Street. (McLEOD *stops typing, listens.*) Her name? Mc . . . ? What . . . ?

McLEOD (*calls across room, sharply*): What was that name?

CALLAHAN (*on phone*): Wait a minute . . . ! (*To* McLEOD.)
What's that, Jim?

McLEOD: You got a jumper?

CALLAHAN: Yeah.

McLEOD: Woman?

CALLAHAN: Yeah.

McLEOD: She killed?

CALLAHAN: Sixteenth floor.

McLEOD: Who is it?

CALLAHAN: What'sa matter with you?

McLEOD: Who is it?

CALLAHAN: Name is McFadden. Old lady. Her son just identified her. Why?

McLEOD (*mops brow with handkerchief*): Nothing. That's
my street. Fifty-third. (CALLAHAN *looks at* McLEOD *with
puzzlement, concludes phone conversation sotto voce.*)

SUSAN (*standing behind ARTHUR's chair and smiling sadly at
him*): A tattoo?

ARTHUR (*sheepishly*): The others all had them. It made me
feel like a real sailor. I was *such* a kid. Seven years ago.

SUSAN: Seven? It was yesterday, Jiggs.

ARTHUR: Seven years. Another world.

BRODY (*finishes fingerprinting* LEWIS): Okay, Lewis! Go in
there and wash your hands. Next . . . ? (LEWIS *walks to
washroom, slowly.*)

McLEOD: Arthur! (ARTHUR *rises, walks slowly up to* BRODY
at fingerprint board. They exchange glances.)

BRODY (*softly*): This hand, son. Just relax it. That's it. This finger. Roll it toward me.

DAKIS (*rises*): Well, three old squeals polished off. I'm clean. (*Crosses into* LIEUTENANT'S *office, leaving door open.*)

CALLAHAN: There's one here I'm sure they did. (*Propels himself in swivel chair, over to* CHARLIE.) Charlie, did you burglarize this apartment on Sixty-first Str . . . (*Silence.*) Why don't you give us a break? You help us . . . we'll help you.

CHARLIE: How the hell you gonna help me? I'm a four-time loser. I'm goin' to jail for the rest of my life. How the hell you gonna help me?

CALLAHAN: You lived a louse, you wanta die a louse?

CHARLIE: Yes! (CALLAHAN *starts to give him the back of his hand.*) Careful! De sign says courtesy.

CALLAHAN: Coitesy? For you, you bum! You want coitesy? Here! (*Tears off sign on* LIEUTENANT'S *door, hits him on head with it.* CHARLIE *laughs.* LEWIS *comes swaggering out of washroom.*)

BRODY (*finishes fingerprinting* ARTHUR): That's all, son. Go inside and wash your hands. (ARTHUR *goes into washroom.* LEWIS *and* MCLEOD *cross to a desk.*)

MCLEOD: All right, Lewis. . . . Sign here. (BRODY *goes to table;* CALLAHAN *crosses to files.*)

SHOPLIFTER (*rises, to* SUSAN): It don't hurt. You roll it. (*Demonstrates.*) Like that. Just gets your hands a little dirty. It washes right off. It's nothing. (SUSAN *crumples into a chair.*) What'sa matter? Did I say something? (SUSAN *shakes her head.*) Are you married? (SUSAN *shakes head.*) Me neither. Everybody tells you why don't you get married. You should get married. My mother, my father, my sisters, my brother—"Get married!" As if I didn't want to get married. Where do you find a man? Get me a man, I'll marry him. *Anything!* As long as it's got pants. You think I'd be here? A rotten crocodile bag? I'd be home, cooking him such a meal. Get married!! It's easy to talk! (*Sits again.*)

JOE (*with* PHOTOGRAPHER, BARNES *and* CHARLIE *goes to desk; to* BARNES): O. K., Steve! Get 'em over here.

BARNES (*moves chair for* LEWIS; *nudges* CHARLIE *with his stick*): Rise and shine, Charlie. (*They line up in front of desk.* DAKIS *crosses out of office, puts coat on and sits.* MCLEOD *sits at desk.*)

JOE (*to* BARNES): Want to stand on the end? (BARNES *does.*)

BARNES: Stand here, Lewis.

LEWIS (*comes close to* CHARLIE, *murmurs in his ear*): You louse! I ought to kill you.

CHARLIE (*mutters*): Me? The thanks I get!

JOE (*to* PHOTOGRAPHER): Wait a minute! I want to line up those bullets. I want 'em in the shot. (*Stands bullets on end.*) Can you get 'em in? (MCLEOD *picks up* ARTHUR'S *"sheet."*)

PHOTOGRAPHER: Yeah! Ready?

LEWIS: Thirty grand, eh?

CHARLIE: Uh!

LEWIS: I saw the list.

PHOTOGRAPHER (*to* BARNES, *posing them for the shot*): Grab him by the arm. Look at him.

CHARLIE (*mutters*): Lists? It's a racket! People get big insurance on fake stuff. They collect on it.

BARNES (*smiling for photo, through his gleaming teeth*): Sh! You spoil the picture. (*The picture is taken.* BARNES' *gleaming smile vanishes.*) Over there! (*He waves them to bench with his club, turns to* JOE *to make sure his name is spelled correctly, fixes chair.*)

LEWIS: What about that fourteen hundred dollars?

CHARLIE (*indignantly*): I had it on me for your protection. If this flatfoot had any sense, he was supposed to take it and let us go . . . Dumb cop! Can I help it? (BARNES *crosses, handcuffs them, goes to door of* LIEUTENANT'S *office.*)

LEWIS: Now, look, I want my share.

CHARLIE: All right, Lewis. I'm not gonna argue with you . . . If it'll make you happy, I'll give you the whole fourteen hundred. Satisfied?

LEWIS (*thinks it over*): Ya.

CHARLIE: Good. (ARTHUR *crosses to* McLEOD.)

BARNES: No talking.

McLEOD (*to* ARTHUR): Your signature. Here! (ARTHUR *glances at card, hesitates.*)

SUSAN (*rises*): Shouldn't he see a lawyer first?

McLEOD: It's routine.

SUSAN: Anyway, a lawyer should . . . (McLEOD *presses his temples, annoyed.*)

ARTHUR: Susan! (*Shakes his head.*)

SUSAN: Excuse me. (*Crosses near* BRODY. McLEOD *hands* ARTHUR *pen.* ARTHUR *looks about for an ashtray for his cigarette butt.*)

McLEOD: On the floor. (ARTHUR *throws it on floor.*) Step on it! (ARTHUR *steps on butt, crosses to* McLEOD.)

ARTHUR: Where do I sign?

McLEOD: Here. (*Indicates line on card.* ARTHUR *signs; sits.*)

SUSAN (*going over to* ARTHUR): I believe in you, Arthur. I want you to know. Deep inside—deep down, no matter what happens—I have faith in you.

JOE (*to* PHOTOGRAPHER): Now, this one. (*To* McLEOD.) You want to be in this?

McLEOD (*pressing his temples*): No! Got an aspirin, Yussel?

JOE (*curtly*): No. (*Walks away.*)

PHOTOGRAPHER (*to* ARTHUR): You mind standing up? (*Flashes picture as* ARTHUR *rises.*)

SUSAN (*hysterical; crosses to* PHOTOGRAPHER, *turns to* BRODY): No! No! They don't have to do that to him! They don't have to. (*Desperately, to* BRODY.) Officer Brody. They're not going to print that in the papers, are they?

ARTHUR (*goes to her*): It's all right, Suzy! Stop trembling. Please. I don't care . . .

BRODY (*beckons* JOE *and* PHOTOGRAPHER *out through gate*): Joe! Teeney! (*They follow him.*)

SUSAN: I'm not . . . really . . . It was the sudden flash! (*Buries head in her hands, turns away to control herself.*)

DAKIS (*putting on his hat and jacket, to* SHOPLIFTER): Well, quarter to nine. Night court'll be open by the time we get there. Come on. (*Crosses around desk to her.*)

SHOPLIFTER (*rising, picking up her bag and scarf*): What do I do?

DAKIS: They'll tell you. Your brother-in-law's gonna be there, ain't he?

SHOPLIFTER: Yeah. All I can do is thank goodness my sister's sexy. Well . . . (*Looks about.*) So long, everybody! Really it's been very nice meeting you all. And I'm sorry I caused you all this trouble! Good-by! (*She and* DAKIS *go off.*)

McLEOD (*crossing to* SUSAN): You better go home now, young lady. It's all over.

SUSAN: May I talk to Arthur? For two minutes, alone? Then I'll go. I won't make any more trouble, I promise.

McLEOD: All right. (*Handcuffs* ARTHUR *to chair at desk.*) Two minutes. (*Goes to* LIEUTENANT'S *office, sits in darkened room, in chair above desk.*)

SUSAN (*going to* ARTHUR, *lips trembling*): Jiggs . . .

ARTHUR (*calming her*): Don't!

SUSAN (*dragging a chair over to* ARTHUR; *sits*): I'm not going to cry. This is no time for emotionalism. I mean we must be calm and wise. We must be realists.

ARTHUR (*smiles*): Yes, Suzy.

SUSAN: The minute I walk out of here, I'm going to call Father.

ARTHUR: No, Susan, don't do that!

SUSAN: But he likes you so much, Arthur. He'll be glad to help.

ARTHUR: I don't want him to know. I'm ashamed. I'm so ashamed of myself.

SUSAN: Jiggs, it's understandable.

ARTHUR: Is it? I don't understand it! I stole, Suzy. I stole money from a man who trusted me! Where am I? Am I still floating around in the middle of the Pacific, looking for concrete platforms that aren't there? How mixed up can you get?

SUSAN: But, Jiggs, everybody gets mixed up, some time or other.

ARTHUR: They don't steal. . . . It's a kind of delirium, isn't it?

SUSAN: O. K. So it is delirium, Jiggs. So what? You're coming out of it fine.

ARTHUR (*shakes his head*): Look around, Susan. Look at this. (*Indicates his handcuffs.*) The dreams I had—the plans I made . . . to end like this?

SUSAN: This isn't the end of the world, Jiggs.

ARTHUR: It is for me. How did this happen—how did I come to this? (*Studies handcuffs.*) All I ever wanted was to live quietly in a small college town . . . to study and teach. No! (*Bitterly.*) This isn't a time for study and teachers . . . this is a time for generals.

SUSAN (*rises, going around chair*): God, I hate that kind of talk, Jiggs! Everywhere I hear it. . . . I don't believe it. Whatever happens to you, you can still pick up and go on. If ever there was a time for students and teachers, this is it. I know you can still make whatever you choose of your life. (*Pauses, sees his anguish.*) Arthur! Do you want Joy? Would that help? Would you like to see her and talk to her?

ARTHUR: No.

SUSAN: I'll go to Connecticut and bring her back.

ARTHUR: I don't want her.

SUSAN: I'll get her here. Say the word. I'll bring her here, Arthur. She'll come. You know she will.

ARTHUR: I don't want her, Suzy. I don't want Joy.

SUSAN: You're sure?

ARTHUR: Yes. I wouldn't know what to say to her now. For five years I've been in love with a girl that doesn't exist. That's finished.

SUSAN: Oh, Arthur! Why couldn't you have fallen in love with *me*?

ARTHUR (*looks at her, then, tenderly*): I've always loved you, Suzy. You were always . . . my baby.

SUSAN: I've news for you. I voted in the last election. I'm years past the age of consent.

ARTHUR: Just an old bag?

SUSAN: Arthur, why didn't you fall in love with me? I'd have

been so much better for you. I know I'm not as beautiful
as Joy, but . . .

ARTHUR: But you are. Joy's prettier than you, Susan, but
you're more beautiful.

SUSAN: Oh, Jiggs, you fracture me! Let us not . . .

ARTHUR: Let us not be emotional. We were going to be
realists, remember?

SUSAN: Yes.

ARTHUR: Suzy, when I go to jail . . . (*Her lips quiver again.*)
Now . . . Realists?

SUSAN: I'm not going to cry.

ARTHUR: Be my sensible Susan!

SUSAN: Jiggs, I can't be sensible about you. I love you.

ARTHUR: Suzy, darling . . .

SUSAN: Jiggs, whatever happens—when it's over—let's go
back home again.

ARTHUR: That would be wonderful, Suzy. That would be
everything I ever wanted.

CHARLIE (*on end of bench; pretends to play violin—screeches
"Hearts and Flowers." Then laughs raucously.*) Hear that,
Lewis? He's facin' five to ten? Wait'll the boys go to
work on him. (ARTHUR *and* SUSAN *look at him; to* SUSAN.)
What makes you think he'll want you then?

SUSAN: What?

CHARLIE: A kid like this in jail. They toss for him.

SUSAN: What do you mean?

CHARLIE: To see whose chicken he's gonna be! Whose sweetheart!

SUSAN (*rises*): What does that mean? What's he talking
about?

ARTHUR: Don't listen to him. (*To* CHARLIE.) Shut up! Who
asked you to . . . ?

CHARLIE: After a while you get to like it. Lotsa guys come
out, they got no use for dames after that.

ARTHUR: Shut up!

CHARLIE: Look at Lewis, there. He's more woman than man,
ain't you, ain't you, Lewis? (LEWIS *grins.*)

ARTHUR (*rises in a white fury, goes for* CHARLIE, *dragging chair to which he is handcuffed*): Shut up! I'll crack your goddamn skull! (BARNES *runs over to* CHARLIE.)

SUSAN: Stop them! Stop! (BRODY *enters quickly.*) Officer Brody, make him stop! Make him stop!

BRODY (*to* ARTHUR): Take it easy! Sit down! (*Kicks* CHARLIE *in shins.*) Why don't you shut up?

SUSAN: Oh, Officer Brody, help us! Help us!

BRODY (*crossing to desk*): Take it easy. He ain't convicted yet. The judge might put him on probation. He might get off altogether. A lot of things might happen.

CHARLIE: Yak! Yak!

BRODY: One more peep outa you! One! (*Slaps* CHARLIE. *To* BARNES.) Take them inside! (BARNES *waves* CHARLIE *and* LEWIS *into next room. As they pass* ARTHUR, LEWIS *eyes* ARTHUR *up and down, grinning and nodding.* CHARLIE *hums his mockery of "Hearts and Flowers."* BARNES *prods* CHARLIE *with his nightstick, muttering "We heard the voice." They exit. To* SUSAN.) If the complainant still wants to give him a break, that'll help. You got a good lawyer? (*She shakes her head.*) I'll give you the name of a cracker-jack! I'm not supposed to, but I'll call him myself. There are a lot of tricks to this business.

SUSAN: Don't let it happen!

BRODY: Here's his picture! (*Crumples up photographic plate, tosses it into wastebasket, goes to his file cabinet, fishes out bottle of liquor.* SUSAN *begins to weep.*)

ARTHUR (*pulls* SUSAN *to chair*): Sh! Sh! Listen. The rest of my life, I'm going to find ways to make this up to you. I swear. Whatever happens . . . (*Puts arms around her, pulls her down into chair alongside him, holds her tight.*)

SUSAN (*clinging to him*): Arthur, I . . .

ARTHUR: Sh! Don't say anything more, Suzy. We've got a minute left. Let's just sit here like this . . . quietly. (CAL-LAHAN *exits;* SUSAN *starts to speak.*) Sh! Quiet! (*She buries her head in his shoulder, and they sit there in a gentle embrace. After a second's silence, she relaxes.*) Better?

SUSAN (*nods*): Mm!

BRODY (*goes into* LIEUTENANT'S *office, looking for* McLEOD):

What are you sitting in the dark for? (*Switches on light.*)
Want a drink, Jim?

McLEOD: No.

BRODY (*pours himself a stiff drink while standing between
door and desk*): Jim, I've been your partner for thirteen
years. I ever ask you for a favor?

McLEOD (*pressing hand to his temples*): What is it, Lou?

BRODY: That kid outside. (McLEOD *groans.*) I want you to
give him a break.

McLEOD: You know better. I can't adjudicate this case.

BRODY: And what the hell do you think you're doing?

McLEOD: What makes him so special?

BRODY: A lot. I think he's a good kid. He's got a lot on the
ball. Given another chance . . . Jim, he reminds me of my
boy.

McLEOD: Mike—was a hero.

BRODY: Why? Because he was killed? If Mike'd be alive today, he'd have the same problems this kid has.

McLEOD: Lou, Lou—how can you compare?

BRODY: Thousands like 'em, I guess. New generation, a new
idea. We don't even understand them, Jim. I didn't Mike,
till he was killed. . . . Too late then. (*Swallows his drink.*)
How about it?

McLEOD: Don't ask me, will you?

BRODY: But I am.

McLEOD (*rises, pushing chair back*): I can't. I can't do it,
Lou. I can't drop the charges.

BRODY: Louder, please! I don't seem to hear so good outa
this ear.

McLEOD: This fellow and Mike—day and night—there's no
comparison.

BRODY: Jim, this is me, Lou Brody. Remember me? What do
you mean you can't drop it? You coulda let him go two
hours ago. You still can. The complainant left it up to you.
I heard him.

McLEOD: Be logical, Lou.

BRODY: To hell with logic! I see you logic the life out of a

thing. Heart! Heart! The world's crying for a little heart.
What do you say?

McLEOD: No, Lou. No dice!

BRODY (*crosses to chair, sits*): My partner! Arrest his own
mother.

McLEOD: I'm too old to start compromising now.

BRODY: There's a full moon out tonight. It shows in your
puss.

McLEOD (*crossing a step*): You shouldn't drink so much, Lou.
It melts the lining of your brain.

BRODY (*pushes bottle to him*): Here! You take it. Maybe
that's what you need. Maybe it'll melt that rock you got in
there for a heart.

McLEOD: Stop it, Lou, will you? My nerves are like banjo
strings.

BRODY: Well, play something on them. Play "Love's Old
Sweet Song."

McLEOD (*crossing to* BRODY): Shut up! Lay off! Goddamn it!
I'm warning you. Lay off!

BRODY (*studies him, then . . . softer*): What's the matter?

McLEOD: I'm drowning, Lou. I'm drowning. That's all. I'm
drowning in my own juices. (*Sits in swivel.*)

BRODY: I wish I could understand what makes you tick.

McLEOD (*as* JOE *enters* LIEUTENANT's *office*): I don't expect
you to understand me, Lou. I know I'm different than the
others. I think differently. I'm not a little boy who won't
grow up, playing cops and robbers all his life, like Callahan; and I'm not an insurance salesman, like you, Lou.
I'm here out of principle!! Principle, Lou. All my life I've
lived according to principle! And I couldn't deviate even
if I wanted to.

BRODY: Sometimes you gotta bend with the wind . . . or
break! Be a little human, Jim! Don't be such a friggin'
monument!

McLEOD: How, how? How do you compromise? How do you
compromise—convictions that go back to the roots of your
childhood? I hate softness. I don't believe in it. My
mother was soft: It killed her. I'm no Christian. I don't

believe in the other cheek. I hate mushiness. You ask me to compromise for this kid? Who the hell is he? Now, right now, Lou, I'm faced with a problem of my own that's ripping me up like a .22 bullet bouncing around inside, and I can't compromise on that. So what do I do? What do I do?

JOE: Try picking up that phone and calling her.

McLEOD: Who?

JOE: Mary. (*Tosses aspirin box onto desk.*) Here's your aspirin.

McLEOD: What are you talking about?

JOE: This ".22 bullet."

McLEOD: You don't know anything about it.

JOE: It's one story I had in my pocket years before it happened.

McLEOD: Listening at keyholes, Yussel?

JOE: No. I met Mary years before you did. The spring of '41 —I was on the *Newark Star*. She didn't remember me. I never forgot her, though. It's one of those faces you don't forget. She's one in a million, your Mary. I know. She's a fine girl, Seamus. She could have had anything she wanted —materially—anything. She chose you instead. Why? What'd you have to offer her? Buttons! These crazy hours, this crazy life? She loves you. You don't know how lucky you are. I know. I'm little and ugly—and because I'm a lover of beauty, I'm going to live and die alone. But you? . . . The jewel was placed in your hands. Don't throw it away. You'll never get it back again! (CALLAHAN *reenters squad room. Offers* ARTHUR *and* SUSAN *cigarettes and lights them for them.*)

BRODY (*softly*): You know what you were like before you met Mary? You remember?

McLEOD: Yes.

BRODY: Like a stick! Thin.

McLEOD (*broken*): Yes.

BRODY: Dried up, lonely, cold.

McLEOD: Yes.

BRODY: And you know what tenderness and warmth she brought to your life?

McLEOD: I know. I know better than you. (MARY *enters squad room.*)

BRODY: So what the hell you asking me what to do? Pick up the phone! Get on your knees. Crawl!

CALLAHAN: Yes, Miss?

MARY: Is Detective McLeod here?

CALLAHAN: He's busy, Miss.

MARY (*wearily*): It's *Mrs.*, Mrs. McLeod.

CALLAHAN: Oh! Yes, ma'am. I'll tell him you're here. (*Crosses. Pokes his head into* LIEUTENANT'S *office, to* McLEOD.) Jim, your wife is out here. (McLEOD *rises at once, comes out of* LIEUTENANT'S *office, to* MARY. JOE *and* BRODY *follow him out, discreetly vanish into washroom.* BRODY *leaves whisky bottle and glass on file near washroom door.*)

MARY (*digs into her purse to avoid his eyes; her voice low, brittle, weary*): I'm leaving now, Jim. I thought I'd come up and tell you. Here are the keys.

McLEOD (*softly*): Come inside.

MARY: My taxi's waiting.

McLEOD: Send it away.

MARY: No. My things are in it.

McLEOD: What things?

MARY: My valises and my trunk.

McLEOD: Oh, Mary, be sensible.

MARY: I intend to. Let's not drag it out, Jim! Please! I don't want any more arguments. I can't stand them. (*Her voice becomes shrill.* CALLAHAN *passes by, crosses to files. She clamps controls on, becoming almost inaudible.*) It's only going to make things worse.

McLEOD: Come inside! I can't talk to you here.

MARY: The meter's ticking.

McLEOD (*firmly*): Let it tick! Come! (*She goes into* LIEUTENANT'S *office with him. He shuts door, turns to her.*) Mary, this isn't the time or place to discuss our lives, past, present or future. I want you to take your things and go home. I'll be back at eight A.M. and we'll work this out then.

MARY: You think we can?

McLEOD: We'll have to.

MARY: I don't think it's possible.

McLEOD: Wait a minute! Wait one minute! I don't get this. What are *you* so bitter about? Who's to blame for tonight? You put me in a cement mixer. And now you're acting as if I were the . . .

MARY: The whore?

McLEOD: Don't say that!

MARY: I didn't invent the word, either, Jim.

McLEOD: I wasn't myself.

MARY: You were never more yourself, Jim, and you called me a whore.

McLEOD: I'm sorry, Mary.

MARY: It's all right. I'm beyond feeling. I'm nice and numb.

McLEOD: You're certainly in no condition to discuss this tonight.

MARY: I've thought everything over and over and over again and I don't see any other way out. I know what I'm doing has got to be. Our life is finished. We couldn't go on from here.

McLEOD: You're married to me. You can't just walk out. Marriage is a sacrament, Mary. You don't dissolve it like that.

MARY: You once told me when you bring a married prostitute in here, if she's convicted, her marriage can be dissolved "just" like that! Well, I've been brought in and I've been convicted.

McLEOD: I don't like that talk. Stop that talk, will you, Mary? I'm trying, I'm trying . . .

MARY: To what?

McLEOD: To put all this behind me.

MARY: But you can't do it. Can you?

McLEOD: If you'll let me.

MARY: Me? What have I got to say about it? I know the way your mind works. It never lets go. The rest of our days

we'll be living with this. If you won't be saying it, you'll
be thinking it. . . . It's no good. It won't work. I don't
want to live a cat-and-dog existence. I couldn't take it. I'd
dry up. I'd dry up and die.

McLEOD: Why didn't you ever tell me? If you'd come to me
once, just once . . .

MARY: What good would it have done? Would you have
understood? Would you have been able to forgive me?

McLEOD: Wasn't I entitled to know?

MARY: Yes, yes!

McLEOD: Why didn't you tell me?

MARY: Jim, I can't go over this again and again and again. I
refuse to.

McLEOD: If I didn't love you and need you so, it'd be simple,
you understand?

MARY: I understand.

McLEOD: Simple. You go home now and wait till morning.

MARY: That won't help us. Please, I'm so tired, let me go now,
Jim.

McLEOD: To what? What'll you go to? You, who turn on
every light in the house when I'm not there!

MARY: Let me go, Jim.

McLEOD: You, who can't fall asleep unless my arms are
around you! Where will you go?

MARY: Jim, I beg you . . .

McLEOD: No, Mary, I'm not going to. (*Grasps her by the
arm.*)

MARY: You're hurting my arm.

McLEOD: I'm sorry . . . I'm sorry. (*Lets her go.*)

MARY: You ripped my sleeve.

McLEOD: You'll sew it up.

MARY: The taxi's waiting. Please, Jim, let me go, without any
more razor-slashing. I hate it.

McLEOD: You'd go without a tear? (CALLAHAN *starts to cross
to* LIEUTENANT's *office.*)

MARY: I wouldn't say that. One or two, perhaps. I haven't
many left. You'll find them all on my pillow.

McLeod: Mary, I . . . (Callahan *enters* Lieutenant's *office, leaving paper on desk; exits.*) Mary, you just don't stop loving someone.

Mary: I wouldn't have thought so. I wouldn't have believed it could happen. But there it is. I suppose in this life we all die many times before they finally bury us. This was one of those deaths. Sudden, unexpected, like being run over by a bus. It happens.

McLeod (*turns her*): Who do you think you're kidding?

Mary: No one! (*Begins to cry.*) Least of all, myself.

McLeod (*takes her in his arms*): Mary, I love you.

Mary (*clinging to him, sobbing*): Then help me! I'm trying to be a human being. I'm trying to bundle myself together. It took every bit of strength to go this far. Help me, Jim. (Callahan *crosses to files.*)

McLeod: It's no use, sweetheart, it's no use. I couldn't go home if you weren't waiting for me with the radio going and the smell of coffee on the stove. I'd blow out my brains. I would, Mary, if I went home to an empty flat—I wouldn't dare take my gun with me. Now powder your nose! Put on some lipstick. (*She kisses him.* Sims *appears at gate, outside of rail.*)

Callahan (*goes to* Sims): Yes, Counsellor?

Sims: I want to see Detective McLeod.

Callahan: All right, Counsellor. Come in. (*Knocks on* Lieutenant's *office door, crosses to files.*)

McLeod: Come in!

Callahan: Someone's outside to see you.

Mary: I'll go home, now.

McLeod: No. Wait a minute.

Mary (*smiles now*): That taxi bill is going to break us.

McLeod (*grins back at her*): Let it break us, what do we care? It's only money. (*He goes out to the squad room, sees* Sims; *his face goes grim again.*) You see, Counsellor? I told you your client was acting.

Sims: He's still in shock.

McLeod: He'll be okay in the morning.

Sims: I suppose so. No thanks to you. When he's brought

back here tomorrow, though, he'd better remain okay. This is not to happen again! You're not to lay a finger on him. If you do . . .

MCLEOD: Then advise him again to keep his mouth shut.

SIMS: You're lucky you're not facing a murder charge yourself, right now.

MCLEOD: I could always get you to defend me.

SIMS: And I probably would. That's my job, no matter how I feel personally.

MCLEOD: As long as you get your fee?

SIMS: I've defended many men at my own expense.

MCLEOD: That was very noble of you.

SIMS: Nobility doesn't enter into it. Every man has a right to counsel, no matter how guilty he might seem to you, or to me, for that matter. Every man has a right not to be arbitrarily judged, particularly by men in authority; not by you, not by the Congress, not even by the President of the United States. The theory being these human rights are derived from God Himself.

MCLEOD: I know the theory, Counsellor. (BARNES, CHARLIE *and* LEWIS *enter;* CHARLIE *sits at bench,* LEWIS *and* BARNES *at table.*)

SIMS: But you don't go along with it? Well, you're not alone. There are others. You've a lot of friends all over the world. Read the headlines. But don't take it on yourself to settle it. Let history do that.

MCLEOD: Save it for the Fourth of July, Counsellor.

SIMS: I'll save it for the Commissioner. I intend to see him about you. I'm not going to let you get away with this.

MCLEOD: As long as Schneider gets away with it, Counsellor, all's well. Why do you take cases like this, if you're so high-minded? Schneider killed the Harris girl—he's guilty. You know it as well as I do.

SIMS: I don't know it. I don't even permit myself to speculate on his guilt or innocence. The moment I do that, I'm judging . . . and it is not my job to judge. My job is to defend my client, not to judge him. That remains with the courts. (*Turns to go.*)

McLEOD: And you've got that taken care of, Counsellor. Between bought witnesses and perjured testimony . . .

SIMS (*stops in his tracks, turns to* McLEOD): If you're so set on hanging Schneider, why don't you ask Mrs. McLeod if she can supply a corroborating witness? (McLEOD *looks a little sick; lights a cigarette slowly; returns to* LIEUTENANT'S *office.*)

MARY: What's the matter, dear?

McLEOD: Nothing.

MARY: This has been our black day.

McLEOD: Yes.

MARY: I'm sorry, darling. And yet, in a way, I'm glad it's out in the open. This has been hanging over my head so long. I've had such a terrible feeling of guilt all the time.

McLEOD (*mutters*): All right! All right!

MARY: I needed help and there was no one. I couldn't even go to my parents.

McLEOD: They didn't know?

MARY: No.

McLEOD: You didn't tell them?

MARY: I didn't dare. I didn't want to hurt them. You know how sweet and simple they are.

McLEOD: You didn't go home then?

MARY: No.

McLEOD: Where'd you go?

MARY: That's when I came to New York.

McLEOD: And how long was that before I met you, Mary?

MARY: Two years.

McLEOD: Who'd you go with then?

MARY: No one.

McLEOD: How many others were there, Mary?

MARY: Others?

McLEOD: How many other men?

MARY: None. (*Alarmed now at look on his face.*) What's the matter with you, Jim?

McLEOD: Wait a minute! Wait a minute!

MARY: No! What's the matter with you?

McLEOD: At an autopsy I witnessed yesterday, the medical

examiner sawed off the top of a man's skull, took out the brain, and held it in his hand. (*Holds out his hand.*) Like that.

MARY (*horrified*): Why are you telling me this?

McLEOD: Because I'd give everything I own to be able to take out my brain and hold it under the faucet and wash away the dirty pictures you put there tonight.

MARY: Dirty pictures?

McLEOD: Yes!

MARY: Oh! I see. . . . I see. (*To herself.*) Yes. That would be convenient, if we could. (*She straightens out, turns to him.*) But when you wash away what I may have put there, you'll find you've a rotten spot in your brain, Jim, and it's growing. I know. I've watched it . . .

McLEOD (*hoarsely*): Mary! That's enough.

MARY (*stronger than he, at last*): No, let's have the truth! I could never find it in my heart to acknowledge one tiny flaw in you—because I loved you so—and God help me, I still do! But let's have the truth, for once, wherever it may lead. You think you're on the side of the angels? You're not! You haven't even a drop of ordinary human forgiveness in your whole nature. You're everything you've always said you hated in your own father.

McLEOD (*throws on his jacket, takes her by arm*): I'm not going to let you wander off in the streets this way. I'm going to take you home myself.

MARY (*screams at him*): What for? To kill me the way your father killed your mother!! There are the keys. (*He takes his hand off her as if he'd been struck. She puts keys down on desk, turns to go off through squad room and door.*)

McLEOD: Where are you going? (*She looks at him, sadly.*)

MARY: Far away . . . you won't find me. I'm scorching my earth . . . burning my cities.

McLEOD: When will I see you?

MARY: Never. . . . Good-by. . . . (*She goes through squad room and off. McLEOD, dazed, walks slowly back to squad room.*)

BRODY (*enters washroom with JOE*): How'd it go?

McLEOD: Fine.

BRODY: I mean Mary.

McLEOD: Fine. Dandy. (*Crossing to* SUSAN.) All right, young lady, your two minutes are up. (LIEUTENANT *enters*.)

LIEUTENANT (*to* McLEOD): What the hell's the matter with you?

McLEOD: Nothing. . . .

LIEUTENANT: Don't you feel well?

McLEOD: Yes, sir. Feel all right.

LIEUTENANT (*to* BRODY): Am I crazy? Look at him.

BRODY: You've gone all green, Jim.

McLEOD: I've got a headache.

LIEUTENANT: You better go home. Buzz your doctor.

McLEOD: I've got a squeal to finish off, Lieutenant.

LIEUTENANT: Brody! You finish it off.

BRODY (*reluctantly*): Yes, sir.

McLEOD: I'd rather do it myself.

LIEUTENANT: You go home. That's an order.

McLEOD: Yes, sir.

LIEUTENANT: Callahan! You catch for Jim tonight.

CALLAHAN: Yes, sir. (*Crosses up to duty chart, takes it off wall.*)

BRODY (*crossing to* McLEOD): What happened, Jim? What's wrong?

McLEOD (*sits down heavily on nearest chair*): Mary left me. Walked out. We're finished.

BRODY: Too bad. She'll come back.

McLEOD: No. . . . This was for keeps. (LIEUTENANT *walks over*.)

LIEUTENANT: What are you sitting there for? Why don't you go home? (LIEUTENANT *exits*.)

McLEOD: Because I haven't got any . . .

JOE (*comes down to him, close*): You drove her away, didn't you? Why? (McLEOD *doesn't answer*.) I tried to warn you, you damn fool. Why?

McLEOD: Why? Why do we do these things, Yussel? Who knows? I built my whole life on hating my father—and all the time he was inside me laughing—or maybe he was crying, the poor bastard! Maybe he couldn't help himself, either. (*An excited woman,* INDIGNANT CITIZEN, *enters.*)

CALLAHAN: Yes, Miss? (*He is at a desk reaching into bottom drawer for celluloid letters to replace name on duty chart.*)

INDIGNANT CITIZEN: Someone snatched my purse . . .

CALLAHAN: Come on in, Miss. We'll take care of you. (*Bends over to pick up a letter.*)

INDIGNANT CITIZEN: This happened to me once before . . . on Seventy-second Street . . . (CHARLIE *lunges for* CALLAHAN's *exposed gun, grabs it, hits* CALLAHAN *on head with butt, knocking him out.* BARNES *raises his club.*)

CHARLIE: Drop that club! (*Aims at* BARNES.)

BRODY: Drop it! He's a four-time loser. He'll kill you. (BARNES *drops club.*)

CHARLIE: Goddamn right. Rot in jail the rest of my life! I take five or six a-you bastards with me first. (BARNES *makes a movement.*)

BRODY: Take it easy! He can't get by the desk.

CHARLIE: Shut up. One word! One move! Anybody! (Mc-LEOD, *seated, laughs.*)

McLEOD: I was wondering when you'd get around to it, Charlie.

CHARLIE: None of your guff, you!!

McLEOD: Give me that gun! (*Rises.*)

CHARLIE: In the gut . . . you'll get it. One step! I'm warnin' you. One!

BRODY: Easy, Jim. He can't get by the desk.

McLEOD (*walks toward him, reaching for gun*): You evil son-of-a-bitch! (CHARLIE *fires point-blank at* McLEOD. *One, two, three quick shots.* McLEOD *staggers back and is whirled around by impact.* BARNES *goes into action, knocks gun out of* CHARLIE's *hand, starts beating him over the head with his club.* O'BRIEN *crosses to* CHARLIE. KEOGH *and* MOTORCYCLE COP *rush in.*)

BRODY (*rushes to him, puts arms around him, supporting him*): Jim! Did he get you? Are you hurt? (CALLAHAN *crosses to washroom.*)

McLEOD: Slightly. . . . (*A little boy for one second.*) Oh,

Mary, Mary, Mary . . . Slightly killed, I should say. . . . (LIEUTENANT *comes running in from door, also a number of* POLICEMEN *crowd in,* GALLAGHER *with* LIEUTENANT.)

LIEUTENANT: What's happened?

BARNES: That son-of-a-bitch shot Jim . . .

LIEUTENANT: Take him inside! Get him into bed, quick.

BRODY (*to* McLEOD): Easy, baby. Come, I'll carry you to bed. . . .

McLEOD: Wait a minute.

BRODY: Now, Jim.

McLEOD: No. Don't! Don't pull at me. . . . (*Sinks back into a chair.*)

JOE: You got to lie down, Seamus.

McLEOD: No. Once I lay down I'm not going to get up again.

LIEUTENANT: Notify the Communication Bureau. Get an ambulance. Quick!

McLEOD: Never mind the doctor! Get a priest.

BRODY: Feel that bad, Jim? (GALLAGHER *goes to phone at desk.*)

GALLAGHER (*on phone*): Communication Bureau.

LIEUTENANT: Why don't you lie down, Jim?

McLEOD: Get me a drink.

LIEUTENANT (*to* BRODY): With a belly wound . . . ?

BRODY (*whispers*): What difference does it make? . . . Look at him. (LIEUTENANT *nods—goes for glass of whisky on files.*)

McLEOD: Don't whisper, Lou. I can hear you.

BRODY: Sure you can. You're all right, baby. They can't hurt you. You're one of the indestructibles; you're immortal, baby.

McLEOD: Almost, Lou. Almost. Don't rush me. Give me your hand, Lou. Squeeze! Harder! (SUSAN *begins to sob.*)

ARTHUR: Don't cry, Suzy. Don't cry! (CALLAHAN *crosses to* CHARLIE, *drags him off.*)

McLEOD (*glances up at* ARTHUR, *shakes head; to* BRODY): Give me Buster's prints! I don't know. I hope you're right, Lou. Maybe he'll come in tomorrow with a murder rap. I don't know any more. Get me his prints. (BRODY *goes for them.* CHARLIE *is dragged off by* O'BRIEN *and* BARNES, *half unconscious, moaning.*)

JOE: How're you feeling, Seamus?

MCLEOD: Yussell Find her! Ask her to forgive me. And help her. She needs help . . . will you?

JOE: Sure. Now take it easy. (BRODY *hands* ARTHUR's *fingerprint sheet to* MCLEOD, *who tears it up; looks at* LIEUTENANT.)

MCLEOD: Tear 'em up. Unchain him, Lou. The keys are in my pocket. We have no case here, Lieutenant. The complainant withdrew. (*Crosses himself.*) In the name of the Father and the Son and the Holy Ghost. Oh, my God! I'm heartily sorry for having offended Thee. I detest all my sins because I dread the loss of Heaven . . . (*Falls.* BRODY *catches him, eases him to the ground, feels for his pulse.*)

BRODY: He's gone!

JOE (*also kneeling*): He's dead.

LIEUTENANT (*completes prayer*): "I firmly resolve with the help of Thy Grace to confess my sins, to do penance and to amend my life. Amen." (*Crosses himself.*)

BRODY (*murmurs*): Amen. (BARNES *uncovers, crosses himself.* BRODY *crosses himself, rises clumsily, goes to* ARTHUR, *unlocks his handcuffs.*) All right, son. Go on home. Don't make a monkey outa me! If I see you . . . up here again, I'll kick the guts outa you. Don't make a monkey outa me!

ARTHUR: Don't worry! I won't.

SUSAN: He won't.

BRODY: Get the hell outa here.

SUSAN: Thank you. (SUSAN *takes* ARTHUR's *hand. They go off.*)

GALLAGHER (*on phone*): St. Vincent's? Will you please send a priest over to the Twenty-first Precinct Police Station to administer last rites?

LIEUTENANT (*on phone*): Communication Bureau? Notify— the Commissioner—the D.A., the Homicide Squad— Twenty-first Precinct. . . . Detective shot . . . killed.

INTRODUCTION

Edward Chodorov was born in New York City on April 17, 1911. This dramatist and director has staged all of his plays except the first, *Wonder Boy* (1931), written in collaboration with Arthur Barton, which was produced and directed by Jed Harris. Besides *Kind Lady* (1935), his plays include *Cue for Passion* (1940), written with Hy Kraft; *Those Endearing Young Charms* (1943); *Decision* (1944); *Common Ground* (1945); *Signor Chicago* (1947); *Oh, Men! Oh, Women!* (1953); *The Spa* (1956), based on Ferenc Molnár's *Olympia; Listen to the Mocking Bird* (1959) and *Monsieur Lautrec* (1959).

Kind Lady was successfully revived in 1940 with the same star, Grace George, and was more highly acclaimed than on its debut. Although *Common Ground,* laid against a World War II background, was no box-office success, his play remains one of the genuinely significant anti-Fascist American plays. He has spent much time in Hollywood both as a writer and a producer. Among his credits on outstanding films, he produced *Craig's Wife* and wrote the screen plays for *Yellow Jack* and *The Hucksters.* In 1952 he wrote a series of twenty-six plays for television under the collective title of *The Billy Rose Show.*

Richard Lockridge, in the New York *Sun* of April 24, 1935, said: *"Kind Lady . . .* is a masterly exercise in the creation of horror; a quiet and reasonable play, which, without resorting to the fireworks of melodrama, manages to curdle the blood and make the hair stand on end."

In the April 24, 1935, New York *American,* the late Gilbert Gabriel wrote: "A pure and simple horror play . . . probably the hardest sort of play to write and act, as well as to see, is *Kind Lady."*

Further Reading

Mantle, Burns. (ed.). *The Best Plays of 1943–1944*. New York: Dodd, Mead, 1944.

Contains an abridgment of the text of *Decision,* pp. 133–63.

Shipley, Joseph T. *Guide to Great Plays*. Washington: Public Affairs, 1956, p. 381.

"One of the most thrilling psychological melodramas is that of the 'kind lady' kidnaped in her own home. . . ."

EDWARD CHODOROV

Kind Lady

based on a story by Hugh Walpole

SCENE: *The downstairs living room in* MARY HERRIES' *house in Montague Square, London.*

The room proper is a large, comfortably furnished living room reflecting the excellent taste and character of MARY HERRIES. *Many of its furnishings, the pictures in particular, are objets d'art. In the right wall are two large casement windows with fine lace curtains and heavy drapes. In the left wall is a large fireplace and a door leading to the dining room. Above the mantel is a large oil painting, a Whistler. In the center of the living room is a large arch. Going through the arch one rises two steps to a platform that extends off to the front hall and door and to the rear of the house. Upstage of the platform two more steps lead to a bay window, and stair landing. Leading from this bay-window landing is a flight of stairs to the upper part of the house.*

*Between the windows at right are a desk and chair, a sofa
with a coffee table in front of it, and against the right section
of the back wall is a chest.*

*In front of the fireplace is a low upholstered fire seat. Two
large overstuffed chairs with a drum table between them
occupy the left side of the stage.*

*Against the left side of the back wall is another chest and
at its right is a low table with a lamp. On the wall above
these are an El Greco and a Whistler. Above the furniture
on the back wall are two more Whistlers.*

PROLOGUE

*There is a slight rearrangement of furniture just described.
On the right and left back walls and over the fireplace the
"old masters" have been replaced by "moderns."*

It is a late afternoon in spring. It is raining outside.

*The curtain rises on an empty stage. The doorbell is heard
ringing. After a moment it rings again. A SERVANT is seen
crossing on the platform from the rear of the house toward
the front door. The doorbell rings again.*

MR. FOSTER (*offstage*): Mr. Abbott, please.

SERVANT (*off*): Mr. Abbott's out.

FOSTER (*entering to center of platform; a small man, carrying
an umbrella, hat and brown paper envelope, and wearing
a coat*): I'm from the bank, Foster's the name. I had an
appointment for four o'clock. (SERVANT *gestures him to
sit down and wait.*) Then, if you don't mind, I'll take off
my coat—it's damp.

(FOSTER *removes his coat, gives it, his hat and umbrella to*
SERVANT *who exits.* FOSTER *in the meantime has come down
into the room proper, gone to the desk and left his envelope
there. He then crosses, glances out the window and then
at the pictures. His attention is drawn to someone coming
down the stairs. It is* MARY HERRIES. *She comes down from
upstairs uncertainly and rather furtively. She steps on the*

*platform and looks off left. She turns and starts off right
on the platform.)*

FOSTER (*stopping her as she reaches the center of the platform*): How do you do? (MARY *stops but doesn't answer.*)
I am waiting for Mr. Abbott, if you please, Madam. I'm
from the bank. I have an appointment for four o'clock, but
since he's not here, perhaps—

MARY: Mr. Abbott—is—not here?

FOSTER: No. Servant said he was out. Perhaps I should come
back later.

MARY (*crossing on platform and looking off left*): They—
don't usually keep people waiting.

FOSTER: That's all right. I don't mind waiting. Only I hope
I'm not in the way.

MARY: No. You're not in the way. Of course not— From the
bank?

FOSTER (*still near desk*): Blakely's, Madam.

MARY: Oh, yes. I know that bank very well. I used to do
business with Blakely's Bank.

FOSTER (*crossing to front of desk*): Excuse me, Madam. But
is there any possibility that Mr. Abbott may not be here
shortly? I'm to see another gentleman at five.

MARY: You've never been here before?

FOSTER: No, Madam.

MARY: Then you've never seen me before. I don't see many
people—from outside.

FOSTER: Oh.

MARY: Don't you think it odd that I never see anyone?

FOSTER: Why—I don't know, Mrs.—

MARY: Miss—Mary Herries.

FOSTER: Oh. (*then suddenly*) Herries? It seems to me I
remember the name, Madam. It's been on our books for
years.

MARY: Yes— It has been. For years.

FOSTER: But I thought—I mean I took it for granted—that
you were away. Abroad, or some place. For several years,
I think?

MARY: No, I've been here—always. (MARY *crosses to dining-room door and closes it. Then comes back to* FOSTER.) Don't you want to know why I never see anyone?

FOSTER: Uh—what is that, Madam?

MARY: It's a very interesting reason. Very interesting. I think you might be very interested. You might be the very one.

(*During this last speech the lights have been slowly fading —and at the end of the speech the stage is in total darkness.*)

ACT I

SCENE 1

SCENE: *The lights fade up very shortly and the stage is set as first described.*

LUCY WESTON is sitting in the chair in front of the fireplace. In another chair is an open suitcase with wrapped Christmas packages in it. There are also some packages on the table and an envelope.

It is late Christmas Eve, several years before. A small Christmas tree is on the chest in the bay window.

ROSE (*entering with a piece of red ribbon and a tray containing a whisky decanter, syphon, and glasses*): This is all I could find, Mrs. Weston.

(ROSE *puts tray on chest and crosses to table to tie up a Christmas package.*)

LUCY: Fine! That will do nicely. Now let me see. Cynthia, Peter, John, Harold, Kitten and Sybil. That's six. Six nieces and nephews. Rose, think of it. And I didn't have to go through a thing to have them! It is quite different when I have my own chickabiddies.

ROSE: Oh—Mrs. Weston!

LUCY: What's this? (*She notices a package which hasn't been*

put in suitcase.) "Rose." Now who in heaven's name! Has
my brother had another child? I mean his wife? Dear me
it's hard to keep track, Rose— (*Looks at her.*) Oh, my
heavens! It's *you!* I nearly packed it with the others. Well,
now the cat's out of the bag. (*Hands package to* ROSE.)
Merry Christmas, Rose.

ROSE (*crossing in front of table*): Oh, thank you, Mrs. Weston.
The same to you and many more.

LUCY: Well—we won't count how many more. And— (*Takes
envelope.*) this. For looking after me so nicely this visit.

ROSE (*takes envelope*): Oh, Mrs. Weston. This is too much!

LUCY: When you open it you won't say that. Well, things
are going to get better some day. Those go in the bag to
take with me tomorrow. Don't let me forget. Am I all
packed?

ROSE (*putting packages in suitcase*): Yes, Madam. Except for
the blouse at the cleaner's. I'll send that on to you the
moment it comes.

LUCY: That's fine. What time is it?

ROSE (*puts suitcase on floor above table*): After eleven o'clock,
Madam.

LUCY: What time are these operas usually over, Rose?

ROSE (*straightens chair*): It's hard to say Mrs. Weston. But
Miss Herries always leaves early when the weather's bad.

LUCY: There's one place I will not be found on Christmas
Eve— And that is an opera house. Well—I have to leave
in half an hour. Miss Herries is sure to be back by then,
isn't she?

ROSE (*going upstairs*): That's hard to say, Mrs. Weston.

(*Front doorbell rings.* ROSE *puts suitcase on landing and goes
to answer it.*)

PHYLLIS (*offstage*): Is Miss Herries in?

ROSE (*offstage*): No, Miss, she's not back from the opera.

PHYLLIS (*enters and stops on platform*): Oh, dear, I was sure
she'd be here. (*Sees* LUCY.) Mrs. Weston! Merry Christmas.

LUCY: Hello, Phyllis, Merry Christmas!

PHYLLIS: I'm doing the rounds of the relatives, bearing gifts. (ROSE *picks up suitcase and is crossing toward stairs.* PHYLLIS *turns offstage.*) Peter! Come in—don't stand out there in the hall. (*To* ROSE.) Don't go, please. (ROSE *stops at foot of stairs.* PHYLLIS *calling.*) Peter!

PETER (*offstage*): Huh?

LUCY (*confidentially*): Is this—

PHYLLIS: I don't know yet, but I think so. (PETER *enters, carrying small package.*) Peter, this is Mrs. Weston. Mrs. Weston, Mr. Santard. (*Takes package.*)

PETER: How do you do?

LUCY: How do you do?

PHYLLIS: Please put this—by the tree tomorrow morning. (*Gives* ROSE *package.*)

ROSE: Yes, Miss. (*Exits upstairs.*)

PHYLLIS: Peter's an American.

PETER: You know—

(*Acknowledging this,* PETER *gives slight Indian war cry.*)

PHYLLIS: Now Peter, not *that* American!

PETER: Sorry.

PHYLLIS: Say something nice, Peter.

PETER (*to* MRS. WESTON): Are you Aunt Mary?

LUCY: No, I'm just—visiting—Phyllis' Aunt Mary.

PETER: I've heard a great deal about Aunt Mary and— (*Brightly, for* PHYLLIS' *benefit.*) I've wanted to meet her! (*Nods to* PHYLLIS *with a "How's that?" expression.*)

PHYLLIS: You see—Peter and I—thought it would be a good idea to *bring* Aunt Mary her present—and now she isn't here! Peter!

PETER (*who has been looking around the room*): Oh! How do you like London, Mrs. Weston?

LUCY: Why—I should be asking that of you!

PETER: I know—that's why I asked you first.

PHYLLIS: Don't mind Peter, Mrs. Weston. No one in New York would dream of giving him a job so his father sent him over here!

LUCY: I think he's very charming. Sit down, and tell me about— (*Sees decanter.*) Oh, would you like a drink?

PETER: Yes, please—and *no* ice.

PHYLLIS: No, Peter. No time.

PETER (*bowing politely to* LUCY): Merry Christmas.

PHYLLIS: Sorry, Mrs. Weston. We have miles and miles of driving to do. (*Telephone rings.*) Good night.

LUCY: Good night. (*Crossing toward telephone on desk.*)

PETER (*going off*): Good-by.

PHYLLIS: Don't tell Aunt Mary we were here. Present— secret. Merry Christmas. (*Exits.*)

LUCY: Merry Christmas, Phyllis. (*At telephone.*) Hello? Hello, Bunny! I'm on my way! Really I am—I thought I might induce Mary Herries to "step out" this once— What do you mean she's "no fun?" Of course you don't know her— The car? Oh, lovely— Yes—half an hour. Right you are. (*Hangs up.*)

PHYLLIS (*calling out*): Merry Christmas.

ROSE (*offstage*): Merry Christmas, Miss.

(ROSE *enters from dining room with a plate of sandwiches on a tray.*)

LUCY: Oh, those look good! (ROSE, *about to put sandwiches on table, comes to* LUCY *and offers them.*) Er—no. Not until I'm down ten more pounds. (*Turns away but looks back at sandwiches.*) Oh, well. Christmas comes but once a year. (*Takes a sandwich.*) Thank you. (*Crosses and sits on sofa.*)

ROSE (*putting sandwiches on table*): Is there anything else, Madam?

LUCY: No—except my trunk. I'm sure I'll be in no mood tomorrow to worry about that.

ROSE (*takes whisky and syphon from chest and puts on table*): The baggage people promised to be here at seven sharp they said.

LUCY: Well, if they're pretty and have curly hair you wake

me up, Rose. Otherwise I'll leave their money on the dressing table.

ROSE (*laughs*): Yes, Madam. (*Exits to dining room.*)

(*The door is heard to open and* MARY HERRIES *enters.*)

MARY (*in arch*): Hello! Head better, dear? (*Rings bell for*
ROSE.)

LUCY: Much.

MARY: Good! (*Speaking off right.*) Come in. (HENRY ABBOTT
*appears. He is tall, handsome, emanates strength and charm
immediately; shabbily, miserably dressed.*) Here's a hungry
young man we've got to feed, Lucy.

HENRY (*very quietly, half smiling*): Just a cup of tea, thanks.

MARY: Oh, nonsense. You've made me take you in here at
this time of night. You'll have to justify it.

HENRY: I'm afraid I couldn't manage much more.

(ROSE *enters from dining room.*)

MARY: Rose, would you make some tea, and let this gentleman have anything else he wants. (*To* HENRY.) If you feel
better.

HENRY: Just some tea.

(*There is a moment's pause.*)

ROSE (*who has been eyeing him*): This way, please. (*He turns
and follows* ROSE *out past arch without any further sign.*)

MARY (*crossing, puts purse on table*): Poor chap.

LUCY: Where did you find him?

MARY: Just outside—I've never done this before! I never
even give— (*Crossing to desk.*) to beggars on the street.
Anyway, all I had was a one pound note. There's something
about him— Don't you think? (*Puts wrap on desk chair.*)

LUCY: Mmm.

MARY: Matter of fact. Made me feel awfully sorry for him.
I just couldn't leave him standing there—but I'd never

have brought him in if you weren't here. (*Laughs.*) Haven't I been trying to convince you that I'm getting sillier all the time! I really should apologize!

LUCY (*taking a cigarette*): What for?

MARY: After all, heaven knows *what* he is.

LUCY: What he looks like probably—a rather charming, hungry young man.

MARY: Isn't he? Striking, I mean.

LUCY: Very.

MARY: So unusual.

LUCY: Very. How was Covent Garden?

MARY (*taking off gloves*): Horrible I thought. The place reeked of mackintoshes and galoshes. I could see the strings resenting it bitterly. I hate London at this time of year.

LUCY: In a few weeks I'll be home—in my garden—with an armful of the loveliest azaleas *you* ever saw.

MARY: What a persistent woman! Oh, I feel so stupid refusing.

LUCY: Well now, why refuse? Now look here! Why shouldn't you give yourself a month of Riviera sun and warmth? What's keeping you here?

MARY: I don't know. It's simply—

LUCY: Simply rot.

MARY: Lucy, I'd love to go back with you—

LUCY: Then why not?

MARY: But I'm just comfortable here, I suppose—

LUCY: Why do you avoid everyone?

MARY (*not listening and looking off left*): You know, Lucy, he didn't ask me for money.

LUCY: What??? Ohh.

MARY: He simply stood there with the most disarming smile and said: "I wonder if I might have a cup of tea on Christmas Eve."

LUCY: Very touching. I asked you why you avoid everyone.

MARY (*crosses to chair and sits*): I? I don't do anything of the sort. I've just been busy—that's all.

LUCY: Don't tell me, Mary Herries. Won't you come with me tonight, just this once? Bunny would love to have you.

MARY: No, thank you, Lucy.

LUCY: Oh, ho! You're going to have a nice little chat with Tiny Tim.

MARY: Who?

LUCY: The striking young beggar you met in the fog—or snow—on Christmas Eve.

MARY: I am not! When he's had something to eat, Rose can let him out through the basement.

LUCY: Aren't you going to give him some money or something?

MARY: No, I am not.

LUCY: At least you must let him thank you.

MARY: Not necessarily.

LUCY: Well—if you want to sit all alone on Christmas Eve —I'll stay with you. I'll ring up Bunny.

MARY (*rises and crosses to* LUCY): No, Lucy. I won't let you. Please go and have a good time.

(ROSE *enters on platform.*)

ROSE: He's finished, Madam.

MARY (*turns to* ROSE): What?

ROSE: He's had his tea.

MARY: Very well, Rose. You can show him out downstairs.

ROSE: But— (*She pauses.*)

MARY: Yes—?

ROSE: He says he wants to thank you.

LUCY: There!

MARY: That's very nice of him. Tell him he's quite welcome.

LUCY: Mary!

ROSE: Yes, Miss Herries.

(*Turns to go—but* HENRY *enters on platform.*)

HENRY (*half smiling, a peculiar somber smile*): I've had my tea. You're very kind.

MARY: I was happy to help you.

HENRY: I wanted to thank you, that's all.
MARY: Of course.

(*There is a pause.*)

HENRY (*sees sandwiches on table*): I—I wonder if I might take a few of those sandwiches.
LUCY (*ill at ease*): Please do!
MARY: Of course.
HENRY (*crosses to table*): I'll eat them outside.

(*Doorbell rings.* ROSE *goes to answer it.*)

LUCY (*mischievously*): Eat them here!

(MARY *looks uncomfortably at* LUCY.)

HENRY: Thank you. I'm able to now, I think. (*Looks at whisky.*)
MARY (*weakly*): Have some whisky if you like.
HENRY: I will.

(ROSE *enters.* HENRY *crosses below table and mixes whisky and soda.*)

ROSE: The car's at the door for Mrs. Weston. (*Exits.*)
LUCY: Oh, dear! Well— (*Mischievously.*) Good night, Mary, and—Merry Christmas.
MARY: Merry Christmas, Lucy. I'll see you in the morning.
LUCY: I hope so. (*She goes out.*)
HENRY (*looking at paintings*): You've a few nice things here. (MARY *smiles nervously—looking covertly back over her shoulder for* ROSE.) That's a good El Greco. (*Points to back wall.*)
MARY (*indicates immediately she is quite astonished*): It's not bad.
HENRY (*going closer*): One of his early ones; they're not common.

MARY: No. There aren't two hundred people in London who'd know that! Are you an artist?

HENRY: Not really. One of many confused talents.

MARY: You talk as if you knew something about painting.

HENRY: I suppose I do. (*He starts toward sandwiches.*)

MARY: Look here—if you really want something to eat now —those stale sandwiches— (*Paces to chair.*)

HENRY: They're exactly right. Again thanks. And again forgive me for disturbing you like this.

(ROSE *enters and gets* MARY's *wrap at desk.*)

MARY: You haven't. It isn't every day one bumps into an El Greco lover on the street.

(ROSE *exits on platform, a bit uneasy.*)

HENRY (*looking around again*): You collect seriously—

MARY (*amused*): How do you tell? Is this room that bad?

HENRY (*quickly—walking around room and pointing*): It's lovely of course— But it takes a collector to jam a Whistler, an El Greco, and a Ming horse all together, doesn't it?

MARY (*after a moment*): Well, whatever you are, you have an educated eye—no question about that! And you're right about the jam. (*Carries horse from one chest and puts it on another chest.*) There seems to be a difference between my maid and myself as to just where this bronze belongs!

HENRY: Your maid is a strong-minded woman.

MARY (*laughs*): You've found that out? Rose is a good soul —and devoted to me. She won't go to bed now until she's quite sure you don't mean to murder me. (*Sits at end of sofa,* HENRY *laughs and drinks.*) What do you do?

HENRY: Nothing. Everything. The last year I've had odd jobs I shouldn't like to mention in this house. (*Crosses to sofa, puts glass on table below sofa.*)

MARY: But you certainly have a good eye—and knowledge. Collecting *is* my one interest.

HENRY: Mine, too, once—and not wasted. (*Sits left end*

of couch.) I find it very comforting to remember, standing
in the line on the embankment.

MARY: The line?

HENRY: The bread line.

MARY: Oh.

HENRY: As a connoisseur of lines—I should say it was the
best in London—and wonderfully philanthropic. I bothered
you tonight because the two odd miles to the embankment
seemed to stretch like eternity in the snow.

MARY: I'm glad you did.

HENRY: I, too.

MARY (*pause*): Are you alone?

HENRY: Alone, as they say, in the world?

MARY: Yes.

HENRY: Practically. I have a wife—and a child.

MARY: Oh—really?

HENRY: A nursing child.

MARY (*very sympathetically*): What do you do?

HENRY: We do rather nicely comparatively. Ada—my wife—
is a delicate creature who scrubs floors occasionally, when
she's lucky, in an office building in the city—a Fragonard
charwoman.

MARY: A nursing child. That's dreadful.

HENRY: Not at all. What Ada makes pays the rent of our
hovel in South Wharf Road—and buys approximately
enough food for herself and the little brute, of course.

MARY: South Wharf Road. You live—

HENRY: In the neighborhood. I've admired the outside of
your house many times—from the drinking trough opposite.

MARY: And I'm going to send you back to your house right
now.

HENRY (*rises*): Of course—I'm keeping you up.

MARY: That's an unkind remark, young man. I could sit here
and tell you how I got that El Greco until you beg for
mercy. But I won't—for a very good reason.

HENRY (*stopping her*): I should like to hear—

MARY: Oh, no. (*Turns back to* HENRY.) All my life the mistakes that I've made—and there have been plenty—have all arisen from the same thing—my heart swamping my good sense. (*She looks at him.*) I'm telling you this because you're obviously a very unusual and intelligent young man —and you've just told me a terribly pathetic story.

HENRY (*smiling*): Thank you. I'm sorry—

MARY: I'm afraid of it—and you. I had a birthday a short time ago, and I thought at last I'm too old to be foolish any more. But here I am—helping an entirely unknown man into my house in the middle of the night and listening to a tale that's going to make me see white-faced babies in my dreams for a week.

HENRY: He's red as a herring—and looks like one.

MARY: Believe me—I don't care. Everything about you conspires to make me help you. Why—you even live around the corner! Well, I'm not going to help you. I'm a selfish old maid—and I never want to see you again—or hear anything more about that young girl you've presented with a baby. You're probably the worst sort of criminal. (*Turns and walks across room as she finishes speech, then turns back quickly.*) Wait a minute.

(HENRY *looks after her quietly. Finishes whisky and puts glass on table below sofa. Then slowly crosses and easily picks up a white jade cigarette case from table, examines it, takes out cigarette, taps it against the case, looks at case again, then puts it in his pocket in the most natural manner in the world—as if it had come from there. He lights his cigarette, crossing to couch. As* MARY *comes down carrying a heavy cloth coat with a fur collar over her arm,* HENRY *puts out cigarette.*)

MARY (*hands him coat*): Give this to your wife.

HENRY: That's good of you.

MARY (*going on as she gets her purse from table*): She'd better let a tailor do the alterations. Here. (HENRY *crosses to her.*) And you'd better get some shoes.

HENRY (*without the slightest emotion*): You're saving our lives.

MARY: Nonsense. (*He looks at the money in his hand.*) It's all I have in the house—so you needn't bother holding me up now, you see?

HENRY: It *was* foolish of you to let a tramp in here at this time of night.

MARY: So I've been told. But an old woman like me—what's the difference?

HENRY: I could have cut your throat.

MARY: You might have—but you'd have been sorry.

HENRY: Oh, no. The police never catch anybody any more.

MARY: Don't let's worry about that.

HENRY: Not tonight. It would be ungrateful—

MARY: Good-by.

(HENRY *crosses to right of* MARY *on platform—turns to her.*)

HENRY: Good night. (*Exits.*)

MARY (*calling off*): Good luck. And—Merry Christmas!

(MARY *comes in, hesitates in arch. Goes to above chair, looks for cigarette case on table, then on chest, then on mantel.*)

ROSE (*enters on platform*): Is there anything you want, Madam?

MARY (*looks for cigarette case*): No, Rose. You can go to bed.

ROSE: Yes, Madam— Good night. (*Starts to go.*)

MARY: Rose— Have you seen my cigarette case?

ROSE (*comes to table*): The white jade, Madam? (MARY *nods.*) It was layin' right there this evening.

MARY: I thought so. (*Pause as they both reflect about* HENRY.) Oh, well—never mind.

ROSE: I'd say he took it, Madam.

MARY: Oh, no, Rose.

ROSE: Do you know where to find him, Madam?

MARY: Mmmmm. It doesn't matter.

ROSE: Oh, dear—that's too bad. (*Puts stopper in decanter on table.*)

MARY: No, Rose—he didn't take it—I remember now—I had it with me in the taxi.

ROSE: I didn't like him at all, Madam. Too good-lookin'.

MARY (*sits in chair*): He was good-looking, wasn't he?

ROSE: Too much so— I don't believe he was hungry at all. The way he sat in the kitchen!—You're not hungry, I said to myself—you're too good-looking. And you're up to something. And sure enough. (*Picks up sandwich plate—crosses toward sofa.*)

MARY: No, Rose. (ROSE *stops and turns to* MARY.) I left it in the taxi, I'm sure.

ROSE (*shaking her head*): Yes, Madam. (*Picks up glass from coffee table and goes to dining-room door.*) Good night. (*Exits.*)

(*Christmas chimes from a church ring out.* MARY *doesn't answer. Looks toward arch, turns front—shrugs shoulders.*)

═══════════════════════════════════

SCENE 2

SCENE: *It is after dinner, two weeks later, in January.* PHYLLIS *is sitting on couch reading,* PETER *is standing in front of Troubetzkoi on table with glass.* PETER *looks at Troubetzkoi for a while, then walks away, half looking at Troubetzkoi; then stops, returns to statue, looks at it again.* PETER *puts glass down deliberately on table. Takes out match, strikes it and holds it to statue.*

PHYLLIS: Peter! Peter, put those matches away and sit down.

(PETER *hastily shakes out match and picks up brandy glass.*)

PETER (*indicates Troubetzkoi*): That—is a woman. Phyllis! We must get one of those.

PHYLLIS: Yes, dear.

(*Looking at her,* PETER *walks imitating a tightrope walker. He stops in front of picture—looks at it for a pause—then suddenly—with extreme deliberation, he puts his glass down on chest.*)

PHYLLIS: Peter, *please* don't set off any more matches!

PETER (*picks up glass and comes toward her*): Phyllis— who's that tall thin girl last night with the— (*Makes series of adenoidal noises, saying*) "So pleased to meet you, so very nice"—can't understand a word she says—who *is* that?

PHYLLIS: That, my dear—will be your cousin Elizabeth.

PETER (*looks at her for a moment*): That'll be nice. And *who* —was the fat gentleman with the— (*Indicates fat stomach.*) and—the— (*Indicates pompous look and monocle.*)

PHYLLIS (*cuts in*): If you're attempting to describe Sir Arthur Verne—he's a *very* dear friend of Mother's—and happens to be a *very* distinguished man.

PETER (*agreeing quickly*): Yes—yes, indeed—I could see that. (*Suddenly gets a glint in his eyes and goes into the next speech as though he were tremendously puzzled.*) But who—*who*—was the little feller! (*He extends his hand about chest high.*)

PHYLLIS: Who?

PETER: You know— (*Drops his hand about a foot.*) The *little* feller.

PHYLLIS: What are you talking about?

PETER (*drops his hand to about a foot from the floor—bending way over—and holding this stance; speaks patiently*): The *little* feller! With the— (*Lifts his hand to pull at his chin.*)

PHYLLIS: With the *what*—?

PETER: The goatee!

PHYLLIS: Peter—get *up!*

PETER (*straightens*): But who *is* he? Really!

PHYLLIS: There's no one like that in our family.

PETER: No? (*He shudders.*)

PHYLLIS: No.

PETER: Funny— I keep seeing him everywhere.

PHYLLIS: Peter, you simply mustn't drink brandy.

PETER: There's only *one* of your family that I really like.

PHYLLIS: Really?

PETER (*pointing wisely upstairs*): Aunt Mary—

PHYLLIS (*rises and crosses behind sofa*): We are rude, Peter, but we simply must dash off!

PETER (*sitting on sofa*): Well, let's not! Let's stay here instead.

PHYLLIS (*with mock weariness, but real annoyance*): Darling —how can we?

PETER: I feel mellow and witty and dignified all at once for the first time in my life! I don't want to go out in the cold world!

PHYLLIS (*patronizingly*): It has been awfully nice—but you have no sense of responsibility.

PETER: I like it here! This is what I call gracious living and it's the first dinner party I've enjoyed in a long while.

PHYLLIS: Much as you hate doing the rounds, you've simply *got* to. I don't like these continual introductions either. But do you make it any easier for me? No! You act as though I were whipping you through hoops or something!

PETER: Can't stand being introduced—wholesale.

PHYLLIS: You spend most of the time standing around and grinning foolishly at everyone.

PETER: I'm not grinning foolishly now. I like Miss Herries— and I'm crazy about this house—and I hope that— (*Closes his eyes.*) the solidification—of our relationship will permit me to run in and out of here at frequent intervals. (*Both laugh.*) Furthermore, she has the best wine I ever tasted. (*He reaches for brandy decanter.*)

PHYLLIS (*taking his glass out of his hand and crossing to put it on table*): Don't imagine you can pop in and out of here whenever you please!

PETER (*lighting cigarette*): Why not?

PHYLLIS: Aunt Mary isn't a very sociably inclined lady.

PETER: She's damn nice.

PHYLLIS: I know. We must see her more often, really. Most of the family don't, you know.

PETER: I'll see her without the family any time.

PHYLLIS: We've all neglected her shamefully.

PETER: Your dear mother.

PHYLLIS: Oh, no—it's not Mother. She couldn't keep me away. I don't know why—I'm so horribly busy.

PETER: Trotting me around to meet cousins and uncles.

PHYLLIS: I hope she doesn't think this was that kind of a duty call. Wonder what she's doing?

PETER: You hinted strongly enough that a wedding present would be acceptable.

PHYLLIS: Now, Peter, that's not done.

PETER: Maybe she's gone to get us a present right now.

PHYLLIS: How many times must I tell you that I'm not showing you off to my relations just to get presents from them?

PETER: Then why visit the Howards tonight? Why not stay here awhile?

PHYLLIS: George Howard's not a relative. He's your best client— (*Crossing in front of sofa.*) Or will be now that he knows you're going to marry me.

PETER: I feel as if I were getting married for business reasons.

PHYLLIS: Marriage *is* a business.

PETER: Yeah!

PHYLLIS: Yes!

PETER: I suppose I'll go to the Howards whether I want to or not. And all the other places. (*Rises and turns to* PHYLLIS.) "How do you do? Yes—I'm the lucky fellow! When? Oh, about the first of June. Yes! The first of June. What? Oh, I'm an American bond salesman. Do you want any nice bonds so I can get married?"

PHYLLIS: Oh! "I want you to meet Peter. I met him in New York, but he's over here now. (*Looks around.*) Oh, where has he gone. Peter, Peter, here Peter! Oh there you are! This is Aunt Evelyn. Oh, he's only joking Aunt *Eve*lyn. He's making believe he's shy. Say something to Aunt *Eve*lyn, Peter."

PETER: "Hello, Aunt Evelyn."

PHYLLIS: There! (*Sits on sofa.*)

PETER: I wish your grandfather hadn't been so prolific.

(MARY *enters from stairs.*)

MARY (*coming between* PHYLLIS *and* PETER): I waited until
the last second with this—because I just want to give it to
you—and let that be the end of it. (*Hands* PHYLLIS *a small
box.*) Don't open it now—your grandfather gave it to me
—long time ago—to wear at *my* wedding. (*Smiles brightly.*)
It's very old—but you'll love it.

(PETER *drifts, looking at statue, puts out cigarette on table.*)

PHYLLIS: I know I shall, Aunt Mary. But why so soon?
MARY: Oh—I don't know—I never know where I'm liable
to be when people get married.

(PHYLLIS *and* MARY *are in front of sofa.*)

PHYLLIS: Oh— (*Very sweetly.*) Thank you, Aunt Mary. I
hope you don't think we came here tonight just to—
MARY: No, no. Even if it were I wouldn't mind. And I know
the next time it will be because you want to come.
PETER: Miss Herries, may I ask who did that?
MARY: Which?
PETER: This one—the statue.
MARY: Troubetzkoi—Mr. Santard.
PETER: Troubetzkoi, eh? What's it supposed to be?
MARY: I really don't know who she is. I think it's listed in the
catalogue as "Figure" or something equally enlightening.
PETER (*crosses to* PHYLLIS): I think it's grand. Phyllis, we
must get one of this fellow's things sometime.
PHYLLIS: Yes, yes—all right, darling. That's the fourth time
tonight you've said that.
PETER: Is it? I must like it.
MARY: Do you like it very much, Mr. Santard?
PETER (*with mock sadness*): Please call me "Peter."
MARY: All right, Peter. I'll tell you what I'll do. I'll give it to
you for a wedding present.
PETER: What—really?

PHYLLIS (*crossing to her*): Oh, no, Aunt Mary. I won't dream of it. You simply mustn't!

MARY (*sits*): No—no. It's all settled.

PHYLLIS: But you must be awfully fond of it yourself.

MARY: I am. But I want you to have it—if you like it too, Phyllis.

PHYLLIS: Oh—I like it. (*Gives a look of disgust to* PETER.)

MARY: It's the best present I can think of for me to give you.

PHYLLIS: Honestly, Aunt Mary—after one drink of cold water, Peter wouldn't know if Troubetzkoi or Madame Toussaud did it.

PETER: What's the difference? And anyway I know very well who did it—Troubetzkoi. (*Snaps fingers and returns to contemplating it.*)

MARY: Then that's that. (*She imitates his finger snap.*)

PETER: Have you any more Troubetzkois in the house?

(PHYLLIS *has crossed to in front of fireplace.*)

MARY: Oh, yes. Didn't you notice the one in the dining room?

PETER: Whereabouts?

MARY: On the sideboard.

PETER (*picking up brandy glass from table*): I'll have another look at it.

MARY: Do.

PETER (*as he passes into dining room, he salutes* PHYLLIS *with the glass*): Troubetzkoi!!

PHYLLIS (*silent for a moment, then very formal*): Look, Aunt Mary. We really *must* go. The Howards will be terribly offended and we can't afford that.

MARY: No, indeed!

PHYLLIS: I didn't mean it that way. Really, Aunt Mary—

MARY: That's all right.

PHYLLIS: *I* want to be friends with you—even if Mother insists on being an idiot!

MARY (*with a laugh*): The Howards are expecting you!

PHYLLIS (*looks for a moment at* MARY; *shakes her head and goes to door*): Peter!

PETER (*off in dining room*): Huh!
PHYLLIS: Say good-by to Aunt Mary.
PETER (*off*): Good-by, Aunt Mary.

(MARY *laughs*.)

PHYLLIS: Peter!
PETER (*enters from door to in front of fireplace*): Yes?
PHYLLIS: We're leaving!
PETER: Oh! Sorry! (*To* MARY, *crossing close to table*.) What
   did you say the name of that fellow was?
MARY: Troubetzkoi.
PETER: Oh, yes.
PHYLLIS (*quietly, shaking her head*): Oh, you *are* a fool!
PETER: What's the matter?
PHYLLIS (*pointing at* MARY): Here's someone with banks full
   of lovely money—and nothing to do with it except buy
   statues—and you go and get us a statue for a wedding
   present!

(*Doorbell rings*.)

PETER (*to* MARY): Don't you think she's a little commercial?
MARY (*rises*): No, Peter— Just frank. All our family is ad-
   dicted to frankness.
PETER: Thanks for the tip. You must tell me all about the
   family.
PHYLLIS: Come on, Peter.

(ROSE *crosses on platform to door off right*.)

MARY: Come and see me in a few months and pick up the
   Troubetzkoi.
PETER: May I come sooner than that and look at it—and look
   at you?
MARY: Do that! And I'll see if I need any bonds.
PETER: Did she tell you you had to buy bonds, too?

PHYLLIS: Why not? She's always buying them from *somebody*.
PETER: My God!

(MARY *laughs*. ROSE *enters on platform*.)

ROSE: Madam!
MARY: What is it, Rose?
ROSE: It's—!
HENRY (*enters*): I beg your pardon. I'll wait outside. (*He goes off*.)
MARY (PETER *and* PHYLLIS *look at each other, a little embarrassed*): That's a young man whom I—never mind—you're in a hurry. It's all right, Rose. Get Miss Glenning's and Mr. Santard's things. (ROSE *exits*. PHYLLIS *looks at* PETER *with a "What do you know."*) And now—run along, you two. Keep your "appointments." I hope I haven't made you too late.
PETER (*crossing to join* PHYLLIS): Of course not. Please forget about it.
MARY (*as she reaches entrance to hall, speaks to* HENRY): Will you come in here?
HENRY (*as he passes*): I'm very sorry.
MARY: Please sit down.
PHYLLIS (*handing* PETER *box*): Put the box in your pocket darling and be very careful.

(PHYLLIS *and* PETER *exit, glancing back at* HENRY.)

MARY (*off*): That's a lovely wrap, Phyllis.
PETER (*off*): I'll remember that hopping in and out business!

(ROSE *crosses past arch*.)

MARY (*off, laughs*): Please do!
PHYLLIS (*off*): Good night, Aunt Mary. I'll ring you up. Honestly!
PETER (*off*): Good night—and permit an old man to bless you.

MARY (*off—laughing*): Good night. (*Door slams.* MARY *enters.*)

HENRY (*rises, takes cigarette case from his pocket and holds it out*): I pawned it.

MARY (*takes it*): What a disgraceful thing to do. And what are you going to steal next?

HENRY: My wife made some money last week. That will see us through for a while.

MARY: Don't you ever do any work?

HENRY: I paint—but no one will touch my pictures. They're not modern enough.

MARY: You must show me some of your pictures sometime.

HENRY: I have some here. They're in the hall. (*Goes toward arch.*) You probably didn't notice. (*He goes out and returns immediately from the hall with two canvases, face to face.*)

(MARY *puts cigarette case on table.*)

MARY: Let's see what you have. (HENRY *places one picture on desk. He holds up another picture showing a cowherd playing his pipes to a group of cows. There is a pause while she looks at them.*) Oh, those are very bad.

HENRY: I know they are. You must understand that my aesthetic taste is very fine. I appreciate only the best things —like your cigarette case. But I can paint nothing but these. It's very exasperating.

MARY: It must be.

HENRY: Won't you buy one?

MARY: You don't mean it?

HENRY: Why not?

MARY: But what should I do with it? I'd have to hide it!

HENRY: Not necessarily. Bad as they are, they have something, I think. (*Puts cow picture on floor against sofa.*)

MARY: I don't see it—whatever it is. I really don't want one.

HENRY (*two paces toward* MARY): Please buy one, anyway.

MARY (*retreating a pace*): No—but of course not.

HENRY (*comes closer to her*): Yes, please. (*She looks at him,*

*disturbed by his peculiar insistence. At any rate there is
something of the rabbit and the snake in this passing
tableau.)* My wife is waiting in the street just opposite—
waiting for me to call her.

MARY (*recovering herself*): What on earth for?

HENRY: She wanted to thank you. And I wanted her to see
some of your lovely things.

MARY: How can you let her wait out in that deathly cold?

HENRY: I didn't like to bring her without your permission.
And I don't like her to see me begging.

MARY: Well, you go straight out and take her home.

HENRY (*not moving*): Can't I possibly persuade you—
(*Crosses upstage a bit.*) this one with the cows isn't so bad.

MARY (*shaking her head as she looks at it*): It's peculiar
enough. What is it supposed to be?

HENRY: It's a Swiss scene. In Switzerland the cowherd pipes
his cows from the pasture! He plays a traditional melody.
"Ranz des Vaches" they call it. I read about it and I thought
it was a rather nice macabre idea.

MARY: You've achieved a sinister quality in it, at any rate.
How much is it?

HENRY: Five guineas. The other one is seven.

MARY (*laughing*): You're really amusing. And quite absurd.
They're not worth anything at all.

HENRY: They may be one day. You never know with modern
pictures.

MARY: I'm quite sure about those.

HENRY (*crosses to picture of cow, takes it to* MARY): But I
must sell one tonight—whatever you think of them. (*Holds
out cow picture.*) Please buy it. (*But he is not pleading.*)

MARY (*after a pause*): I'm a perfect fool. (*She is crossing
toward desk.* HENRY *puts picture behind chair, then crosses
to desk for check.*) What's your name? (*Writing check at
desk.*)

HENRY: Henry—Abbott. The baby's Henry, too.

MARY (*hands him check*): Here—and please understand that
I never want to see you again. Never. You will not be

admitted. It's no use speaking to me in the street. If you bother me, I shall tell the police.

HENRY (*in spite of this he has not let go of her hand which he took when he reached for the check; he does so now, folding the check and putting it in pocket*): Hang that in the right light and it won't be bad. (*He crosses down a step.*)

MARY: You didn't get those shoes. Those are terrible.

HENRY: I'll be able to now.

MARY: The first thing you do is rescue that poor girl. You're a thorough brute, young man.

HENRY: She's used to it—

MARY: More shame to you!

HENRY: You can see her from here. (*He crosses to window.*) There she is.

MARY (*goes to window*): With the baby! Oh!! (*Gasps.*)

HENRY: Ada!!! My God!! (*He runs out.*)

MARY (*running to arch*): Rose! Rose!

ROSE (*running from arch*): Yes, Madam!

MARY: Run out and help him—the baby!!! (*As ROSE half turns.*) Never mind! Take my coat! Run! (*Almost pushing her; ROSE runs out, MARY goes to window, thrusts shade aside, watches.*) Oh. (*Suddenly goes quickly out to hall again. After a second HENRY enters, carrying ADA. MARY follows to arch.*) On the sofa!

(ROSE *enters with baby, crosses to chair. MARY follows. HENRY carries ADA to sofa and places her on it. HENRY has taken ADA's head in his hands, shaking it, drops it, grabs her hands, almost immediately lets go, pours drink of brandy from decanter on coffee table, puts it to her lips; it dribbles back.*)

HENRY: Ada! Ada! (*Again tries unsuccessfully to give her brandy. To MARY.*) What shall we do?

MARY (*quietly holds her heart—crosses to ROSE*): Isn't there any doctor near here—somewhere, Rose?

Rose: Yes, Madam. In the block of flats at the top of the street.

Mary: Get him! Get someone—the nurse—if there's no one there, call an ambulance—

Rose: Yes, Madam. (*Gives baby to* Mary. *Starts to go.*)

Henry (*rises and meets* Rose; *holding* Rose *with one hand*): I'll go. (*Rushes out.*)

Rose (*looks after* Henry—*steps toward* Ada—*turns to* Mary): Miss Herries—

Mary (*almost simultaneously*): Get that bottle of smelling salts. . . .

Rose: Yes, Madam.

Mary (Rose *runs out upstairs;* Mary *tries to rub* Ada *and hold baby. She looks helplessly from* Ada *to the baby, puts baby in chair, returns to* Ada, *crosses to window—then to baby.* Rose *rushes in with smelling salts which she puts in front of* Ada's *nose.* Ada *stiffens but does not come to*): It's all my fault—all my fault for letting him—

Rose: What's the matter with her, Madam? (*Crosses to* Mary.)

Mary: Go on, go on!

(Rose *administers smelling salts, rubs* Ada *in a very inexperienced manner.* Henry *and* Doctor *enter.*)

Henry: Here! (*He does not take baby from* Mary, *but crosses to above sofa.* Doctor *crosses below sofa and looks at* Ada.) Ada! Ada!

Rose: I'll take it, Madam.

(Mary *gives baby to* Rose.)

Doctor (*to* Henry): Exposure. (*Picks up* Ada.) You'd better put her to bed at once.

Mary: Bed? She—

Henry: You see, Doctor—

Doctor (*to* Rose): Where's a bedroom?

Mary (*looks at* Rose): Why—

DOCTOR: Upstairs? (*This spoken to* ROSE *with the baby. He carries* ADA *out.*) Don't worry. Nothing serious. Needs rest and nourishment. (*To* ROSE.) Some hot soup. Chicken broth.

(DOCTOR *exits upstairs, followed by* ROSE. MARY *goes up onto platform and turns back to* HENRY *who is walking unconcernedly, lighting a cigarette.* MARY, *greatly agitated, hurries upstairs.* HENRY *calmly walks looking at room. Sees his painting of the cows. Picks it up. Looks about the room. Selects the mantel. Puts his picture there. Stands back looking at it. Sits in a chair admiring his picture. He is totally unconcerned about what has just happened.*)

ACT II

SCENE: *Two weeks later in January, an afternoon.*
The scene is the same. However, the desk is now behind the sofa. The coffee table is to the right of the sofa. A side chair is behind the desk and another is between the windows. HENRY *is at the desk. The doorbell rings—*HENRY *looks up from a paper he has been writing on—then resumes.* ROSE *comes in and crosses the room. She is dressed in street clothes. She walks, looks straight ahead, her hands folded before her.*

HENRY (*speaking just as she reaches the center of the room—not looking up*): Rose. (ROSE *stops, facing him but not looking at him. He looks up now.*) You're all dressed up, Rose. Why?
ROSE: I think you *know* why, Mr. Abbott—
HENRY: Leaving us?
ROSE: I think you know I *am*, Mr. Abbott.

(*She stands there as if anxious to continue the conversation—to get something off her chest. But after a moment, he looks down at his paper.*)

HENRY: Answer the bell.

(*She hesitates for a moment, then pressing her lips, walks off.*)

MR. EDWARDS (*offstage*): Mr. Henry Abbott here?
ROSE (*comes into room, and, not looking at* HENRY, *starts to cross toward dining room*): People outside.
HENRY: Who are they?
ROSE (*not stopping*): I don't know.
HENRY (*gently, as if admonishing a child*): Rose! Ask them to come in.

(*She stops, hesitates as though she were inwardly undergoing a struggle. Then turns and goes to left arch.*)

ROSE (*standing in arch*): Come in. (ROSE *exits.*)

(MR. EDWARDS *appears, followed by "his wife and daughter,* AGGIE." MR. EDWARDS *is a thick-set, reddish and bulbous-faced man with a hearty hoarse voice.* MRS. EDWARDS *is short, black-clad and eminently respectable looking.* AGGIE *is a thin, sharp-faced girl whose eyes and hands are rarely still.* MR. EDWARDS *is carrying a portable gramophone.*)

MR. EDWARDS: Hello, Henry.

(HENRY *gets up.*)

MRS. EDWARDS: How's Ada, Henry?
HENRY: Much better.
AGGIE: Hello, Henry.

(HENRY *nods.*)

MRS. EDWARDS: We brought Aggie with us.
MR. EDWARDS: We thought we'd better—
MRS. EDWARDS: How's the baby, Henry?
MR. EDWARDS: Doing well, Henry?

HENRY (*nods*): Ada will be glad to see you all.

MRS. EDWARDS: And we'll be awfully glad to see her—poor Ada.

MR. EDWARDS: I brought the gramophone. Thought she might like to hear some music.

MRS. EDWARDS: Layin' up in bed, you know—

HENRY: Sit down, and I'll call Miss Herries—

MRS. EDWARDS: Oh, Henry—the way I look—

(*Crosses and sits.*)

HENRY: I shall have to ask permission to bring you upstairs.

MR. EDWARDS: Sure, Henry—that's only right!

HENRY: Sit down. (*He goes upstairs.*)

MR. EDWARDS (*looking over the room; AGGIE goes and picks up bronze on table*): Very nice layout. (*Puts gramophone on coffee table and hat on end of desk.*)

MRS. EDWARDS: I should say it is. My—isn't it pretty!

MR. EDWARDS: Looks like a house I stayed in once—in Melbourne in Australia.

MRS. EDWARDS: Put that down, Aggie!

MR. EDWARDS: Same layout. I'd be able to tell better if I saw the whole house. (*To AGGIE, who is touching things on mantel.*) Aggie! I wish you would talk to her, Mother. Nice thing if somebody saw her. (*Crosses and sits on sofa.*)

MRS. EDWARDS: Father's right, Aggie. You ought to learn to behave yourself in a decent place.

(AGGIE *walks to arch. They watch her; she looks out and returns to room crossing to desk.*)

MR. EDWARDS (*after another moment*): You notice how nobody has pianos any more?

MRS. EDWARDS (*nodding*): If you lived in a house with a court you'd hear the children practicing, all day long.

MR. EDWARDS: It's the wireless that's spoiled it for pianos.

MRS. EDWARDS (*not looking at daughter*): Sit down, Aggie. Didn't you hear Henry say to sit down?

(AGGIE *crosses to end of sofa to fool with gramophone on coffee table.*)

MR. EDWARDS: Yep—now it's the wireless. But anything that's pushed out of a wire—sounds like it.

(AGGIE *is opening gramophone.*)

MRS. EDWARDS: Ts, ts. Oh, leave it be!

MR. EDWARDS (*has risen with surprising swiftness to* AGGIE *and stands over her*): Don't you realize there's somebody sick around here?

(AGGIE *looks frightened, stops playing with gramophone and examines other objects on coffee table. After a moment* MR. EDWARDS *starts toward arch.*)

MRS. EDWARDS: I'll warrant we'll have to take you off your job, Aggie, and put you back in school, to learn some manners.

MR. EDWARDS (*looking upstairs in arch*): That staircase—just like this house in Melbourne—in Australia. A very good sign.

MRS. EDWARDS: I never *knew* you were in Australia, Father.

MR. EDWARDS: Sure—I must have told you. Been everywhere. (*Crosses to* MRS. EDWARDS.)

MRS. EDWARDS (*shaking her head, puzzled*): Perhaps you did.

MR. EDWARDS: Didn't I ever mention about staying in this house that used to belong to Lord—Greville? Something like that.

MRS. EDWARDS (*thinking*): I don't remember the name.

MR. EDWARDS: Fine feller—black sheep. (AGGIE *crosses.*) Came to Australia and made a pile of money.

MRS. EDWARDS: Never got married!

MR. EDWARDS: No—real black sheep. Lived all alone. Got peculiar in his old age with all that money. Used to keep it around the house, they said.

MRS. EDWARDS: Must have been a tough customer.

MR. EDWARDS (*nodding, lips pursed*): That's what they said—

MRS. EDWARDS: All that money around the house, ts, ts—

MR. EDWARDS: In gold—gold bars. (AGGIE *crosses to look through arch.*) Some of 'em as long as your arm.

MRS. EDWARDS: Ts, ts. I suppose they found it all after he died?

MR. EDWARDS: No—I can't say they did. No. (*Laughs.*) Stop worryin' about it, Mother!

MRS. EDWARDS: Well, it's interesting! My goodness!

MR. EDWARDS: I hope Ada ain't too sick to see us—

(AGGIE *crosses to painting.*)

MRS. EDWARDS: Henry said she was all right—she was much better, he said—

MR. EDWARDS: Yep—but you know Ada ain't a strong girl. If she's been layin' in bed for two weeks—there's something wrong with her.

MRS. EDWARDS: Very nice of this lady, isn't it, Father?

MR. EDWARDS: I should say. She sounds like a real fine woman.

MRS. EDWARDS (AGGIE *has wandered around and is touching the things on a table*): Keep your hands off, Aggie!

(HENRY *comes downstairs.*)

HENRY (*stops, speaking from landing*): Miss Herries begs to be excused. She hopes to meet you all some other time.

MRS. EDWARDS (*rises*): I hope she ain't sick, Henry?

HENRY: No. (*Gestures them to go up.*)

MR. EDWARDS: Should I bring up the gramophone, Henry?

HENRY: I don't think so—no.

MR. EDWARDS (*setting it at back of sofa*): I'll just set it here out of the way then.

MRS. EDWARDS (*crosses between chair and table toward stairs;* AGGIE *drifts behind her*): Oh—this is certainly a *beautiful* house, Henry!

MR. EDWARDS (*crosses below sofa—propelling* AGGIE): Go on, Aggie.

(*Doorbell rings when* MRS. EDWARDS *is at foot of stairs,* AGGIE *behind her on bay-window landing,* MR. EDWARDS *on hall platform. Bell rings second time. For some reason the four of them stop dead still. There is a pause.*)

HENRY (*indicates*): Two flights up—the little room at the head of the stairs.

(*Slowly they move up again.*)

MR. EDWARDS (*the last*): Lots of visitors today, Henry.

(*He is off.* HENRY *waits on the landing.* ROSE *enters and crosses. He watches her. She goes off. A moment later.*)

LUCY (*offstage*): Hello, Rose. Is Miss Herries in?
ROSE (*offstage*): Yes, Madam.

(LUCY *enters room, followed by* ROSE. *She stops on seeing* HENRY.)

HENRY: How do you do? (LUCY *nods in surprise.*) I'll tell Miss Herries, Rose. (*To* LUCY.) Excuse me. (*He goes upstairs.*)
LUCY (*crossing into room, stopping* ROSE *as she starts off behind arch*): Rose! Isn't that the young man Miss Herries brought in here one night?
ROSE: Yes, Madam—it is.
LUCY (*as if she knew something*): Oh—

(ROSE *goes off on platform.* LUCY *crosses to desk to remove her gloves.*)

MARY (*coming down*): Lucy!
LUCY (*meets* MARY *below platform*): Mary, dear.

MARY: Not even a picture postcard! (*Kisses her.*)

LUCY: Didn't you get my letter?

MARY: No.

LUCY (*disturbed*): Oh, that's too bad!

MARY: Forget about it. Have a good time?

LUCY: That letter worries me.

MARY (*laughs*): Really? You probably addressed it wrong. (*Crosses to end of sofa and sits.*)

LUCY: No. Oh, well. (*Crosses to desk above couch, takes off gloves.*) How are you, Mary?

MARY: Oh, fairly well. *You* look splendid.

LUCY: Thanks. I feel as though I'll never get warm again!

MARY: Just an excuse to get back to the Riviera, isn't it?

LUCY: I'm leaving this afternoon. I'm flying to Paris. (*Crosses to other end of sofa—a bit away.*)

MARY: Oh, I'm sorry!

LUCY: That's what I wrote. I didn't think I'd have a chance to see you. Then I decided to come around for a minute anyway.

MARY: I'm glad you did!

LUCY: I just couldn't write you as I did and let it go at that. And when you didn't answer—I knew something was wrong.

MARY: What are you talking about?

LUCY: I'll tell you simply and to the point—if you'll tell me what's been going on here.

MARY: Going on? (*After a moment she sits back.*) Please say what you have to say, Lucy, before I go completely out of my mind—

LUCY: All right. Some days after we got to St. Moritz, a lady joined us. She had just arrived—and she had it on *excellent authority*—steady on—that you had taken a man to live with you—

MARY (*after a moment, as though this were the last straw, murmurs*): What?

LUCY: I laughed her down of course—told her she was a silly woman, I insulted her frightfully—(*Slowly.*) It didn't do much good.

MARY: But who would say a thing like that?

LUCY: She from whom all such blessings flow—your sister Emily.

MARY: Emily! It's incredible! How would she know?

LUCY: She didn't say.

MARY (*very puzzled—thinking*): Emily—

LUCY: Women like that make mountains out of blades of grass—you know that.

MARY: Oh ho!

LUCY: You've traced it!

MARY: No. My niece Phyllis—and her fiancé—were here one night. They saw him—but why would they—? Oh, no!

LUCY: Saw who?

MARY: Lucy—it's true.

LUCY: What?

MARY: I have taken a man in to live with me—and his wife and child.

LUCY: That one—you brought in here on Christmas Eve?

MARY: Hmmm. He came back with his wife. She fainted and I put her up for the night. She's been here ever since.

LUCY (*crosses to sofa and sits; after a pause*): Oh, Mary, Mary. My poor Mary!

MARY: That's only part of it. My cook left me last week—and Rose gave me notice. I've been on my knees to her in the kitchen. She insists on going.

LUCY: Who are those people?

MARY: I don't know. It's become nightmarish. What will I do without Rose? I'll never replace her.

LUCY (*dismissing this*): Rose! Throw those people out! How ill is she?

MARY: I don't know—I can't tell. I know *I've* been feeling badly the past few days. My heart has been raising red hell.

LUCY: Oh, Mary! (*Pause, then decisively.*) It's insane! You're being used in the most ridiculous and criminal manner.

MARY: Well, goodness knows, I begged for it!

LUCY: I know you! Throw them out! You've simply *got* to!

MARY: I suddenly feel very old and helpless. (*Doorbell rings.*)

LUCY (*quietly*): You fool, Mary—I haven't the heart to scream at you.

MARY: Now they've got friends upstairs—visiting. I don't know why that should bother me. But it does—intensely.

LUCY: Will you please get rid of them—and take a plane tomorrow with me? I'll wait on.

MARY: A plane?

LUCY: A train then.

(ROSE *crosses to door on platform.*)

MARY: I never felt more like it. I really want to.

LUCY: Fine!

MARY: Not tomorrow of course. I've got to clean up this mess. And if I go I'll close the house.

LUCY: Next week then—

MARY: Perhaps, in a week or so.

DOCTOR (*offstage*): Good afternoon.

ROSE (*offstage*): Good afternoon.

MARY: Now who? (*Rises, crosses to archway.*)

LUCY: You certainly have a busy house.

ROSE (*entering*): It's the Doctor, Madam.

MARY: Oh! Go straight up, Doctor.

(ROSE *starts to lead way, getting to landing.*)

DOCTOR (*to* MARY): Thank you. (*To* ROSE.) That's quite all right. I know the way.

(DOCTOR *goes upstairs.* ROSE *goes off past arch on platform.*)

LUCY: I should go—but I'm not going to—until you promise to close this house and get out of here.

MARY: All right, I promise.

LUCY: Good. (*She rises.*) I must rush. (*Crosses to desk and*

gets gloves.) I expressed everything through the St. Moritz.
But there's a coat I want—and some shoes.

MARY: Go on, then. (*Smiles wanly, speaks simply.*) And
thank you.

LUCY: Now remember—you've *promised!*

MARY: All right!

LUCY: Well—good-by—and God bless you. (*Starts off.*) Get
rid of those strange leeches.

MARY: I will. (*As she goes through the arch.*) Give my love
to Phil and the children.

LUCY: Thank you, dear. (*Offstage.*) When will I hear from
you?

(ROSE *enters.*)

MARY: I'll write—

LUCY: The minute you've decided—I wish you could come
and tell me what you think of this coat. I'm spending far
too much. Good-by—

MARY: Have a nice trip, Lucy. (*Door slams.*)

ROSE (*as* MARY *comes in*): Miss Herries—

MARY (*surprised as she looks at* ROSE's *clothes*): Going already, Rose?

ROSE: Yes, Madam. I was just waiting to say good-by.

MARY (*after a moment—as if tired of the whole thing, crosses
to desk*): Well—I suppose if you've made up your mind to
leave, you'd better.

ROSE: Yes, Madam. I'm sorry. I'd like to come back in a while.

MARY: Let me have your address?

ROSE: It's on the bill hook—in the pantry.

MARY (*sees* EDWARDS' *hat on desk and distastefully puts it on
chair between windows*): All right—

ROSE: Good-by, Miss Herries.

MARY: Rose, I wish I really knew why you were leaving. Is
it the work, Rose?

ROSE: I told you, Madam.

MARY: What's the matter?

ROSE: Nothing, Madam, I told you—I want to visit my sister in Newcastle.

MARY: I don't believe that. You've never *mentioned* a sister all the time you've been with me. (*Walks toward* ROSE.) Now look here, Rose, I didn't intend to plead with you to stay on. But I've decided to close the house. If you'll wait a week you can go where you like and I'll be glad to take you back in about three months.

ROSE (*with trace of eagerness*): You're closing the house, Miss Herries?

MARY: This week.

ROSE: But excuse me, Madam— What's happening to them?

MARY: The Abbotts? They're leaving, of course.

ROSE: They are?

MARY: Oh. So it *is* the Abbotts. Why didn't you say so?

ROSE: Miss Herries—! (ROSE *cannot speak.*)

MARY: What is it? What are you crying for?

ROSE: Miss Herries— I don't want to go!

MARY: Then why?

ROSE: It isn't the work, Madam, I don't mind that—

MARY (*close to* ROSE): What's wrong then? You must tell me!

ROSE: Are you sure they're leaving, Madam?

MARY: Quite sure.

ROSE: Him, too?

MARY: Yes! What *is* it, Rose? (*Taking* ROSE's *arm;* ROSE *pauses uncertainly.*) Has Mr. Abbott said anything to you?

ROSE: No, Madam. (*Bursts out.*) It ain't what he says! I can't explain what I mean, Miss Herries! There's something about him! I'm afraid—

MARY: Afraid of what?

ROSE: I don't know. I'm afraid to stay here.

MARY: What is it, Rose? Try to tell me.

ROSE: That Mrs. Abbott—

MARY: Yes.

ROSE: She's not ill, Madam. She lays up there in that bed—lookin' like she's dyin'. But she ain't ill—and never was!

MARY: Never was?

ROSE: No, Madam! There's some people always look that way
—an' she's one of 'em. But I know she's not ill!

MARY: *How* do you know?

ROSE: I just do, Madam. She's been putting it on all the time!

MARY: Putting it on?

ROSE: Yes. And the baby! Did you notice something funny
about it?

MARY: No.

ROSE: Did you ever hear it cry?

MARY (*after quite a pause, as if she just realized*): No.

ROSE: Neither did I! Never! I never heard it make a sound. I
think it *can't*, Miss Herries. It wants to—but it can't.

MARY (*a quick involuntary phrase*): Oh, no.

ROSE: Yes, Madam—that's what I think. And something else
—it don't look like her. It looks foreign—like an Italian
baby. But it's not hers.

MARY: How can you tell? It's just an infant.

ROSE: No, it's not. Not as young as he said! Oh, I don't know,
Miss Herries! I'm just scared to death—! (*She cries again.
There is a pause.*)

MARY: Rose, please stop crying.

ROSE: I'm sorry, Madam.

MARY: I want you to pack up whatever belongs to the baby
—at once.

ROSE: Yes, Madam.

MARY: Then take a directory and see if you can find some
private hospital which has an ambulance we can hire to
call for Mrs. Abbott.

ROSE (*turns*): Yes, Madam?

MARY: Wait a minute. (ROSE *turns*. MARY *crosses to her*.)
Tell them we don't want anyone taken to the hospital. We
just want to hire the ambulance and an attendant for about
an hour.

ROSE: I will, Miss Herries.

MARY: Tell them we'll ring up again—and let them know—
will you, Rose?

ROSE: Yes, Madam.

MARY (*ushers* ROSE *onto platform*): Straight away. Now go on and don't be afraid of anything.

ROSE (*turning to* MARY): I don't want to be foolish, Madam — As long as they're goin'.

MARY: It's all right. I'm sorry you didn't tell me all this before.

ROSE: I didn't want to interfere, Miss Herries. I thought perhaps you had some special reason.

MARY: I've just been very stupid, Rose. Now please go and do as I asked.

ROSE: Yes, Madam.

(*Turns and goes off.* MARY *watches her off—then suddenly goes to stairs, reaches landing and is about to go up when she pauses as the sound of voices reaches her. She hesitates for a moment then returns to room, standing by fireplace. Lights dim on stage.*)

MRS. EDWARDS (*off*): Good-by. Aggie, say good-by to Ada.

AGGIE (*off*): Good-by, Ada.

MR. EDWARDS (*off*): That's a good girl.

MRS. EDWARDS (*off*): Mind your manners and you'll keep your friends. Ha! Ha!

MR. EDWARDS (*off*): Good-by, Ada. (*Door slams.*)

MRS. EDWARDS (*offstage*): We shouldn't have come, Father.

MR. EDWARDS (*offstage*): She's a pretty sick girl.

MRS. EDWARDS (*offstage*): Ts, ts. I hope we haven't done any harm.

MR. EDWARDS (*off*): Country air—that's what she needs.

MRS. EDWARDS (*off*): Leave that alone, Aggie!

MR. EDWARDS (*off*): There ain't an ounce of flesh on her. (*As he finishes talking he comes into view.*)

MRS. EDWARDS: You'd hardly know what was whiter—her or the sheets. I—

(*She, too, has come into view and stops, seeing* MARY. *Behind* MRS. EDWARDS *is* AGGIE; *from dining room comes* HENRY.)

HENRY: Miss Herries, these are Ada's friends, Mr. and Mrs. Edwards and their daughter, Aggie.

(MARY *nods.*)

MR. EDWARDS: How do you do, Ma'am?

MRS. EDWARDS: We've just been up to *see* Ada. My—she's a sight, isn't she?

HENRY (*crosses to* MRS. EDWARDS): I'm afraid the excitement was too much.

(AGGIE *drifts to above desk.*)

MRS. EDWARDS: I hope we haven't done any harm—

MR. EDWARDS (*crosses to above table*): She's just all in! Not an ounce of flesh on her, Ma'am.

HENRY (*paces floor*): It occurred to me upstairs. We're looking for a cook. If I may take the liberty of recommending Mrs. Edwards—

MRS. EDWARDS: Now, Henry.

HENRY: I know she's worked in the very best homes.

MRS. EDWARDS: As a cook only, Ma'am.

HENRY: And with Aggie to help—if Rose insists on going— I thought we could struggle along for a while.

MARY: Thank you. I won't need anyone. I'm closing the house.

HENRY (*paces toward* MARY): Really, Miss Herries?

MARY: I'm not well, either. I need a rest.

HENRY: That's too bad.

MARY: I'm glad your friends are here. They can help move Ada. I'm hiring a private ambulance.

HENRY: You mean move her today?

MARY: Oh, yes!

HENRY: Where shall I take her?

MARY: Take her home!

HENRY: I would—willingly—but, we have no home. (MARY *starts to speak.*) We were so far behind on the rent—we were dispossessed a week ago, I thought I told you.

MARY: I'm afraid your troubles can't concern me any longer. Take Ada any place you please.

MRS. EDWARDS: That's a pretty hard way to talk, Miss Herries.

MARY: You must understand, I don't want to seem brutal —but I think Mrs. Abbott is well enough to go now—and I wish you all good day.

MRS. EDWARDS: I'm sure you've been kindness itself, Miss Herries. Ada knows that, I'm sure. But to move her now would be to kill her, that's all. Any movement and she'll drop at your feet.

HENRY: Besides we have no place to go—as I've told you.

MARY (*controlling herself*): But this lady—

MRS. EDWARDS: Oh, Lord, Miss Herries—we only have two rooms—

MR. EDWARDS: That's a good idea, Ma'am! There ain't space now to swing a cat in!

AGGIE: Popper coughs all night, anyway.

MRS. EDWARDS: Keep still, Aggie.

MR. EDWARDS: And then there's the kid, mind you!

MARY (*to* HENRY): I don't care to discuss it! You will get Ada out of here today!

(HENRY *looks at her steadily.*)

MRS. EDWARDS: It might be life and death you know. Do you think she ought—?

MARY: I told you I didn't care to discuss it! (MR. EDWARDS *crosses to fireplace.* MARY *crosses to* HENRY.) I believed your bad luck stories—and I've done everything in my power to help you! I think it's pretty obvious that you've imposed on me in the crudest way!

HENRY: I'm sorry you think that.

MARY: You will please oblige me by getting out of here as quickly as possible.

HENRY: That's more easily said than done.

MARY: Why you—! Leave at once, all of you!

(*They do not move.* MRS. EDWARDS *looks about her.*)

MRS. EDWARDS (*after pause, crosses to desk— AGGIE drifts*): Such a fine big house, Ma'am. It's wonderful how clean it is with only one help.

MR. EDWARDS (*crosses to MARY one step*): Yep. I was telling Mother—that's my wife, Mrs. Edwards over here, how much it looks like a house I stayed in once in Melbourne, in Australia.

MARY (*to HENRY*): Will you please—!

MR. EDWARDS (*makes small movement toward MARY*): It's the staircase made me think of it—same layout. Used to be a private house. Turned into a lodging house later—when I stayed there.

MARY (*to EDWARDS*): Leave immediately, or I shall call the police!

MR. EDWARDS: Lady who ran it—she was a leftover from the old day. A real character, Ma'am. I stayed on the top floor— (*MARY crosses to ring bell. MR. EDWARDS follows.*) That was the cheapest in those times.

(*MARY goes to the bell. Just before she reaches it, HENRY puts his hand out gently and covers it. They have somehow formed a semicircle about her.*)

MARY (*to HENRY*): How dare you!

(*Doctor comes down stairs and stands below platform with the rest. MARY sees him.*)

MRS. EDWARDS (*as MARY reacts to DOCTOR's entrance*): Would you believe it, Miss Herries—he's never told me a word of this!

MR. EDWARDS: Well, the old lady used to start from the bottom floor in the morning. (*MARY turns to see MR. EDWARDS coming toward her.*) Knock, knock, knock—how do you like your ham and eggs this morning, sir? Thank you, sir. (*MARY starts backing away.*) Second floor. Knock, knock, knock. How do you like your ham and eggs this morning, sir? (*As MARY has backed down center, HENRY, MRS.*

EDWARDS *and* DOCTOR *have joined* MR. EDWARDS *in their slow walk forcing* MARY *downstage. They have her surrounded.*) Thank you, sir. Third floor.

MARY (*to* HENRY): This is monstrous. What do you want of me?

MR. EDWARDS: Well Ma'am, by the time she reached me— I was mighty glad to get myself a cup of tea! (*Laughs.*)

MRS. EDWARDS: He was a one when I married him, Miss Herries!

MARY: What do you want?

HENRY: What about my pay for all these weeks?

MARY: Pay—?

HENRY: My pay.

MRS. EDWARDS: His pay.

MR. EDWARDS (*sings*):

> "When the time comes to pay—
> You must pay."

(*Staggers slightly, looks around at them.* MARY *starts to speak, but doesn't. She puts her hand to her heart—then looks around at the others. They are all watching her; quietly, she starts to speak again—then bends over slightly as if in pain, stands gasping*): Oh! (*Then groans and staggers to couch, moves toward desk with arm outstretched but suddenly sinks to couch—half lying.*) Oh, please! In the drawer—the green bottle—! (*Tries to point to the desk drawer.*) Oh, quickly, please! (*She is choking. Suddenly with a deep groan she collapses in the couch. They look at her.*)

MRS. EDWARDS: Ts, ts, ts—poor woman.

MR. EDWARDS: Luck—! The minute I laid eyes on that staircase I knew it!

(HENRY *snaps fingers to* DOCTOR, *who bends and touches her heart.*)

DOCTOR: Still going.

HENRY: Take her upstairs. (*He gives* EDWARDS *the key.*)

MR. EDWARDS: Sure, Henry—you bet.

(*Bends to pick her up.* DOCTOR *helps.* AGGIE, *who has been standing over her, now kneels and claws at* MARY's *bracelet.*)

AGGIE: Gimme that!

MR. EDWARDS (*pushes her away*): Why don't you behave yourself?

MRS. EDWARDS: You're just like a little *animal*, Aggie!

MR. EDWARDS (*takes bracelet, looks at it, starts to pocket it*): It's a cheap one.

HENRY: Let me see. (*Looks and throws it to* AGGIE.) There now be quiet.

MR. EDWARDS (*pulls* MARY *to sitting position;* DOCTOR *takes her under arm,* EDWARDS *by feet*): Upsa-daisy!

MRS. EDWARDS: Don't hurt yourself, Father.

MR. EDWARDS (*as he goes up to landing carrying* MARY): Oh, you're not such a heavy old lady. Say good-by to everybody. (*As he goes up sings under his breath.*)

"Where are the friends that—that we used to know
    Long long ago—long long ago.
    Where are—"

HENRY (*crosses to bell*): Sh, sh, sh, sh, sh.

(DOCTOR *and* MR. EDWARDS *go up carrying* MARY.)

MRS. EDWARDS (*sits on sofa*): Came awful sudden, didn't it, Henry? Very unexpected. Saved a *lot* of trouble I should say.

HENRY (*rings bell, to* AGGIE, *who is examining bracelet*): Put that away, please!

MRS. EDWARDS (*settling herself on the couch properly*): Sit down, Aggie.

(AGGIE *sits in desk chair.* HENRY *takes bills from pocket and counts some off. Holds bills in his hand.* ROSE *enters, stops level with* HENRY *and looks around.*)

HENRY: Miss Herries asked me to give you this, Rose. Unless you changed your mind and stayed.

ROSE: Why—Miss Herries wanted me to stay on a week—she asked me to.

HENRY: I know—we thought of taking Mrs. Abbott home today—but that's impossible. (*Watches her face.*) I know you complained about us, Rose. Miss Herries told me. I convinced her that you were wrong. Well, which is it? Will you stay? If not—this lady is ready to take your place.

ROSE (*after a pause*): I'll go.

HENRY (*hands her money*): Here, then.

ROSE: I've *been* paid.

HENRY: I persuaded Miss Herries to give you this—in place of the extra week. (ROSE *takes the money.*) I'm not as bad as you think, Rose. But as long as you can't bear the sight of us—you'd *better* go. (ROSE *turns uncertainly and starts out.*) Did you order the ambulance?

ROSE (*stopping*): No.

HENRY: Whom did you call?

ROSE: St. Mary's Hospital—

HENRY: As long as you've spoken to them—would you call again before you leave and ask them not to come on—Never mind, I'll call them myself. St. Mary's Hospital. Thank you, Rose.

(ROSE *does not leave immediately.*)

HENRY: Good-by.

(HENRY *watches* ROSE *off.* AGGIE *follows her to arch, stands looking after her.*)

MRS. EDWARDS: Very nicely done, Henry. Come away from there, Aggie!

(AGGIE *crosses to window.* DOCTOR *comes in from stairs.*)

HENRY (*taking money out—to* DOCTOR): The maid, Rose. (*To* MRS. EDWARDS.) Call St. Mary's Hospital. Paddington.

MRS. EDWARDS: Yes, Henry. (*Crosses to desk as she speaks to* DOCTOR.) The maid will be coming out of the basement.

HENRY (*gives* DOCTOR *money*): Here.

DOCTOR: 'k you.

HENRY: Don't lose her.

(DOCTOR *goes off.*)

MRS. EDWARDS (*looking in phone book*): Aggie, come away from that window.

HENRY: Sit down!

(AGGIE *sits in chair, scared.* HENRY *crosses to fireplace. Downstairs comes a strange white figure. It is* ADA *in a nightgown. She comes into the room, doing almost a little dance. A sharp laugh from* ADA *draws* MRS. EDWARDS' *attention to her.*)

MRS. EDWARDS (*at phone*): Ada—you're going to catch your death of cold walking around here barefoot! Paddington 7831, please. Thank you. (ADA *really begins to dance, around center of the room. She takes a little springing sidestep around the room, holding the sides of her nightgown.*) Now that's enough, Ada—the floor is awfully draughty! (ADA *suddenly begins to laugh—a strange animalic laugh.*) Ada!

(ADA *dances toward* HENRY.)

HENRY: Keep still!!

(HENRY *almost simultaneously has hit her across the mouth with the back of his hand. She gives a low cry, clasping both her hands to her mouth, and almost doubled up,* ADA *whimpers. She looks very much like an animal looking for a place to hide.* HENRY *has gone to* MRS. EDWARDS. *Down the stairs comes* MR. EDWARDS *heralding his approach by whistling "Long, long ago."* HENRY *crosses to foot of stairs, takes key from* EDWARDS.)

MR. EDWARDS (*crosses to window above desk and looks out*):
Oh, that's fine. There goes Rose and there goes Doc. (*He
leaves the window and crosses to gramophone. Picks it up
and crosses above desk to table—where he places it,
cranks it.*)

HENRY: What's the matter, don't they answer? (*Crosses to
MRS. EDWARDS.*)

MRS. EDWARDS: Ringing. Hello? St. Mary's Hospital? This is
the maid who called you a little while ago about an ambulance for an invalid. Montague Square? Yes.

HENRY: Never mind, they took her in a taxi.

MRS. EDWARDS: Well please never mind—they took her in
a taxi—

HENRY: To her own Doctor.

(EDWARDS *puts gramophone on table. Takes crank out of
pocket and winds.*)

MRS. EDWARDS: To her own Doctor.

HENRY: Make sure the ambulance hasn't left.

MRS. EDWARDS: The ambulance hasn't left, has it? Thank you.
(*Hangs up. To* HENRY.) No. They take their time.

MR. EDWARDS (*having placed the gramophone on table,
winds it*): What's the matter, Ada?

HENRY (*going to* ADA, *who meets him*): Never mind. (*Puts
his arm around her. She responds but he quickly turns to
business. To* MRS. EDWARDS.) Get the baby out of here.
(*He crosses to window.*)

MR. EDWARDS (*unlocking clasps on gramophone*): That's the
trouble, Henry. Can't you just forget about it?

MRS. EDWARDS (*rises*): No, Henry's right, Father. It's just a
nuisance here, poor little thing.

MR. EDWARDS: What about Ada, Henry?

HENRY: Ada stays.

MRS. EDWARDS: What for, Henry? She's done her job.

MR. EDWARDS: Henry's right, Mother. You wouldn't want
Ada roaming around the streets.

(MRS. EDWARDS *exits upstairs.*)

HENRY (*crosses to* MR. EDWARDS): See that the Italian woman gets the baby back tonight.

MR. EDWARDS: Whatever you say, Henry.

HENRY: Shutters nailed in her room?

MR. EDWARDS: Coming up, Henry. (*Lifting lid of gramophone as if it were uncovering a big surprise. And that's the way he talks.*) *There* you are, Henry! Ain't that nice?

(*Without replying* HENRY *takes a hammer and some nails out of record compartment in gramophone.*)

MR. EDWARDS (*taking a record from cover slot, puts it on the disc. Calls up the stairs*): I'm going to board over the window tomorrow anyway, Henry——! (*Returns to gramophone, starts it going. It is an orchestra playing—*MR. EDWARDS *leans over, listening—*ADA *listens.*) I'm crazy about that record— Ain't it nice, Ada? (ADA *who has been listening and moving her head to the rhythm now starts to dance again.* MRS. EDWARDS *is heard coming down the stairs.*)

MRS. EDWARDS: Oh, he's a sweet little feller— Oh, he's a sweet little feller. (AGGIE *meets* MRS. EDWARDS, *trying to see baby.*) Go away, Aggie! Frightening the poor little chap. (MRS. EDWARDS *goes to sofa, sits, talking to baby.*)

MR. EDWARDS (*whistling he goes to* MRS. EDWARDS): Cootchie —cootchie—coo. (*Tickles baby.*)

MRS. EDWARDS (*slapping* MR. EDWARDS' *hand*): Now, now, now! (AGGIE *is listening to music.* ADA *has come to center, swaying to the music.* MR. EDWARDS *goes to* ADA. MRS. EDWARDS *continues her baby talk throughout.*) Oh, isn't he a sweet little baby. Whoooo. Sweet little feller. Whoooo —et cetera, et cetera.

(ADA *and* MR. EDWARDS *start dancing—*ADA *breaks out into an exultant laugh.*)

ACT III

SCENE: *It is an afternoon during the following summer. The same room. The arrangement of the furniture is the same as in the Prologue. The only exception is that there are no "moderns" on the back right wall. There is a solitary "old master" there.*

MRS. EDWARDS *is seated in chair left of desk, peeling potatoes.* MR. EDWARDS *is reading a newspaper.* MARY HERRIES *sits in a half-daze, an unbelieving dream. The other two pay no attention to her as long as she keeps quiet. Finally, she attempts, slowly, to rise.* EDWARDS *notices this, pays no attention, lets her struggle and rise.* MRS. EDWARDS *rises.* MARY *looks at* MRS. EDWARDS *and sits. Then* MR. EDWARDS *resumes his reading.*

The doorbell rings, followed by two knocks on the door knocker. A trace of a glance passes between the EDWARDS, *a ray of hope is visible in* MARY. MRS. EDWARDS *goes to the window and then goes to the door. There is a pause, then she returns with the mail.* MR. EDWARDS *has risen and crossed to meet* MRS. EDWARDS. MARY's *eyes follow the letters as they pass from* MRS. EDWARDS *to* MR. EDWARDS *and then back to the desk, in a neat pile.* MR. EDWARDS *returns to his newspaper.* MARY *looks for a time at the letters on the desk and finally at* EDWARDS *who nods a solemn* "No, no." MRS. EDWARDS *takes her potatoes out. That closes the incident and there is inaction until the door is heard to open.* MRS. EDWARDS *goes to door and meets* HENRY, *who enters.* HENRY *pays no attention to* MARY, *but ques-*

258

tions MRS. EDWARDS. *What they say is as much for* MARY's
benefit as for anyone else's. HENRY *carries a portfolio.*

HENRY: Is Miss Herries in?

MRS. EDWARDS (*a pause, during which* MR. EDWARDS *slowly
rises and looks at* MARY): Oh, no, sir—Miss Herries is
traveling.

HENRY: Is that so? I had no idea.

MRS. EDWARDS (ADA *enters slowly and sits in front of fireplace*): Yes, sir. She left for America three weeks ago.
From there she was going to South America—and from
there to Australia.

HENRY (*looking about the room*): Really! Strange she didn't
let us know.

MRS. EDWARDS (*very quietly and for* MARY's *ears*): Miss
Herries had a bad nervous breakdown, sir. She wouldn't
see anyone. She left very suddenly.

HENRY: Well! I'm sorry to hear it.

MRS. EDWARDS: Yes, sir. We're closing the house for the time
being.

HENRY: You are the—?

MRS. EDWARDS: Housekeeper, sir.

HENRY: Thank you. Very good! (*Crosses to desk, puts portfolio on desk, looks at mail, never looking at* MARY. MARY
looks at HENRY *in the manner of a paralytic almost—an
unwavering, dull stare, her head moving very slightly from
side to side.* HENRY *addresses* MARY *as if she had just ap-
peared, very much as if he were dealing with a child.*)
Well! How do you feel, Miss Herries? (*She gives no sign
she has heard.*) How do you feel?

MARY (*after a long time, very low*): Let me go!—

HENRY: Let you go where, Miss Herries?

MARY (*after another long time*): What do you want?

HENRY: We want you to get well as soon as possible, Miss
Herries. You know that. (*A slight pause, after which he
looks up at* MRS. EDWARDS.) I'm afraid she's not much better, Mrs. Edwards.

MRS. EDWARDS: No, sir, I'm afraid not.

HENRY (*to* MARY): The nurse tells me you haven't been
eating well. (MARY *slowly looks at* MRS. EDWARDS, *then
back to* HENRY.) You should, you know. It's very important.

MARY: What do you want?

MRS. EDWARDS: I do think she seems to be more herself, sir.

HENRY (*nods*): Do you understand what we are saying, Miss
Herries?

(*After a pause,* MARY *slowly nods grimly. There is an immediate reaction on all of them.*)

MR. EDWARDS: Well, that's fine!

MRS. EDWARDS: I knew it!

HENRY: I'm so glad. You're pulling through at last, Miss
Herries. You'll be up and about in no time now.

MARY: Let me go! Let me go!! Let me go!!!

(HENRY *looks at* MRS. EDWARDS *and shakes his head.*)

HENRY (*takes pen and paper from pocket*): Will you sign
this paper, Miss Herries? (*She looks at them, uncompre-
hendingly.* MR. EDWARDS *crosses between chair and table
with his newspaper. He places newspaper on* MARY's *lap
and stands at her left.*) Will you sign it now so your affairs
can be taken care of? Here, please. (*Points out place.*)

MRS. EDWARDS (*crosses to* MARY, *takes pen from* HENRY):
I'll help, dear. (*Puts pen in her hand, and holds the back
of her fist.*) Go on.

(MARY *remains motionless; only her heavy breathing can be
heard.*)

HENRY: Sign, Miss Herries. It's best.

MARY: Will you let me go? I won't tell—

HENRY: Go on, Miss Herries.

MRS. EDWARDS: Here we go. "Mary," a nice "M" now.

MARY: No. No—

HENRY: You must, Miss Herries—do you hear?

MRS. EDWARDS: "Mary"— (*Trying to guide pen.*)

MARY: No— No— (*Suddenly she gets up—screaming, spilling pen, paper and newspaper on floor.*) No—! (MRS. EDWARDS *grabs* MARY'S *shoulders and forces her to sit again.*)

MRS. EDWARDS: Stop it, you old—

(HENRY *almost hits* MRS. EDWARDS *for being so rough with* MARY. MRS. EDWARDS *goes near* MARY'S *chair.*)

MR. EDWARDS: Here we are now. (*Picking up pen, paper, newspaper from floor. He places them on* MARY'S *lap. Puts pen in her hand. Prompts.*) "Mary"—

MARY (*with every bit of resolution and finality but still in a dull, weak voice*): No. No.

(*There is a pause. All look at* HENRY *except* MARY.)

HENRY (*quietly*): Tomorrow, then. Or the day after. (*He takes pen, paper and newspaper from* MARY. *To the others.*) Take her out. (*He goes to desk, puts pen and paper there.*)

MRS. EDWARDS: Don't be afraid, Miss Herries, I'll take care of you. I'm here.

(*They help her to rise and help her towards the stairs.*)

MR. EDWARDS: That's a good girl.

MRS. EDWARDS: We'll have a nice little walk.

(MRS. EDWARDS *and* MARY *go upstairs.* MR. EDWARDS *stops on landing.* HENRY *returns to papers at desk.* ADA *lingers, crossing to center.* HENRY *looks up and talks to her in somewhat the same way he has talked to* MARY.)

HENRY: Hello, Ada. Everything all right?

ADA: Yes, Henry!

HENRY: You like it here?

ADA: Yes, Henry!

HENRY: So do I. (*Pause.*) Ada.

ADA: Yes, Henry?

HENRY (*crossing to* ADA, *as if he were suggesting a game*):
  Go upstairs and watch—and listen!

ADA: Yes, Henry! (*She goes, eager to do what he asks.*)

(HENRY *crosses to get picture and places it in front of fireplace—then crosses to desk and sits.* EDWARDS *looks back
  up the stairs—turns to* HENRY—*shakes his head.*)

HENRY: Don't be impatient, Edwards.

MR. EDWARDS: Whatever you say, Henry.

HENRY: Miss Herries is a very fine woman. She has character.
  She has *strength*—

MR. EDWARDS: That's true—but—

(HENRY *is reading the mail.*)

HENRY: Imagination—hope. She still has hope, Edwards.

MR. EDWARDS: Stubborn.

HENRY: *Time*, Edwards.

MR. EDWARDS: Perhaps.

HENRY: There is a dealer from Paris coming this afternoon to
  look at the Whistler. (*Gestures to the picture propped
  against the fireplace.*)

MR. EDWARDS: Here?

HENRY: He will also see Miss Herries—talk to her.

MR. EDWARDS: *Talk* to her, Henry!

HENRY: It would be comforting to have Miss Herries realize
  that if she ever should be in a position to appeal to anyone
  —no one would believe her.

MR. EDWARDS: Don't like it.

HENRY: Well, I'm going to try it, Edwards. (*Looks through
  letter.*) Ah! Lucy Weston is returning to London. (*This
  announcement worries* EDWARDS, *who crosses away a bit
  and turns back to* HENRY.) Dear Lucy. I shall look forward
  to seeing her again. (*He notices* EDWARDS' *worry.*) What is
  it, Edwards?

EDWARDS: It's about leaving this place.

HENRY: *You* may, if you want to.

EDWARDS: I didn't mean that. (*Pause. Pulls chair of desk up a bit and sits.*) How was Paris?

HENRY: Very nice.

EDWARDS: Buy any pictures?

HENRY: Sold a few.

EDWARDS: Mind if I see the list?

HENRY: All right. (*Gives list to* EDWARDS.)

MR. EDWARDS (*he is impressed by list*): Quite right, Henry. There's a time to. After a while the odds keep stretching.

HENRY (*quietly and patiently*): We *live* here, Edwards. We are Miss Herries' best friends—her only friends—in London. The only ones who have cared for her since her—illness. I should think that idea would appeal to *you. Steady* employment. (*Doorbell.*) That should be the man from Bernstein et Fils.

MR. EDWARDS (*crossing up into bay window and calling upstairs*): Mother!

HENRY (*who has crossed to the window*): Wait! It isn't. It's Peter.

MR. EDWARDS: Peter!

(MRS. EDWARDS *comes down the stairs.*)

HENRY (*picks up portfolio and papers*): Show him in.

(HENRY *exits to dining room.* MR. EDWARDS *goes upstairs.* MRS. EDWARDS *waits until* MR. EDWARDS *is on the way, then goes to the hall. All this is done casually.*)

MRS. EDWARDS (*off*): Yes, sir?

PETER (*off*): I'm Mr. Santard.

MRS. EDWARDS (*off*): Oh, yes, sir. You rang up several weeks ago.

PETER (*off*): That's right.

MRS. EDWARDS (*off*): Will you come in, sir?

PETER (*off*): Thank you. (*He enters.*) You are the—

MRS. EDWARDS: The housekeeper, sir. Mrs. Edwards.

PETER: I told *Mrs.* Santard, Miss Herries' niece, what you said and we all thought it would be a good idea for one of us to hop around sometime and get the details.

MRS. EDWARDS: Yes, sir.

PETER: America, you said?

MRS. EDWARDS: Yes, sir. I believe she had a friend there—in California.

PETER: You don't know who—or where? We're going to America ourselves—

MRS. EDWARDS: She didn't say.

PETER: She left no forwarding address of any kind?

MRS. EDWARDS: Only Thomas Cook in Melbourne, sir—in April.

PETER: Australia?

MRS. EDWARDS: Yes, sir. She's going around the world.

PETER: And nothing until then?

MRS. EDWARDS: Not that I know, sir. I mean not with me.

PETER: Do you know why Miss Herries left so suddenly?

MRS. EDWARDS: No, sir. Her heart was bothering her I think —and the maid told me she was awful nervous.

PETER: Do you know where that maid is?

MRS. EDWARDS: With Miss Herries I believe, sir.

PETER: Was Miss Herries being treated by a doctor?

MRS. EDWARDS: Not that I know, sir. I came just before she left—and all I was told was to close the house and wait till Mr. Henry Abbott dismissed me.

PETER: Mr. Henry Abbott? Who's that?

MRS. EDWARDS: He's the agent, sir, in charge of the pictures.

PETER: What do you mean—in charge of them?

MRS. EDWARDS: I believe he's selling them, sir.

PETER (*after a pause*): Is he here now?

MRS. EDWARDS: Yes, sir. Would you like to see him?

PETER: Please.

(*She goes out.* PETER *takes a cigarette from a case in his pocket, lights it.* HENRY *comes in.*)

HENRY: Mr. Santard?

PETER: How do you do? I believe I saw you here one night—some time ago.

HENRY: Oh, yes. I brought some of my pictures to show Miss Herries—

PETER: Can you throw light on her mysterious disappearance?

HENRY (*laughs*): I think so. Please sit down. (*Indicates chair.*)

PETER: Thank you. (*Sits in chair.*)

HENRY: I'm sorry I wasn't here when you rang up this morning.

PETER: You see, my wife sent her aunt an invitation to our wedding and received a letter from the housekeeper!

HENRY (*crosses to desk, makes notations on paper on desk*): I'm awfully sorry. I must have been away—on the Continent. Had I been here when your invitation came, I—

PETER: That's all right. What's the old lady up to—sneaking away like that?

HENRY: She did, didn't she? (*Laughs.*) But I can't say I blame her.

PETER: What happened?

HENRY: Well—nothing particularly. She had been fed up for a long time, I think, and she had been planning this trip.

PETER: I understand you are selling her pictures?

HENRY: Just a few—I am also buying others. But I want you to believe that financially I have no interest in the matter.

PETER: Of course.

HENRY: I mean, I am doing this for nothing.

PETER (*slight pause*): Do you know why she didn't come to the wedding?

HENRY: Yes. (*Smiles.*) It isn't difficult. I feel greatly responsible, to an extent. (*Pause. Crosses in front of desk and sits on it.*) I'm afraid we'll have to turn psychological for a beginning.

PETER: Whatever you say.

HENRY: Well then—you know something about Miss Herries—

PETER: I met her only once. I liked her immensely.

HENRY: A very fine, gentle, sweet woman.

PETER: That's what I thought—

HENRY: But a lonely woman. I seem to be delivering a lecture on—

PETER: No—go ahead.

HENRY: An old maid, afraid of being a polite nuisance to her friends. A sensitive middle-aged woman— No relative but a sister— Emily—

PETER (*nods*): My mother-in-law.

HENRY: Whom she hasn't seen for years.

PETER: I wish I could say the same. I can understand that.

HENRY: Well, Miss Herries had a great fondness for my wife—

PETER: Oh—

HENRY (*crosses to center*): I should explain my position here —Miss Herries is a very generous woman. You probably know that she befriended both my wife and myself—

PETER: No, I didn't.

HENRY: She lent us money—enabled me to make a few commissions—and when my wife was ill kept her here. (PETER *nods.*) I stayed too, of course, and here's where I come in, and why I say I feel great responsibility.

PETER (*leans forward*): I think I understand!

HENRY (*sparring*): Really?

PETER: Please go on.

HENRY: In some way I was seen here, casually by someone, who immediately spread the most damnable silly rumor, that Miss Herries had taken a man to live with her.

PETER: I know. That was Phyllis—my then fiancée. My now wife.

HENRY: I'm sorry.

PETER: You're right. *She's* damned sorry about it now. Her mother knew she had been here and kept pumping her until Phyllis happened to mention it—just gossip, I thought.

HENRY: I'm afraid so. One of Miss Herries' friends told her and that hurt her so, I believe, that it was the real reason for her "mysterious disappearance," as you say.

PETER: Yes, yes, I see.

HENRY (*crosses to desk—gets list*): So—she went, leaving
   me certain items in her collection to dispose of. I'm to
   deposit the money in Blakely's Bank and send a report to
   Australia in April. It's quite a responsibility.

PETER: Sounds like it.

HENRY (*crosses to center—*PETER *rises and crosses to meet
   him*): Here's her list. You can see she's stipulated the
   minimum amounts to be obtained on each—and quite a
   few of these prices are prewar.

PETER: I wouldn't know a thing about it—except that she has
   some pretty fine stuff.

HENRY (*nods*): Most of it is extremely desirable. But art
   collectors don't pay as much as they used to.

PETER: I guess you art collectors were the first to feel the
   pinch of hard times.

HENRY: Both as artist and agent I can tell you, Mr. Santard.
   You're most emphatically right.

(*They both laugh.*)

PETER: Great stuff, anyway. (*Giving list back to* HENRY—
   crosses left.) I had a fine time here, picking out things I'd
   like to own.

HENRY: I know! If ever temptation worried me, it did in this
   house. (*Puts list back on desk.*)

PETER (*pointing to upper left wall*): There was a swell looking painting on that wall—

HENRY: An El Greco. That unfortunately was sold to a mu-
   seum in Brussels.

PETER: Oh, yes. And a Ming horse.

HENRY: Alas, that too is gone.

PETER: There were a few other things that hit me. I remember those two particularly.

HENRY (*smiling*): Well— (*Getting list from desk.*) There are
   a few things, if you feel inclined—

PETER: Not a chance—but let's see anyway. (*Takes list from
   * HENRY, *looks at it and whistles.*) Whew— I'm just a poor
   bond salesman—

HENRY (*laughs*): I think Miss Herries might consider a reduction—for a relative.

PETER (*laughs*): Yes, I suppose she might. Oh, say—there's one thing I could be interested in. There was a statue on this table. I forget who did it. (*Points to table.*)

HENRY: A statue?

PETER: I remember—Troubetzkoi!

HENRY: Oh, yes.

PETER: Does that happen to be in stock?

HENRY: Oh, yes. There it is.

PETER (*crosses*): Oh, there. Yes. Isn't it funny I thought it was—no you're right. I was a little—you know, the night I was here. (HENRY *smiles.*) In fact, I thought I remembered Miss Herries promising to give it to us for a wedding present. But—I suppose she changed her mind after Phyllis spilled that gossip.

HENRY: I'll be glad to remind Miss Herries if you could suggest some tactful method.

PETER (*laughs*): Never mind. Anyway it doesn't look as nice as it did the night I first saw it. The hell with it.

(*Snaps his fingers. Doorbell rings.* MRS. EDWARDS *crosses toward the front door.*)

HENRY: I shall tell Miss Herries in my next letter that you called.

PETER: Do that. (*Reflects.*) No—you'd better not. The other half of the family have all decided not to—bother her—until she asks them to.

HENRY: I'm extremely sorry. (MRS. EDWARDS *brings in cable, hands to* HENRY, *who opens it.*) Excuse me.

(MRS. EDWARDS *leaves.* HENRY *reads cable without any sign of emotion, and puts it in his pocket.*)

PETER (*crosses to desk—puts out cigarette*): Well, I'm off. My —wife and I are going to live in America, you know.

HENRY: Indeed.

PETER: I'm going to take charge of a branch out in Kansas City. Ever hear of it?

HENRY: Oh, yes.

PETER: God help me!

HENRY: Good luck, sir!

PETER: Thank you, sir! Well, I'll tell the—family about Miss Herries—not that it matters much, I suppose.

HENRY (*follows* PETER): I shall be here until Miss Herries returns and I'll be glad to do anything I can—

PETER (*laughs*): That's all right. Good-by.

(HENRY *see* PETER *out.* MR. *and* MRS. EDWARDS *come on and wait until* HENRY *returns. They enter from dining room.* HENRY *re-enters, still fingering the cablegram. He looks at them a bit triumphantly.*)

MR. EDWARDS (*as* HENRY *enters*): Nicely done, Henry.

HENRY (*crossing to window to watch* PETER *leave*): Yes, I think so. (*Then, handing cable to* EDWARDS.) This is interesting.

(EDWARDS *reads.* HENRY *sits at desk.*)

MRS. EDWARDS: What is it, Father?

MR. EDWARDS: Feller named Weston cables that his wife, Lucy, was killed in an airplane crash near Marseilles.

MRS. EDWARDS: My goodness—

(MR. EDWARDS *hands cable back to* HENRY.)

HENRY: That settles it. I think that when Miss Herries hears of *this*, things will be much simpler. (*Pause.*) It also adds a note of permanency to the whole venture. For now, Miss Herries has no one but me. (*Bell.*) That should be Rosenberg. (*Crosses to window and looks out. Then to* EDWARDS.) Let her come down. I want her to meet this chap.

MRS. EDWARDS: Oh, Henry—

HENRY: I'll go out through the basement and come around

and let myself in—in a few minutes. Show the man in here.
Then you let Miss Herries into this room. Listen carefully.
Don't let the man get away if she starts anything. (HENRY
rearranges things on desk.)

MRS. EDWARDS (*a little fearfully*): Who is it, Henry?

MR. EDWARDS: It's a dealer from Paris.

(*Nodding that it's all right. Doorbell again.*)

HENRY (*crossing to dining-room door*): Go on. (MR. ED-
WARDS *goes upstairs.* MRS. EDWARDS *again waits until he
has gone up. She looks back at* HENRY *as if a little afraid of
this step.*) All right.

(MRS. EDWARDS *goes to the door;* HENRY *lingers until he
hears* ROSENBERG'S *voice, then goes out through the door.*)

MRS. EDWARDS (*off*): Yes, sir?

MR. ROSENBERG (*off*): Monsieur Henry Abbott.

MRS. EDWARDS (*off*): Yes, sir.

MR. ROSENBERG (*off*): Monsieur Gustav Rosenberg, Bernstein et Fils. My card.

MRS. EDWARDS (*off*): Come in, sir. (*Shows in* MR. ROSEN-
BERG, *a Frenchman.*) Mr. Abbott is expected. Will you
wait here, sir.

MR. ROSENBERG: Thank you.

(MR. ROSENBERG *looks around the room, spots the Whistler
and walks over to it, putting his hat on table.* MRS. ED-
WARDS *backs out. He glances at the windows and sees the
shutters and realizes that he cannot get more natural light
—examines the canvas—front and back. He takes out his
handkerchief, spits on it, and rubs the lower right, then
the lower left corner of the canvas. He does not find any
trace of a signature—which doesn't bother him particularly, however. What does disturb him is the fact that his
handkerchief is black with dirt. He is putting his handker-*

chief back in his pocket, and sitting in a chair as MARY HER-
RIES *enters the room from the stairs.*)

MARY (*stops on platform—sees* MRS. EDWARDS *go off, then
looks into room*): Who—who are you?

(*She knows that the* EDWARDS *are listening and that she must
play the part she is expected to play. This man, however,
is a perfect stranger—he may be one of* HENRY'S *satellites
—this may be another trap.*)

MR. ROSENBERG (*rising*): Good afternoon, Madame. I am
Monsieur Gustav Rosenberg, Bernstein et Fils.

MARY (*crossing*): What are you doing here?

MR. ROSENBERG (*a little puzzled*): I—I am Monsieur Gustav
Rosenberg. Monsieur Abbott has invited me to look at this
painting.

MARY: Painting?

MR. ROSENBERG: Yes—this painting—this Whistler.

MARY (*hurt*): No! Oh.

MR. ROSENBERG: What is it, Madame; are you ill?

MARY: Oh, no. I'm quite all right. Only sometimes—I forget.
(*She must make sure who he is.*) I've even forgotten who
you said you were.

MR. ROSENBERG (*now beginning to worry*): Monsieur Rosenberg, Madame. Bernstein et Fils, Paris.

MARY: Oh, yes. But are you *really*? (*Suddenly, with more
intensity.*) How do I know you are Monsieur Rosenberg,
from Paris?

MR. ROSENBERG (*presenting business card*): My card, Madame.

MARY (*indicating this is not enough identification*): No!

MR. ROSENBERG: My passport. (*Shows it to her.*)

MARY (*looks at it quickly, realizes that here may be a friend,
then she senses that the others are listening and speaks for
their benefit*): Oh. Well, it doesn't make any difference.
You'll forget me. *Everybody's forgotten me. I'm supposed
to be away.* Henry writes all my letters.

MR. ROSENBERG (*a bit puzzled*): Pardon, Madame?

MARY: *No one else sees me.* (*She takes a letter from her dress.*) How do you like that picture? (*Points to* HENRY's *painting of the "Ranz des Vaches" on left wall.*)

MR. ROSENBERG: That? Oh, yes—yes—yes.

MARY (*points at letter which she has taken out of her dress*): *Please look at this!* (*Then for the benefit of the others.*) It's Henry's picture. (*Puts the letter in his pocket.*) Henry Abbott did it all. *Do you see?*

MR. ROSENBERG: I—I don't know— (*Reaches into his pocket.*) Madame—what is *this?*

MARY (*pulls his hand away from his pocket*): The cowherd is playing the flute. And the cows are listening. (*Points to the arch.*) *They're listening very carefully, do you see?*

MR. ROSENBERG: Yes—to be sure—

MARY (*points to his pocket*): *You must look at it.*

MR. ROSENBERG: Oh—yes—yes, of course—

MARY: Henry isn't a very good painter. (*Low and pleading for* ROSENBERG *to believe her.*) He's the very worst sort— (*Her voice rises so the others may hear.*) of a painter.

MR. ROSENBERG: Yes—yes, indeed! (*He looks around, hoping someone will enter.*)

MARY (*pointing to letter*): *I'd tell that to anyone*—even to *Lucy Weston*—who lives in *Mentone*—*Mentone*— (*Then for the benefit of the others.*) But she's too far away. Do you agree with me?

MR. ROSENBERG: Yes, Madame—yes. (*Anything to quiet her.*) Please sit down.

MARY (*sits quietly in chair*): Are you going to wait for Mr. Abbott? Or— (*Rises and draws* ROSENBERG *toward her.*) Will you *go away now* and come back later?

MR. ROSENBERG: I was told to wait here, Madame.

MARY: You could come back later.

MR. ROSENBERG: I am sorry, Madame. I have other appointments. I am in London for a few hours only. Please sit down, Madame.

MARY (*sits in chair*): But you will remember what I've said about— (*Pointing to letter in his pocket.*) the picture?

MR. ROSENBERG: Yes, Madame.

(*The front door is heard closing.*)

MARY: Please—help me—*do something!*

(ROSENBERG *crosses.* HENRY ABBOTT *enters the room.*)

HENRY: Mr. Rosenberg! (*Shaking hands.*)
MR. ROSENBERG: Ah! Mr. Abbott!
HENRY: You've had a look at the Whistler, I suppose?
MR. ROSENBERG: Yes—I—I have. I am glad you are here.
HENRY (*sees that everything has gone as planned, crosses to fireplace*): Yes. (*Crosses to the Whistler.*) Well—what do you think of it?
MR. ROSENBERG (*crosses after* HENRY; MARY *gives* ROSENBERG *a look of pleading*): Oh, yes—yes.
HENRY: Do you think Bernstein et Fils will be interested?

(*All through this* MARY *is sitting quietly without making a move, watching* MR. ROSENBERG *with desperate hope.*)

MR. ROSENBERG (*a bit distracted by* MARY, *but forces himself to discuss the picture*): As I have told you, Monsieur Abbott, Bernstein et Fils are not interested in Whistler—except for this one client.
HENRY: Yes, of course.
MR. ROSENBERG: Like so many Whistlers, it has sunken in and darkened to an extraordinary degree.
HENRY: Undoubtedly a good cleaning and one coat of mastic will bring out any details—
MR. ROSENBERG: Of course—this light— (*He shrugs, turns, sees* MARY, *turns back to* HENRY, *picks up hat.*) Might I suggest that you have it sent to our London correspondent —Leicester Galleries, Leicester Square for further examination.
HENRY: Oh, it's genuine, all right.

MR. ROSENBERG: Of course. You will also accompany the
painting with the history and the letter of authenticity.
HENRY: Oh, yes.

(MARY *looks pleadingly at* ROSENBERG.)

MR. ROSENBERG: *Au revoir*, Monsieur. (*Crosses up between
Left Center chair and table.*)
HENRY: Good day, Mr. Rosenberg.
MR. ROSENBERG (*crosses up to Arch, stops, turns back*): Ah
—uh—Mr. Abbott—
HENRY (*goes to him*): Yes?
MR. ROSENBERG: The lady gave me this. (*Produces letter.*)
Perhaps it would be better—
HENRY: Oh, yes. Thank you for understanding.
MR. ROSENBERG: *Au revoir*, Monsieur Abbott.
HENRY: *Au revoir.*

(MR. ROSENBERG *goes.* HENRY *follows him off.* MR. EDWARDS
enters, MRS. EDWARDS *enters, then* ADA.)

MR. EDWARDS: Well!
HENRY (*re-enters—nods—a close call—then gives letter to*
MARY): Here's your letter.
MARY (*low—with despair, still sitting*): God!
MR. EDWARDS: From listening, I'd have sworn she was—
HENRY: You are to be complimented, Miss Herries. (*Then
to* MRS. EDWARDS, *crossing.*): Take her upstairs.
MARY (*gets up and faces* HENRY, *firmly, resolutely and with
as much strength as she can muster; she speaks evenly and
quietly*): Don't be too sure, Henry Abbott. Things end
somehow—sometime—Someone— It's been too easy for
you. How you must despise yourselves! (*Almost a whisper*)
You wretched people—

(*There is a pause.* MARY *starts upstairs.* MRS. EDWARDS *offers
to help, but* MARY *draws away. Then as* MARY *goes up the
stairs—*)

SCENE: *The lights dim up and we find the scene as it was at the end of the Prologue.* MARY *is seated, talking to* MR. FOSTER.

MR. FOSTER (*greatly agitated*): Good God—I beg your pardon, Miss Herries—but I mean—

MARY: You do believe me, don't you?

MR. FOSTER: Miss Herries! Really, I—I—I—

MARY: The rain has stopped. Henry will soon be here.

MR. FOSTER (*rising and pacing*): This is dreadful—dreadful. What's to be done?

MARY (*hands him note*): Please take this. Take it.

(FOSTER *looks at the note—then hears door slam—*FOSTER *hurriedly puts away note.* HENRY *enters and sees* FOSTER.)

HENRY: Hello, Foster. You waited, thank you. I'm sorry to be late. (*He turns on lights and then notices* MARY.) Oh, Aunt Mary! (*He crosses to her.*) Down for your tea, dear?

MARY: Yes.

HENRY: Where is it?

MARY: No one was here.

HENRY: No one here? I don't understand. (*Crosses and rings bell, then crosses to desk.*) Now, Mr. Foster. You want me to sign these papers, don't you?

MR. FOSTER: The signature required by the Inland Revenue.

HENRY: Fine. Where do I sign, Mr. Foster?

MR. FOSTER: Here, sir. This will clear your income tax through June of this year.

HENRY: Till June. (*He starts signing.*)

MR. EDWARDS (*who has entered and put coffee table in front of* MARY—*is in the uniform of the traditional butler*): You rang, sir?

HENRY (*crosses to* MARY *with a protective air*): Yes, Edwards. I will not have you all away from the house at the same time. Miss Herries should never be without someone at her call. I've told you that before.

MR. EDWARDS: We are very sorry, sir, but the rain held us up. I had to take Mrs. Edwards to the doctor. She's not feeling well, sir. And we thought —

HENRY: I want it definitely understood that Miss Herries is not to be left alone at any time. You were engaged to attend to Miss Herries' wants at all hours. If that isn't plain I shall have to get someone who will. Make it clear to Mrs. Edwards. And we'll have tea now.

MR. EDWARDS: Yes, sir. Mrs. Edwards is preparing it.

(*He goes toward dining room—stands aside so* MRS. EDWARDS *can come in with tea tray, which she places on coffee table before* MARY. MR. EDWARDS *exits.* HENRY *has gone back to desk, immediately.*)

HENRY: Now, then, Mr. Foster. Sorry. (*Resumes signing income tax blanks.*)

FOSTER: That's all right, sir.

MRS. EDWARDS (*after she has placed tea in front of* MARY): I'm sorry about being out, Mr. Abbott.

HENRY: All right, Mrs. Edwards. (*He finishes signing—to* FOSTER *as* MRS. EDWARDS *exits.*) Thank you, Mr. Foster.

FOSTER (*picks up papers and puts them in his envelope*): Not at all. (*Crosses to* MARY.) Good day, Madam.

MARY: Oh, you're leaving? Good day, then.

FOSTER (*turns to* HENRY, *who has risen and is at desk*): Good day, Mr. Abbott.

HENRY: Good day, Mr. Foster. (MR. FOSTER *starts out.* HENRY *lets him go almost out, then stops him.*) Mr. Foster. (FOSTER *stops—looks at* HENRY—*then slowly comes back into room to* HENRY *in front of desk.*) You've never been here before, have you?

FOSTER: No, sir.

HENRY: I'm sorry there was no one here.

MR. FOSTER (*after a moment*): Oh—I understand, Mr. Abbott.

(ADA, *in the costume of a trained nurse comes downstairs.*)

HENRY: I thought you might not know.

MR. FOSTER: That's quite all right, sir. (*He sees* ADA *arranging* MARY's *shawl—*ADA *exits.*) She had me going for a few moments, Mr. Abbott.

(MARY *registers despair.*)

HENRY: Ah, yes. (*He crosses to* MARY—FOSTER *starts out.* HENRY *stops him.*) Mr. Foster, my aunt is sometimes left alone—as she was today. Carelessness on the part of the servants. (*Then a deliberate statement—not a question.*) She gave you something—a note. (*He holds out his hand.*)

MR. FOSTER: Oh! (*This is an ambiguous "oh"—and there is life and death in the balance. A look passes between* FOSTER *and* MARY.): No, sir! Good day, Mr. Abbott.

(*He exits. The door slams after him.* HENRY *slowly turns and crosses to* MARY *and stands looking at her. After a moment* MR. EDWARDS *enters from dining room. Crosses on platform. He, too, is puzzled and nervous. With his head he beckons* MRS. EDWARDS *on. She joins* MR. EDWARDS *and both look at* MARY. *When* MRS. EDWARDS *has joined* MR. EDWARDS, ADA *is heard running down the stairs. She stops at* MR. EDWARDS' *right, frightened. She slowly goes to the right side of the arch. Then* MR. EDWARDS *comes down behind* MARY. *He looks at* MARY, *then at* HENRY.)

MR. EDWARDS: What do you think, Henry?

(HENRY *does not answer. He is still watching* MARY. MR.
EDWARDS *starts toward the upper window. Just before he
reaches the window—doorbell.* MR. EDWARDS *hurries to
upper window, followed by* ADA *and* MRS. EDWARDS.
HENRY *hurries to downstage window. They all look out.
The doorbell rings, and there is knocking. Slowly the*
EDWARDS *and* HENRY *straighten up and look at each other
—then at* MARY. *Doorbell and knocking again.* MARY *slowly
rises from her chair. She seems to grow in stature. She
throws off her shawl.*)

MARY: I'll answer.

Production Notes

This anthology is designed for your reading pleasure. In most instances a performance fee is required from any group desiring to produce a play. Usually the organization that handles such performance rights also publishes individual production copies of the plays. Any group interested in additional information concerning performance fees or production copies of the plays in this anthology should apply to the following companies:

Arsenic and Old Lace   Dramatists Play Service, Inc.
                              14 East 38th Street
                              New York 16, N.Y.

Detective Story   Dramatists Play Service, Inc.
                              14 East 38th Street
                              New York 16, N.Y.

Kind Lady   Samuel French, Inc.
                              25 West 45th Street
                              New York 36, N.Y.

Classics
That Will
Delight Readers
Of Every Age!